PRAISE FOR H. PAUL JEFFERS

"This book is a spirited, affectionate tribute to a gallant American officer who led from the front. . . . Gracefully written and engaging—a topnotch study on an American icon."
—MICHAEL D. HULL, *WWII* magazine, on
Theodore Roosevelt, Jr: The Life of a War Hero

"A handsome narrative of a crucial period in the career of one of our country's most colorful politicians."
—*Publishers Weekly* on *Colonel Roosevelt:
Theodore Roosevelt Goes to War, 1897–1898*

Also by H. Paul Jeffers
Theodore Roosevelt, Jr.: The Life of a War Hero

ACE OF ACES

The Life of Capt. **EDDIE RICKENBACKER**

H. Paul Jeffers

BALLANTINE BOOKS • NEW YORK

FOR SID GOLDSTEIN,
*who's always ready to fly me anywhere
in his beloved Mooney.*

CONTENTS

ACE OF ACES

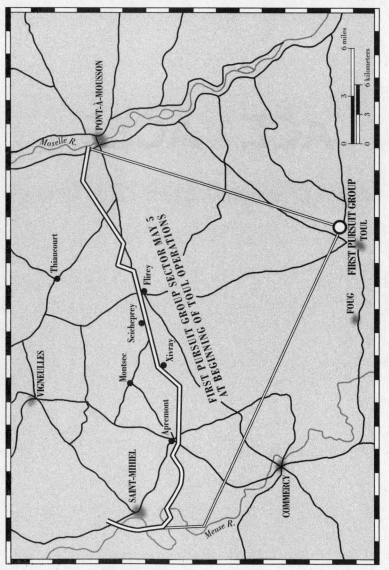

PONT-À-MOUSSON

Moselle R.

Thiaucourt

VIGNEULLES

Montsec

Seicheprey

Flirey

Xivray

Apremont

SAINT-MIHIEL

Meuse R.

COMMERCY

FOUG

FIRST PURSUIT GROUP
TOUL

FIRST PURSUIT GROUP SECTOR MAY 5
AT BEGINNING OF TOUL OPERATIONS

6 miles

6 kilometers

Patrol area of 94 Squadron from May 5 to July 1, 1918

America Holds Its Breath

THE NEWSPAPER HEADLINE ON SATURDAY MORNING, OCTOBER 24, 1942, was a shocker:

RICKENBACKER'S PLANE MISSING
Pacific Hunt Started for Noted Air Ace

The United Press story below the headline, filed from Washington, reported, "Captain E. V. Rickenbacker, the United States' greatest air ace in World War I and confidential advisor to Secretary of War Stimson, is overdue on a flight between Oahu, Hawaii, and another Pacific island." A few days later, a sorrowful editorial in the *New York Daily News* was headlined:

GOOD-BYE RICKENBACKER

How was it possible? How could the wartime flying hero and civilian aviation pioneer "Captain Eddie" be missing and presumed dead? A famous race car driver in his youth, he'd become a World War I fighter pilot whose gallantry as the highest scorer of American aerial victories over the Germans had earned him the title "Ace of Aces" and the Medal of Honor. Considering himself the "luckiest man alive," he'd counted 135 brushes with death in the skies and on the ground. Between the world wars he'd been a forceful advocate of a strong U.S. Air Force, a dashing pioneer of civilian aviation, founder of Eastern Air Lines, and proud owner of the Indianapolis Motor Speedway.

What was a man of his age, a gentleman who had to walk with the help of a cane, doing on a military plane over the middle of the Pacific Ocean?

In a double-breasted suit and fedora, Eddie Rickenbacker had stood out like a sore thumb among men in uniform on October 21 as he scanned the Hawaiian night sky and judged that the weather was perfect for flying. High, thin clouds. A three-quarter moon. He'd hoped for a B-24 because the interior of the Liberator bomber was roomier. But the plane he'd been assigned was a tactically obsolete Boeing B-17 Flying Fortress that had been earmarked to be sent back to the mainland for use as a trainer. According to Brig. Gen. William L. Lynd, commanding officer of Hickam Field, the crewmen were experienced members of the Army Air Transport Command. Before the war, some had flown for airlines.

The pilot was Capt. William Cherry. A Texan, he'd been a baby while Rickenbacker commanded a pursuit squadron in France in 1918 and earned the title "America's Ace of Aces" in dogfights with Germany's justifiably famed "Flying Circus," a child when "Captain Eddie" had barnstormed all around the country to give speeches promoting civilian aviation, and a teenager when Rickenbacker was building Eastern Airlines into an innovative leader in the passenger air travel business. The navigator, Lt. John J. De Angelis, was age twenty-three, short, wiry, with black hair, who struck Rickenbacker as a thoughtful kid. Private John F. Bartek, the flight engineer, was the same age. The radioman, Sgt. James W. Reynolds, was tall and skinny and a few years older. Copilot Lt. James C. Whitaker was heavyset, self-assured, and looked to be around forty years of age. In civilian life he'd been a contractor. An unexpected passenger was Alexander Kaczmarczyk. A ground crew chief who had been in an army hospital in Hawaii with a bad case of jaundice and appendicitis, he was now on his way to Australia to rejoin his unit. Because his last name was hard to pronounce, he told Rickenbacker to call him Alex. The last man to get on board the B-17 was Col. Hans Adamson. An old friend of Rickenbacker's since Adamson had been an aide to the assistant secretary of war in the administration of President Herbert Hoover, he was to accompany Rickenbacker to provide "the necessary amount of gold braid" to cut the red tape and satisfy protocol on a mission that the president of the United States and his secretary of war, Henry Stimson, had assigned to a portly, fifty-three-year-old civilian who walked with a slight limp.

If one of the young men had asked, Rickenbacker could have explained that the leg had gotten banged up two years earlier in a crack-up when he was a passenger on Eastern Flight 21 and the left wing clipped a tree while making a turn to land in bad weather in Atlanta. He also could have told the young airmen that he considered himself "the luckiest man alive" because he had gotten through plenty of brushes with death in racing cars and airplanes.

Concerning exactly why a civilian was being afforded the use of a B-17, except for its routes and destinations, Rickenbacker could not, of course, tell the men anything. The "special, wonderful job," as chief of the Army Air Forces, Lt. Gen. Henry H. "Hap" Arnold called it, had begun with a phone call from Arnold to the Miami headquarters of Eastern Air Lines on a Friday in March 1942. If Rickenbacker was interested in undertaking the job, he'd been told, it couldn't be explained on the telephone. He'd have to go to Washington to find out what Arnold had in mind.

At a meeting on Sunday evening, General Arnold extended an "invitation" to visit the various Army Air Force units being assembled for overseas action so the men could have "the benefit of your knowledge of combat psychology that you gained in the last war."

During the next thirty-two days, Rickenbacker visited forty-three training bases to give talks to crews learning to fly fighter planes and heavy, medium, and light bombers. "The results were evidently useful enough," Rickenbacker noted, "to induce Mr.

Stimson to offer me a worldwide mission to inspect United States air combat groups, both fighter and bomber, in all theaters of war. The assignment called for a report on the comparative values of United States aircraft and those of the enemy, together with my own opinions on air-fighting techniques. I was to be paid one dollar a day, and at the request of Mr. Stimson, I was appointed special consultant to him. This gave me the independence I wanted. In a way, I was the people's representative on American air power."

For two weeks in England he'd met and talked with all the high-ranking commanding officers of U.S. fighter and bomber groups as well as their pilots and mechanics, and the high command of the Royal Air Force (RAF) and ranking British government officials. During one visit to an RAF base he chanced to meet Prime Minister Winston Churchill and found himself riding back to London with him and having lunch at the prime minister's home and office at No. 10 Downing Street. Exhibiting detailed knowledge of bombers and warships, and keenly aware that his guest would report everything said at the lunch to President Franklin D. Roosevelt, Churchill declared, "Give me another thousand heavy bombers and two hundred more destroyers, and while I won't promise to change the trend of the war, I will promise to shorten it."

The trend of the war when the inspection trip ended in mid-October 1942 provided some basis for guarded optimism. On April 18 a fleet of Gen. James Doolittle's B-25 bombers had pulled off an aviation miracle by flying from the aircraft carrier *Hornet* to bomb Tokyo and other Japanese cities, doing little damage but sending homefront morale soaring. American soldiers were flooding into England in preparation for an invasion of North Africa and a fight with tanks and infantry against Germany's Afrika Korps, under command of the "Desert Fox," Field Marshal Erwin Rommel. In Russia the Germans were being bled white at Stalingrad. And Rickenbacker found himself with a new mission. He was to visit combat air bases in the Pacific, question the commanding officers, the pilots, and ground crews, and "make up my mind as to the good and the bad." His principal destinations on the trip, said Arnold, would be Australia, New Guinea, and Guadalcanal. But there was more.

At the request of President Roosevelt, General Arnold gave Rickenbacker a message for General MacArthur that was "so secret that it couldn't be written down." With it memorized, Rickenbacker left immediately with Colonel Adamson for Los Angeles and a brief stopover to visit Rickenbacker's eighty-year-old mother. The following evening he continued on to San Francisco to board a Pan American Airlines Clipper for Honolulu.

The graceful seaplane made the flight to Hawaii in record time—fifteen hours. But the plane awaiting him at Hickam Field was capable of no such speeds. First flown in 1935, the four-engine Boeing B-17 was so heavily armed that it was nicknamed the "Flying Fortress." Its 1,200-horsepower engines could make a maximum 320 miles per hour at 25,000 feet, but its usual cruise rate was 160 miles an hour with a range of 3,400 miles—more than enough to carry Rickenbacker to his destinations. Although more than half of the B-17s in the American arsenal were destroyed in the Japanese sneak attacks at Hickam Field and on air bases in the Philippines, the remainder of the B-17s in the Pacific had fought in gallant rearguard actions, helping to buy time for the U.S. to regroup in Australia.

A tired survivor of those perilous months, the B-17 that Rickenbacker boarded on the night of October 21, 1942, was parked near a second Flying Fortress that also looked as if it had been through a war. Loaded with the luggage of the three passengers, the gear of the five-man crew, and a dozen sacks of high-priority mail for the several headquarters that Rickenbacker would be visiting, the plane assigned to Rickenbacker carried no bombs as it taxied for takeoff. But as it rolled down the runway at eighty miles per hour, Rickenbacker felt it lurch to the left, the result, although Rickenbacker didn't know it, of a blown tire. As the B-17 hurtled toward a line of hangars, he remembered newsreels of the Japanese attack on the air base on December 7, 1941, and thought, "Hickam gets another blitz and Rickenbacker's part of it."

Fighting to retain control of the bomber, Captain Cherry managed to swing it back onto the runway, then wheel it into a vio-

lent loop that kept it from plunging into the bay. Examination of
the plane revealed a broken hydraulic line on the starboard brake
system, rendering the B-17 unusable. With a glance at the worry
on Rickenbacker's face, Cherry pointed to the second B-17 and
said in his happy-go-lucky Texas drawl, "We got another one,
Captain. The crew and I will stand by until it's ready."

Rickenbacker muttered, "Well, it had better not be like the
first."

As the replacement plane took off at a few minutes past midnight, Cherry predicted a smooth, quiet flight of 1,800 miles to the
island he knew only as "X," but known to Rickenbacker by its
real name, Canton Island. Estimated flying time: ten hours. Captain Cherry put the plane on automatic pilot. Rickenbacker decided to take advantage of one of the cots that had been set up for
him and Adamson in the rear, and try to get a little sleep for the
first time since he'd left San Francisco. By then the plane was at
10,000 feet. Wrapped in his trenchcoat and a blanket, he was too
cold to sleep more than a few minutes at a time. As dawn broke
at 6:30, he was up and having orange juice and coffee from ther-
mos jugs, and a sweet roll. Entering the cockpit, he was told by
Cherry that their expected arrival time was 9:30.

At 8:30, Cherry had the B-17 off autopilot and was starting
"downhill" from 9,000 feet to 1,000. The sun was high in the port
quarter of a sky with stretches of heavy clouds. But at 10:15,
three-quarters of an hour beyond the e.t.a., with no land in sight,
Rickenbacker asked Cherry, "How much fuel do you have left?"

With a glance at the gauge, Cherry replied, "A little over four
hours."

A few minutes later, Rickenbacker asked how much tailwind
they were supposed to have. Cherry said, "Ten miles." Rickenbacker said nothing, but he was certain they'd had more tailwind,
had been flying faster than Cherry believed, and that they'd over-
shot Island X and were moving away from it and into open ocean.
At the speed they were making, he figured, the plane had already
passed the island when Cherry began the descent to a thousand
feet. All this time the radio operator had been in contact with Island X, and the navigator had been charting their course by try-

ing to "shoot" the sun through breaks in the cloud cover. When Rickenbacker asked radioman Reynolds to request bearings from the radio post on Island X, he was told that the island had no equipment to provide bearings.

Contacting an American outpost on another island east and north of X, they were told to climb to 5,000 feet and circle for thirty minutes, sending out a radio signal while that outpost took a bearing. Following a compass course provided by the island, they flew on at better than three miles a minute, but all that could be seen below was water and more water. It was plain to Rickenbacker, and beginning to dawn on the crew, that they were lost. Over the next few hours, everything anyone could think of was tried to establish their location. Island X was requested to fire antiaircraft guns and send up search planes.

As the fuel level in the tanks dropped, Reynolds repeated calls for bearings, hoping that someone would be able to take a cross bearing. At 1:30 P.M., Cherry turned east, doubling back on their course and climbing to 5,000 feet. To save gasoline, he shut down the two outboard engines. Reynolds radioed that they had only an hour of fuel, then began sending "SOS."

"Rick, I hope you like the sea," said Colonel Adamson. "I think we're going to spend a long time on it."

When news flashed across the United States that "Captain Eddie" Rickenbacker's plane had gone down at sea and a search was under way, America crossed its fingers and held its breath.

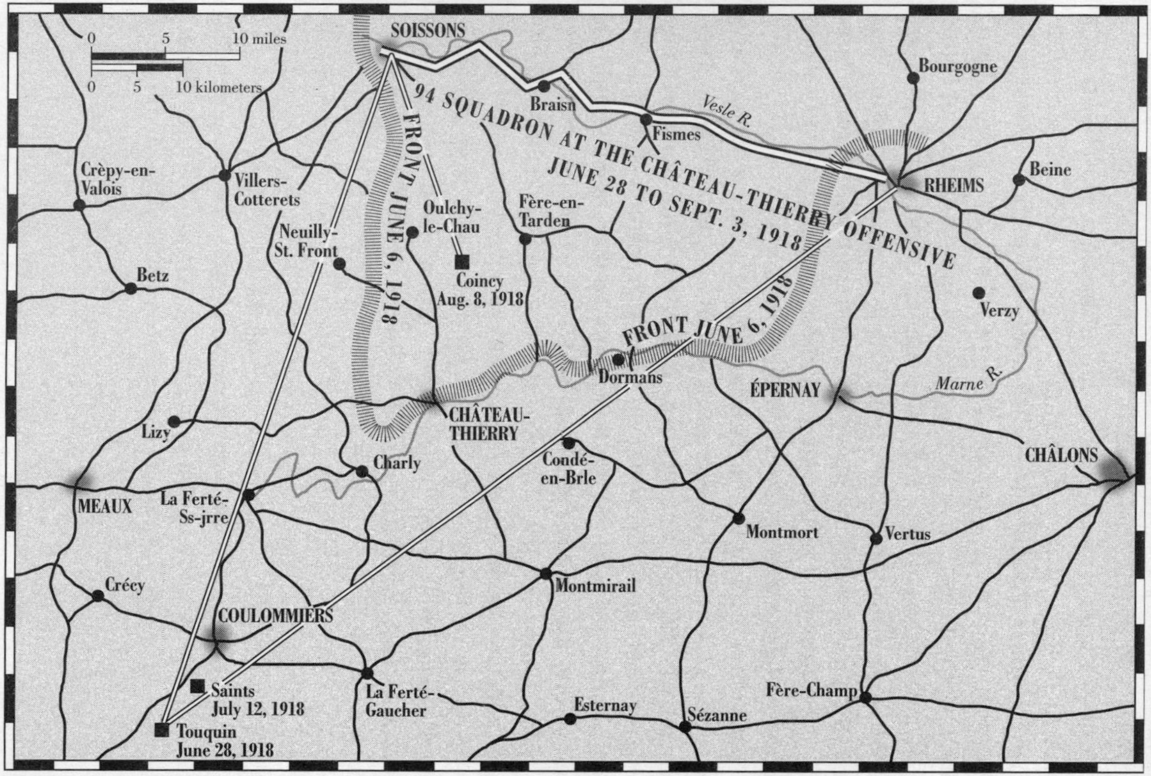
0
5
10 miles
0
5
10 kilometers
SOISSONS
94 SQUADRON AT THE CHÂTEAU-THIERRY OFFENSIVE
JUNE 28 TO SEPT. 3, 1918
FRONT JUNE 6, 1918
FRONT JUNE 6, 1918
Braisn
Vesle R.
Fismes
Bourgogne
RHEIMS
Beine
Verzy
Crèpy-en-
Valois
Villers-
Cotterets
Neuilly-
St. Front
Oulchy-
le-Chau
Coincy
Aug. 8, 1918
Fère-en-
Tarden
Betz
Dormans
ÉPERNAY
Marne R.
CHÂTEAU-
THIERRY
Lizy
Charly
Condé-
en-Brle
CHÂLONS
MEAUX
La Ferté-
Ss-jrre
Montmort
Vertus
Montmirail
Crécy
COULOMMIERS
Saints
July 12, 1918
Touquin
June 28, 1918
La Ferté-
Gaucher
Esternay
Sézanne
Fère-Champ
94 Squadron's sector of the Château-Thierry offensive, June 28 to September 3, 1918

CHAPTER 1

Harum-Scarum

B EING VERY, VERY BLOND, HE WAS SADDLED BY OTHER KIDS WITH
the nickname "Towhead." the second son of Swiss immi-
grants, and speaking English with a thick accent, he was also
called "Dutchy" and "Kraut." His given name was Edward, but
family and close friends called him Rick or Eddie. Given no middle name, he would eventually adopt one: Vernon. Rickenbacher
would also be changed to alter the German-appearing name by
substituting "k" for the "h." The taunting names of the schoolyard
usually provoked a number of fistfights. But no matter how much
fun anyone made of his looks and the way he talked, there was no
getting past the fact that when it came to displaying sheer guts,
eight-year-old Eddie left them all in the dust.

One of the payoffs of his courage was being the unchallenged
leader of "the Horsehead Gang," a name inspired by a horse's head
painted on a sign above the entrance to a racetrack on an outskirt
of Columbus, Ohio. Another attractive feature of the local landscape for boys was a rock quarry with a hundred-foot-deep pit. To
bring stones up a steep incline, the workers used a small steel-
sided cart that was hooked to a cable and ran on rails. They per-
formed this labor from early Monday morning till noon Saturday,

when they left the cart at the bottom. Gazing down at it on a sultry summer afternoon in 1898, the leader of the Horsehead Gang saw it as a beckoning thrill.

Pushing and straining, seven boys inched the cart up from the pit and held it in place with wooden chocks. With his followers inside, Eddie knocked away the chocks and yelled, "Here goes nothing!" As he jumped in, the cart began rolling. Rocketing downward, it careened and jerked. Uncontrolled, unstoppable, and top-heavy, it flipped. Six of the seven riders flew out and away. Eddie landed under its wheels. As it sped forward, one of the steel wheels passed over his leg and cut it open to the bone. Many years later, he took pride in noting that the scar "was one of my first."

Another memory was of a day when he was four or five years old and helping his mother plant potatoes. "She, standing, would make a little hole with the hoe," he recalled, "and I, on my hands and knees, would put the cone-shaped pieces of potato in, then push the dirt over them. I must have moved too quickly toward the new hole she was digging, for instead of the hoe hitting the ground, it hit me, right in the head. One of the prongs actually pierced my skull. Mama picked me up and ran to the house. There she washed my scalp and treated it with healing oil, then rocked me in her arms. What could have been a serious injury is now only a pleasant memory of being nestled in Mother's arms."

When Elizabeth Baker married William Rickenbacher in 1885, she was twenty-one and had been in Columbus, Ohio, for three years. Fair-skinned, red-haired, and of French descent, she had been working as a housemaid. Seven years older, William had emigrated from Switzerland in 1879. Of German stock, tall, strong, black-haired, and with a lush mustache, he had been an apprentice in construction work in Switzerland, but found work in Columbus as laborer for a railroad. Their first child was named Mary. Next came William, Edward, and Emma. The next four children were born in a house that was built by their father on a lot in east Columbus. The fifth child, Louisa, died in infancy. Three boys followed: Louis, Dewey, and Albert.

"From the Old World my parents had brought a sense of duty

and a tireless willingness to work," Capt. Eddie Rickenbacker would write about his boyhood years. "The New World provided what was to them a lavish amount of fertile soil, opportunity and promise. I was a fortunate boy indeed in that I was able to pass my formative years in that favorable atmosphere of industry, production, gratitude and appreciation."

The capital of Ohio, Columbus in 1893 was a thriving city with a population of about 88,000, on the east bank of the Scioto River. Its landmarks were the State Capitol building, Ohio State University (seven hundred students), the State Penitentiary, the Central Ohio Lunatic Asylum, a U.S. Army barracks, and Goodale Park. The main thoroughfare, Broad Street, was paved with asphalt and tree-shaded. Offering railroads running to Cleveland, Toledo, and Indianapolis, Columbus was a vital commercial, agricultural, and manufacturing center for iron and steel goods, farming equipment, and carriages that were renowned in the cities of the East for their elegance and comfort.

When Edward Rickenbacher was born on October 8, 1890, the president of the United States was Ohio-born Benjamin Harrison. But as the family moved into the house that William had built on East Livingstone Avenue, the man in the White House was Grover Cleveland. He had come back from a defeat by Harrison in 1892 to claim the distinction of being the only man to be elected to two nonconsecutive terms and find himself listed as the twenty-second and twenty-fourth president. By 1893 the flag had forty-four stars. Unfortunately, it flew over a country suffering from the effects of a stock market crash, bank failures, wage cuts, labor strife, and economic depression that most Americans blamed on Cleveland. As these conditions dragged on into 1894, an Ohio farmer named Jacob Coxey led the "Army of the Commonwealth of Christ" on a march to Washington, D.C., with a petition to Congress for the government to issue $500 million in bonds to build highways and put men back to work. For his efforts, he and the ragtag group that was now known as "Coxey's Army" were arrested for trespassing on the Capitol lawn, fined five dollars, and run out of town.

For the Rickenbacher family, settling into the new house had been "the beginning of a reality." On the day they moved in, Papa Rickenbacher had quit his job and gone into business subcontracting small jobs, mostly putting down pavements and building foundations. "It was a brave move to make," Eddie recalled, "but he was a man of great self-confidence."

The land surrounding the house provided food. The family raised vegetables, including cabbage for sauerkraut, kept chickens and pigs, and got enough milk from a small herd of goats. Eddie delivered the excess to paying customers in the neighborhood. "America the bountiful" to him was symbolized by what seven cents could do. It was the price of both a dozen eggs and a pound of sugar, so that when the chickens were laying well and produced an extra dozen eggs, they could be traded for a pound of sugar. With a little flour and apples from an orchard, Mama could bake apple pie. Where else but America, asked Papa, could a man begin with nothing and feed his children apple pie for dessert?

"Above all," Eddie would write of his boyhood, "our parents taught us to love America."

Lessons having nothing to do with patriotism were taught with a fatherly use of a switch. It was applied when he and older brother Bill were caught in the barn puffing away on cigarettes made from a five-cent bag of Bull Durham tobacco. Another whipping followed a police report about an attack by the Horsehead Gang on the globes of gas streetlights. But the sting of the switching was forgotten with Eddie's discovery of his mother crying in disappointment over her son's behavior and acknowledging that her son "deserved every lick."

One morning in 1894, as he accompanied her across a street to a peddler's cart, he dashed ahead of her. Unaware of an approaching horse-drawn streetcar, he slammed into its side and barely escaped being run over. Bounding up from the street, he ran home, rushed up the stairs, crawled under a bed, and stayed there until his mother assured him he was safe. The collision left him with a lump on his head, two black eyes, and relief that he had escaped the clutches of "the grim reaper." Another brush with death resulted from curiosity about a hole that had been dug by some workmen for a cistern. Deciding to inspect the progress of the project, he leaned over too far and fell in. Stunned from landing on his head, he "lay there, limp as a broken toy" until a passerby pulled him out and carried him home. He was unconscious for two hours.

Like all boys of his era, and almost all boys of the previous half century, Eddie was fascinated by trains. Behind huge, smoke-belching steam locomotives, they rattled westward from the coal-fields of Pennsylvania to bring fuel for the furnaces of Columbus steel mills and factories of cities beyond in a country bristling with the exuberance of an industrial boom and motivated by its "manifest destiny" to master a continent that Theodore Roosevelt envisioned holding "in our hands the hope of the world, the fate of coming years." But the railroads passing through Columbus came carrying not only the promise of America's future, but heaping mounds of coal from which fell bituminous lumps that were free for the taking by enterprising boys who had the nerve to grab them for the purpose of replenishing kitchen coal bins at home. With trains of the New York Central line passing just seven blocks from the Rickenbacher house, Eddie and Bill set out one summer day in 1896 to collect as many lumps as they could carry to fire the kitchen stove. As an engine lumbered past, Eddie jumped onto the trailing tender with the intention of helping himself to chunks of coal. But the moment he bounded aboard, the locomotive jolted to a stop, hurling Eddie to the roadbed. As the locomotive began backing up, Bill barely managed to drag Eddie from the tracks. In another hairbreadth escape while scav-enging coal, his foot caught in a switch in a railroad yard as an engine barreled toward him. Again Bill rushed to the rescue, yanking him free but leaving Eddie's shoe to be crushed. In a cri-sis that did not involve trains, Eddie ran back into a burning schoolhouse to retrieve a hand-me-down coat and hat, emerging with them and singed hair and able to proudly tell his horrified mother, "I saved my cap and coat."

These brushes with death left Eddie with an unusual recogni-tion for a ten-year-old that "one day I would die and that the world would go on without me." It happened, he wrote, "out of the blue." What he felt, he recalled, "was not merely fear of death or dying; it was more sensitively metaphysical. It was a cry of despair for the entire universe, centralized in the susceptible mind of a nine-year-old child. I could see time stretching on endlessly. As it continued, more and more wondrous marvels would be developed and become realities. But at some point along this interminable path, my life would stop, and time would flow on without me. In my despair, I would go off alone to the barn and sob for hours at a time."

On one of these morbid occasions, his father discovered him "sprawled on my face and crying my heart out." Asked what was wrong, Eddie answered as best he could, choking out the explanation between sobs. "Papa's reaction was typical, fitting and effective," Eddie recalled. "He grabbed a switch. 'You're too young to think things like that,' he said. (*Whack!*) 'Life and death are my worry, not yours. Don't ever let me catch you crying about such foolish things again.' (*Whack!*)"

The whipping did not dispel a sense of loss over what Eddie would never see, but it did impress him with "the futility of despair over the inevitable." Resolving to "enjoy life as long as the good Lord" would let him, he vowed to never cry again over "unseeable occurrences." It was, he said, "the first turning point in my life." His "days of rebellion, of destruction and meaningless mischief, were gone and gone forever."

Under Papa's influence and encouragement, Eddie began to accept more and more responsibility for the work that had to be done around the home. "Though all those tasks were hard work and Papa was a stern taskmaster," he remembered, "I still loved to work alongside him. He would constantly advise me on why something was done this way and not the other. Through his own personal example, he inspired me to do the right job to begin with. He taught us to respect and take care of our tools. He had a phobia against leaving things lying around, and I caught it from him. My father taught me never to procrastinate, to *do it now.*"

While Papa Rickenbacher often resorted to the switch to teach the lessons of life, Mama was a believer in redemption through prayer. She saw to it that each little Rickenbacher knelt by the bedside each night and said the Lord's Prayer. "Mama taught us," Eddie recalled, "that the Lord above was a friendly God, a great Presence who was interested in our problems and was sympathetic to them." Sundays, the family put on their best clothes to go to St. John's Lutheran Church in the south end of Columbus.

A friend found Eddie to be a bundle of contradictions: tender and sensitive within, but tough when a situation required. In those times he could be a "holy terror" in whom neighbors saw a bleak future and probable imprisonment. What else should one expect of the leader of a bunch of ruffians like the Horsehead Gang, a boy who was ready to start a fight at the drop of a hat and regularly sneaked off to smoke Bull Durham? Yet, he was a hard worker at home who collected money owed the family for goat's milk and eggs, got out of bed at two in the morning to deliver the *Columbus Dispatch* newspaper, and from time to time worked on farms and at construction jobs carrying water for the men, with all of his earnings turned over to his mother.

To put a few cents in his own pocket to buy a pouch of Bull Durham tobacco, Eddie saw opportunity in a grizzled junk collector named Sam. The discovery that Sam would give him money for rags, bones that could be ground up for fertilizer, and old pieces of metal was, he said years later, the beginning of his business career. Before long he had put the Horsehead Gang to work on his behalf, collecting junk, pulling nails out of old boards, and scavenging in vacant lots for items to sell to Sam the Junkman, with a healthy percentage of the proceeds going into his pocket and later into his mouth and lungs in the form of Bull Durham smoke. Another source of revenue was the Columbus Derby. When the horse races were on, Eddie and the gang sneaked through the fence at the track to earn a little money by wandering through the crowd selling soda pop for a soft-drink vendor.

Summer also brought Barnum & Bailey's circus to town, but the attraction that riveted Eddie's attention on that occasion in his sixth year was not elephants, lion tamers, or sideshow freaks. He gazed in awe at a demonstration of a Duryea "horseless carriage." The automobile had won the first auto race in America, zooming around a fifty-four-mile course in Chicago at the breathtaking speed of seven miles an hour. Always interested in mechanics, Eddie was fascinated by the noisy contraption, but the closest he could come to experiencing such a thrill was by building a "push-mobile." A long board mounted on wheels sawed from wood with water-pipe axles greased with lard, it had a two-man team—a driver and a pusher. When the Horsehead Gang had several assembled, racing began on a track behind the Rickenbacher home. Recalling the contests, he would write, "We would go around and around our rough little track, jockeying for position, bumping and shouting. Sometimes we would wind up in a free-for-all." Dissatisfied with the performance of wooden wheels, he got his hands on a discarded baby carriage thanks to Sam the Junkman. Rolling smoothly on wheels with ball bearings and rubber tires, he called his new pushmobile "Mile a Minute Murphy," after Charles Murphy, who had pedaled a bicycle at that rate on Long Island and become the first man to travel on land or in the air at that terrific pace. Many years later, when Eddie Rickenbacker was world famous as a race car driver, he would tell officials of the Chevrolet Company about the pushmobile of his boyhood days and witness the birth of the Soap Box Derby.

On another summer day of his childhood, he joined the citizens of Columbus as they looked skyward to watch a dirigible sailing silently over the city. The sight led to talk among some in the crowd about a pair of obviously crazy bicycle-making brothers named Wright, sixty miles away in Dayton, who were said to be working on a "flying machine." The consensus was that they would end up like a man in Paris who had strapped on leather wings, launched himself from the Eiffel Tower, and been killed. A story that would have chilled the imagination of other boys, it sparked Eddie to make a set of canvas wings, attach them to his bicycle, and fly from the roof of a barn. A pile of sand was arranged to soften the landing. "Thanks to the sand and the good Lord," he noted, his first flight left him "only stunned." The bike was smashed.

Papa Rickenbacher's advice was that Eddie never get mixed up with a machine he didn't know how to control. He also told him, "You're a lucky boy to be born when you were. There are a lot of new things in the making, and you ought to be ready to have a hand in them."

Of the future heroic figure that Americans in World War I would hail as the "Ace of Aces" and later generations would know as the pioneer of the skies they called "Captain Eddie," aviation historian Robert J. Serling (brother of Rod) wrote, "It is not true that Eddie Rickenbacker inspired the Horatio Alger stories of Poor-Boys-Who-Made-Good, Rising-From-Poverty-Through-Diligence-and-Hard-Work. But it should have been true. For no man in American history personified the American Dream better than Rickenbacker; his name belongs with those of the Edisons and the Fords and all the others who turned the Horatio Alger fable into fact."

Provided by parents with the sturdy pilings of God, family, patriotism, hard work, and ambition that were deemed necessary for the foundation of proper manhood in the United States of America in the late-nineteenth century, young Eddie had added a zest for adventure and risk-taking that often left his mother and father despairing about whether he would live long enough to become the adult they hoped to shape. A "cagey youngster" by his own definition, he seemed to fear nothing. But most of his adventures were over so quickly, he noted, "that I didn't have time to be scared." Although these scrapes with death and other less perilous daredevil acts were rewarded with a walloping from his father, Eddie knew Papa as a dependable, industrious, hardworking builder who was proud to be helping his chosen country grow and prosper.

"He had come from a tiny country in which three languages were spoken," Eddie wrote many years later. "Now he was in one great country with one language, one common goal."

In 1900 the United States was, in the words of Theodore Roosevelt, the "young giant of the West," standing on a continent and clasping the crest of an ocean in either hand, "glorious in youth and strength" as it looked into the future with eager eyes and rejoiced "as a strong man to run a race." Symbolic of that country were bridges that Papa Rickenbacher was building to span streams and rivers in central Ohio. A foreman and equipment operator, he took Eddie along to his job one day to show him "the meaning of the work." Leaning over the edge of a half-built bridge, he pointed out marks left by steel-rimmed wagon wheels in the rock of the riverbed. It was, he told Eddie, the way early pioneers had come, crossing the river to build the nation. He went on talking about horses and wagons that soon would cross it, and how the bridge would shorten journeys and bring people closer together. One day, he predicted, the new horseless carriages that interested Eddie so much would also use it. "And mark my words, Eddie," he said, "you're going to see more and more of them."

On a July night in 1906, as Papa was on his way to run a pile driver, he stopped for a moment to see what Eddie was up to in a workshop at the back of the house. The project he was tinkering with, Eddie explained, was a perpetual motion machine. It consisted of billiard balls and a wheel that turned as the balls dropped into cups fastened to the rim. After observing the demonstration, Papa turned to go. "I'd give most anything to have my life to live over again," he said, "if I could only start at your age."

That night, a workman with whom Papa had an argument flew into a rage, grabbed up a three-foot level made of hardwood and tipped with brass, and struck him on the head. Rushed to a hospital with a fractured skull, William was in a coma. He lingered in and out of consciousness for a month. When he died on August 4, 1906, with Elizabeth and the seven children gathered at his bedside, he was forty-nine years old. Eddie was almost sixteen. He was laid out at home so neighbors and friends could pay their last respects to him and offer condolences to the family, but on that night, Eddie's attention was directed to Mama's words. "She spoke quietly but very seriously," he recalled. "In the years ahead, some of us might be more fortunate than others; she asked each of us to promise her definitely that those who were successful would share with those who were not and would see that they would never be in want or need of anything within rea-son. We all gave our solemn promise."

Whatever the others thought, Eddie knew on that day that he had turned from a harum-scarum youngster into a young man serious beyond his age.

CHAPTER 2

The Daredevil

T OO YOUNG LEGALLY TO HAVE A PAYING JOB, EDDIE LIED HIMSELF into employment with the Federal Glass Factory. He also attested that he had finished school. Another lie. He was in the eighth grade. But the hardest part was getting his mother to see that bringing in money for the family was more important than studying. "In the long history of boys talking their mother into acquiescence," he remembered about that discussion, "none was ever more persuasive than I."

The factory made handblown glass tumblers. Eddie's job was carrying the hot glasses on a heavy steel platter with a long handle to tempering ovens. He worked a twelve-hour shift six nights a week for three and a half dollars. When he handed Mama his first pay packet, it was, he said, "the proudest day" of his life. But after a few months of backbreaking labor at night, he decided to take a day job at the Buckeye Steel Casing Company that paid six dollars a week. It lasted three months, replaced by a job with shorter hours. Capping bottles at a brewery, he put up with the sickening smell of hops until he learned of an opening at a shoe factory.

His next job provided a bizarre episode in a young life that

might have fired the vivid imagination of the author of the popular Horatio Alger books, or have come from the pages of a Charles
Dickens story. Hired by a cemetery monument maker to polish
stones with water and sandstone, he was so diligent at the wet,
sloppy, and cold work that the firm's owner offered him the opportunity to learn how to engrave monuments. The Alger or
Dickens twist was the fashioning of the marker for his own
father's grave. It was a large marble stone with FATHER carved in
block letters across the top and WILLIAM RICKENBACHER set below.
Enjoying working with stone, he carved a Bible out of white
marble, then sculpted a small stone angel that he presented to
his mother. While she was grateful for the money he was earning, she expressed concern to Eddie's employer that Eddie's
breathing in stone dust was not good for his health. "There was
tuberculosis in my family," she said, "and I've often been afraid
that he has a tendency toward it. Sometimes I don't think Eddie
will live to be a man."

Pondering the remark the rest of that day and most of the
night, Eddie knew that the dust stonecutters constantly inhaled
damaged their lungs and curtailed their life spans. Since taking
the job, he'd developed a slight cough and had a constant tingle
in his throat. "By the time the morning sun came up," he wrote,
"the stonecutting profession had lost Eddie Rickenbacher."

The day after quitting the job, while downtown, strolling
around and thinking over his unemployed state, he noticed a
small crowd gathering at High and Broad Streets. Hurrying to see
what was going on, he discovered a brand-new, two-passenger
Ford runabout. The first one in Columbus, it was a turtleback
roadster, sleek, shiny, and built for speed. The man who'd
brought it began talking about the automobile's performance and
said that for just five hundred dollars practically everyone could
soon own one. When the man finished talking, Eddie blurted,
"Mister, do you ever take anyone for a ride?"

After thinking for a moment, the auto salesman said, "Sure,
kid. Hop in, and we'll go around the block."

Eddie scrambled into the passenger seat on the left. The salesman set the levers on the steering wheel column, turned on the

ignition, and spun the crank. The motor started with a series of
explosions that had the people in the crowd holding their ears.
The little Ford cruised at ten miles an hour as Eddie contemplated what a lucky boy he was, and that not one kid in a million
had such an opportunity. But when the ride ended, he still needed
a job.

Taken on as an apprentice in the machine shops of the Pennsylvania Railroad at one dollar a day, he first cleaned out passenger cars and discovered that on some days there was more money
to be had in coins that had slipped behind seat cushions from
pockets and purses of Pennsy passengers. This often amounted to
two or three dollars. But his greatest discovery was the "beauty of
machinery" and the "creativity of machine design and production" that he saw around him every day. With this came an appreciation of "beautiful, functional, precision-made parts" that
lay beneath the shiny black hood of the little Ford runabout in
which he'd been privileged to ride, if only for a few minutes.
Spinning in his mind was Papa's prediction that one day America's roads and streets in towns and cities would be crowded with
automobiles. Emboldened by his new understanding of the creativity and the functionalism of mechanics and feeling the "irre-
sistible pull" of the exciting promise of the internal combustion
engine, he made up his mind to become part of a burgeoning automobile industry that traced its origins to Karl Friedrich Benz
and Gottlieb Wilhelm Daimler. Working separately at about the
same time in Germany, each had designed and built the first
commercially successful automobiles. Benz's first creation was a
fragile three-wheel carriage that had a tubular framework and a
one-horsepower, single-cylinder engine. Though awkward and
frail, it had an electrical ignition, differential, mechanical valves,
carburetor, engine cooling system, and a lubrication and braking
system. He obtained a patent in 1886. Daimler's was a gasoline-
fueled engine mounted on the frame of a two-wheel bicycle at
first, then a four-wheeled, two-passenger vehicle that included
the first example of a high-speed internal combustion engine.

Although the first automobiles were called "horseless carriages," they were closer to the bicycle than the buggy. As the

result of a "bicycle craze" in America in the early 1890s, and a need for better roads, the U.S. government created the Office of Road Inquiry in the Department of Agriculture that evolved into the Bureau of Public Roads. Among the numerous pioneers in automobiles were bicycle makers Charles and Frank Duryea, one of whose autos had been seen by young Eddie Rickenbacher. In 1897, Alexander Winston, another bicycle manufacturer, made the first American high-performance auto, a twelve-horsepower model that tested out at 33.7 miles per hour. Using bicycle parts, including a saddle, Henry Ford introduced the "quadricycle."

Because the first auto dealers were recruited and converted from bicycle dealers, the best place to see a really fine example was at the local bicycle shop. In Columbus the place was on Chestnut Street. Owned by a man named Evans and called Evans Garage, it was a bicycle repair shop that had been expanded to accommodate covered parking space for the few daring individuals who owned automobiles. Peering into the garage on the day he quit working for the Pennsylvania Railroad, Eddie gazed admiringly at a Waverly electric and a single-cylinder, gas-powered Packard. Walking in, he asked Evans for a job. Told that he could clean up the place and mind the bicycle shop when Evans was otherwise occupied, he was offered seventy-five cents a day, a huge cut from what Eddie had been earning. Even with his responsibilities to his mother and younger siblings, he decided that it was the future that counted, and the chance to work around automobiles.

"You have yourself a boy, mister," he said. "Where do you want me to begin?"

Quickly recognizing Eddie's willingness to work hard and to learn, Evans shared all that he knew about the three types of automobile engines—steam, gasoline, and electric. The first were clumsy and cumbersome, and sometimes blew up. The internal combustion engine was in its infancy and it was complicated. Electric power was safe, smooth performing, and accelerated by simply moving a lever. Its drawback was that the batteries had to be constantly charged. With Eddie watching the shop, Evans went out to solicit business. This provided Eddie the chance he had been waiting for to climb into one of the autos, first pretending to drive it, then starting it up and moving it back and forth in the small, gloomy garage.

When Evans left him in charge while he traveled to Toledo on business, Eddie took advantage of the opportunity to actually drive the Waverly on the streets. Closing the shop early, he "went toward home, sitting high and proud," parked it smoothly at the curb in front of his house, announced his arrival by sounding the machine's warning bell, strode into the house, and invited his mother to join him in a drive around the neighborhood. "We skimmed along at ten miles an hour," he recorded about "the kind of experience that happens often in daydreams, but so rarely in real life."

With the demonstration of his driving skill completed and on his way back to the garage, he was horrified to find that the Waverly's battery was petering out. Left powerless, with night coming on and no wrecker service to rescue him, Eddie faced the certainty that Evans Garage would be minus one employee should Mr. Evans return to find that the employee had taken out a customer's car. Remembering that Evans had said that a dead battery might regain power if it sat idle for a while, Eddie took out his Ingersoll watch and waited. Exactly an hour later he tried the starting lever and felt a satisfying lurch. But several blocks farther, the car stopped again. After another hour of waiting, the Waverly came to life, only to slow to a stop after a few blocks. As the night wore on, the intervals of forward motion shortened until the garage was reached at three o'clock in the morning. He hooked the battery to a charger, then went home. He was at the garage again in the morning to greet Evans with a broad grin, knowing that the Waverly was "as good as ever."

Realizing after six months that repairing cars, charging batteries, and patching bicycle tires did not satisfy his expanding ambitions to design and build automobiles, Eddie looked for a college or university that offered automotive courses. Finding none, he wrote "in a fairly good hand but in seventh-grade English" to the International Correspondence School in Scranton, Pennsylvania. To his delight, the school offered a course in mechanical engineering, including a special section on the automobile and internal combustion engines.

"The first lesson," Eddie recalled, "nearly finished my correspondence-school education before it began. It was tough, and I was a little rusty when it came to formal education. I had to teach myself to study all over again, and, furthermore, I had to teach myself to think. I did not realize it then, as I laboriously worked away at the lessons all alone, that I was receiving a greater benefit from them than I would have received from the same courses in a classroom. As there was no teacher to whom I could ask an explanation, I had to work out the answers myself. Once I reached the answer through my own individual reasoning, my understanding was permanent and unforgettable."

Considering himself "in the automotive business," he found himself "itching to see what was going on" at a small auto factory only two blocks from the Evans Garage. Turning out one auto a month, the Frayer-Miller Company produced every part of a gasoline-powered touring car except its tires. In addition to that model, the firm's designer and chief engineer, Lee Frayer, was supervising the building of three racing cars to be entered in the Vanderbilt Cup Race. He did this mostly on Sunday mornings. Abandoning "the regularity of attendance at Sunday school," Eddie began hanging around the auto shop and watching Frayer at work. Although "on fire" with the allure of being part of the excitement of racing automobiles, the boy who had dared to ride into a rock quarry in a cart and had put ball bearing baby-carriage wheels on a pushmobile to go faster, found himself timid about bothering a "hardworking, ambition-driven man."

After being watched for a few Sundays, Frayer startled Eddie by demanding, "What do you want around here, kid?"

"What I want," Eddie answered nervously, "is to help you build automobiles."

Frayer smiled. "Sorry, kid," he said, turning away. "Nothing here that you can do."

Looking around the cluttered, messy shop, Eddie recognized opportunity in its grease-spotted cement floor, a litter of metal shavings, junk piles, and the most untidy workbenches he'd ever seen. "Mr. Frayer, I think there is," he blurted. "And first thing to-morrow morning, you'll find out what I mean."

Out of bed before dawn, Eddie showed a character trait in adults of the period that novelist Edith Wharton would one day chronicle in *The Age of Innocence*, and that admirers of the heroes of Horatio Alger's stories valued as "pluck," "grit," "good old American get-up-and-go," and a "lift yourself by your own bootstraps" spirit. On the way to Frayer's factory, he left a note on the door of Evans Garage:

> *Dear Mr. Evans:*
>
> *I quit.*
>
> *Resignedly yours,*
> *Eddie Rickenbacher*

Arriving at the Frayer-Miller plant at seven o'clock, he found a broom and heavy floor brush in a corner and began working. When Frayer appeared at 8:30, he had finished about a third of the main floor, leaving it "as clean as our floors at home." By contrast, he thought, the remainder of the space "looked like a pigpen." Surveying the workshop, Frayer said, "You sure as hell meant what you said. Keep up what you're doing. You've got a job, kid."

With three floors of the building cleaned, Frayer told Eddie to report to a toolmaker to help make carburetors. Observing Eddie's eagerness and ability, and impressed that his new employee was using his lunch hours to study a correspondence course in engineering, Frayer moved him to engine assembly and then to chassis assembly. Just under sixteen years old, he was five feet, nine inches tall and weighed 165 pounds. Cheerful and easygoing, always with a joke or amusing story to tell and ever ready to flash an ear-to-ear, dimpled, infectious smile, he was also the inventor of a labor-saving device for the plant's drills that he called a "gimper." Bored with having to drill four holes, one at a time, in a casing called a blower, he made a jig that completed the task in a single action.

After working in every phase of the mechanical department from grinders to lathes, shapers, and drill presses, Eddie heard Frayer speak words that "opened up a new world." "Eddie," he announced, "I want you to go into the engineering department."

The task of the four engineers at that time was designing and setting specifications for each part of the Frayer-Miller entries for the Vanderbilt Cup Race to be run in the fall of 1906 on a course on Long Island, New York. Started by the New York millionaire and racing enthusiast William K. Vanderbilt, the contest was an incentive to the American automobile industry to challenge the supremacy of European carmakers. The prize was a huge sterling silver goblet and a purse of ten thousand dollars. The race was also a laboratory for auto design. Run on a three-hundred-mile course, over a period of five hours, it was a test of a car's durability equal to one hundred thousand miles of routine driving. The races of 1904 and 1905 had been won by the French.

The pride of the Frayer-Miller Company, each of the three racers was little more than an engine and a pair of bucket seats set on a frame with wheels. Each part was built for speed and endurance. "As the race grew nearer," Eddie recalled, "it was all we talked about." Frayer's plan was to take the three cars to Long Island by train. But as the cars were being loaded onto a freight car, he turned to Eddie and asked, "How long would it take you to run home and get your bag? I want to take you with me."

When they arrived in New York and unloaded the cars, Frayer sprang another surprise. Handing Eddie a leather helmet and a pair of Zeiss goggles, he said, "I want you to ride with me as my mechanic. I know that you're young, and this is new to you, but you've got a good head on your shoulders, and I think you're going to make a good mechanic."

Standing by the powerful little car, Frayer explained Eddie's role. His major concern was oil and gasoline pressure. If either fell below the minimum, he would have to pump it back up. Watching the tires for wear was also a task, especially the rear pair. He would know if the rubber began to wear down because the underlying fabric was a different color. With Frayer's eyes concentrated on the roadway, Eddie would have to alert him to cars trying to pass. A single tap on Frayer's knee would signal someone was attempting to go by. Two meant tire trouble. In ordinary use a tire could be expected to last for two thousand miles. The maximum speed in a race was one hundred miles an hour. Maximum rate of the Frayer engine was eight hundred to one thousand revolutions per minute at a top speed of seventy miles an hour.

The first practice run went smoothly, with Frayer feeling his way around the course as Eddie sat in the right-side bucket seat, the wind hitting his face, leaning with Frayer on each turn and watching the pressure gauges and tires, and exulting in the joy of motion. On the second day of testing on a stretch of Jericho Turnpike, Frayer opened the car up. As they entered a turn, Eddie sensed they were going too fast in a car with no brakes. Frayer yelled, "Hold on!"

Careening off the road, the car dipped hard into a ditch, bounded out, and headed for a sand dune. Frayer tried to steer around it, but the wheels bit into the sand, flipping the car over and hurling Frayer and Eddie out. To Eddie's amazement, he and Frayer got only a few bruises and the upturned car sustained easily repairable dents and scratches. It was ready for the next day's test run, again on Jericho Turnpike. This time it took the curve smoothly at fifty miles an hour and clocked a long stretch of straightaway at seventy. "The sensation of speed," Eddie noted, "brought intense exhilaration."

Then he saw in front of them "a guinea fowl with an unfortunate sense of timing" as the bird led a flock of hens across the road. When the car mowed them down, bits of birds and feathers flew into the air. Sucked into the air-cooled engine's blower, one of the birds was defeathered, broiled, and carved into bits in a split second. With the blower also torn to pieces, the car had to limp back to the shop. "Stinking to high heaven," Eddie recorded, "every square inch of surface had to be scraped and cleaned."

On the day of the race, Eddie saw twelve cars from the United States that would compete with those of France, Germany, and England. He was fascinated by a chain-driven Locomobile, a huge Pope-Toledo, and a modified stock model of Oldsmobile. From France came a Panhard and a Darracq, and from Germany

a "monstrous" De Dietrich and a Mercedes. Italy's entry was a
Fiat. Each nation was limited to five entries. At the drop of a flag
by well-known starter Fred Wagner, they would enter the course
at thirty-second intervals. When Wagner flagged Frayer's racer
onto the track, Eddie sat beside him "as tight as a spoke in wire
wheel." Oil and gas were okay. The tires looked fine.

Eddie vividly recalled his first auto race this way more than
forty years later:

> *Frayer got everything out of the car that it could
> give. Perhaps he asked for a little too much on one
> curve, for the right rear tire blew out. Our rear end
> swung to the right, then fishtailed down the road at 60
> miles an hour as Frayer fought the wheel to keep from
> pulling into the trees. When he had the car under con-
> trol, he pulled to the side. In a road race, one changed
> a tire whenever it blew. We had rehearsed the procedure
> over and over and were soon rolling again.*
>
> *We hadn't continued much farther before I saw that
> the temperature gauge was in the red. I could sense
> Frayer's eyes flicking over it. I made certain the oil pres-
> sure was up, but there was nothing further either of us
> could do. The pressure against my face decreased.*
>
> *At first I heard only a faint knocking. It became
> louder and louder. Something was pounding in the en-
> gine. We were losing speed quickly. Behind us a car was
> coming up fast. I tapped Frayer on his knee. He nodded
> and gave way, and the big Loco thundered by at a
> steady roar.*
>
> *Mr. Frayer continued on. He knew the race was over,
> but it hurt too much to quit. The pounding grew worse.
> Any second now the piston would freeze tight to the
> cylinder wall. He sighed, let up on the accelerator,
> pushed in the clutch, turned off the ignition and coasted
> to a stop by the side of the road. We sat there for a long
> moment, and then he sighed and looked at me.*

"We're through," he said.

That was all. A year of seven-day weeks, an outlay of $50,000, or more, and he hadn't even finished the elimination run. Yet his only remark was that quiet "We're through." I never forgot it. Gradually, over the years, the significance of that remark sank in, and I drew inspiration from it. To spell it out:

Try like hell to win, but don't cry if you lose.

One of the Frayer-Miller cars, driven by Frank Lawell, survived the elimination race and competed for the Vanderbilt Cup. It ran well until the seventh lap, when the crankshaft broke. It was the last race for a Frayer-Miller car, but most of the automotive features Lee Frayer had pioneered became standard in race cars: left-hand drive, wire wheels, low-slung chassis, and an air-cooled engine.

About a year later, Frayer was asked to join the Columbus Buggy Company. One of the city's major industries, it was nationally renowned for carriages and bicycles, but it was about to get into the automobile business with an electric coupe that was simply a motorized version of the famous Columbus high-wheeled buggy. The offer came to Frayer from the president of the company, Clinton D. Firestone. Frayer would be chief engineer with full authority to design and build "an honest-to-God automobile." Accepting the job, he invited Eddie to come along for a "whopping" twenty dollars a week. At the age of seventeen he was put in charge of the firm's experimental department, with full authority over a staff of fifteen men.

Testing "those interesting little buggies over the streets of Columbus and out into the countryside," Eddie discerned ways to improve the performance of the five-passenger Firestone-Columbus touring car, a "mechanical masterpiece" that would sell for under two thousand dollars. Its formal introduction was at the Chicago automobile show in January 1909. Appointed "demonstrator-driver," Eddie took potential customers for rides through the city streets. The result was eleven sales, with three going to the Fife and Miller Company of Dallas, Texas. But a week after they arrived in June, Firestone received a telegram furiously complaining that all three cars had been taken on test runs and each engine had frozen after going only ten miles.

Dispatched to Dallas, Eddie saw immediately that by adding cold water to overheated engines the pistons shrank to a tolerance at which they would function with sufficient clearance even in the extreme summer heat of Texas. With the three cars sold, the dealer agreed to order more, but only if Eddie remained in Dallas to help sell them. Delighted with Eddie's successes, Firestone appointed him manager of the firm's north central region. Based in Omaha, Nebraska, with a sales staff of six men, at a salary of $150 a month, he took immediate interest in a new sport racing that was increasingly popular throughout the Middle West: dirt track racing.

Carmakers saw speed events with stock cars as a means to promote sales, so it was natural that Eddie should strip one of the CBC's cars to little more than a framework and an engine on wheels. Then he rebuilt some of the weaker parts of the car, redesigned others, put a bucket seat on the chassis, and gave the car a coat of white paint. He drove it wearing white linen overalls. Grown two inches and with added weight, at nineteen he was six feet, two inches and well over two hundred pounds. Driving his Firestone-Columbus and winning every race he entered, he found that victory translated not only into sales, but prize money. In two days of racing at the Aksarben Festival (Nebraska spelled backward), he made close to fifteen hundred dollars. The combination of his salary and winnings provided enough money to pay off the mortgage on the Rickenbacher house in Columbus and retire all other family debts. But all his races weren't easy. "Some of the tracks," he was quick to note, "amounted to invitations to commit suicide."

In July of that year he received a telegram from Lee Frayer. It asked, "How would you like to swap dust with Barney Oldfield?" Would Eddie be at all interested, Frayer wondered, in coming to Columbus to take on Oldfield in a hundred-mile event on the

Columbus Driving Track in August? When Eddie Rickenbacher was thirteen years old, Barney Oldfield was already hailed as "America's premier driver" for having become the first man in America to drive a gasoline powered automobile around a dirt track at a mile a minute. The car was named "999" after a record-breaking locomotive of the New York Central Line. Built by Henry Ford, the vehicle had been given to Oldfield, a twenty-four-year-old bicycle rider from Toledo, Ohio, in hopes that it would result in sales of Ford cars. In August 1903, at "A Carnival of Speed at Yonkers Track" in New York, Oldfield had clocked 64.52 miles an hour. Two years later he held most of the dirt track speed records. Boys in race car goggles everywhere hero-worshiped him and recited a bit of doggerel that declared:

> *We love his grimy, goggled face,*
> *His matchless daring in a race.*

Eager to test his skills against Oldfield in their home state, Eddie arrived in Columbus to be greeted by Frayer and a Red Wing race car with a fifty-horsepower engine. With Frayer in another Red Wing, Oldfield would be driving a one-hundred-horsepower Knox. Frayer's strategy was for Eddie to "make the most speed on the inside fence without skidding or slowing down." Pushing hard, Eddie would force Oldfield to start pressing. "My guess," Frayer said, "is that his tires won't be able to stand the gaff like yours will. We'll call it the Rickenbacher Razzmatazz."

On race day, the largest crowd in the history of the track awaited the contest between the premier racer in America and the hometown duo of Frayer and Rickenbacher. Eddie wrote of the showdown:

> *It went just the way Frayer had predicted. Well before the midpoint of the race, Oldfield blew a tire. He was a lap ahead, but, by the time he had changed the tire and gotten back on the track, I was even with him. Again he pushed past me, and again blew a tire. At 75 miles I was leading. Oldfield was catching up fast and Frayer was*

*holding a steady third. Oldfield blew another tire. Now
I had him. Our plan was working fine, except that I was
going to be first and Frayer second. But, with only a few
laps to go, one of my connecting rods broke and, clat-
tering and banging, I had to pull over to the side.
Frayer came on strong, and Oldfield could not catch
him. Our combination had won the race. The Columbus 100-mile race was my first big event. I hoped it
would not be my last.*

With racing season finished, Eddie faced a long winter of selling cars back in Nebraska. Then came a letter from Frayer about
"a big new Indianapolis Speedway" that had its debut in 1909
"with a mishmash" of forty-two events in a three-day schedule on
a racecourse made of crushed stone and tar. But in 1911, Frayer
reported, the track was planning to feature a five-hundred-mile
race to be held on May 30. Frayer planned to enter it, with Eddie
as relief driver. Thrilled, Eddie looked forward to "rubbing el-
bows with the great racing drivers" of the day, including Spencer
Wishart, David Bruce Brown, Wild Bob Burman, Ralph De Palma,
Louis Chevrolet, Ralph Mulford, and the chief engineer of the
Marmon Motor Company, Ray Harroun. They would be competing on a new surface consisting of 3.2 million paving bricks that
was two and a half miles around, with two long and two short
straightaways that were 50 feet wide, but 60 feet in four corner
turns pitched at nine degrees.

When Eddie and Frayer arrived at Indianapolis, they learned
that Ray Harroun had come to the race with two innovations. He
would be in his car without a riding mechanic to keep an eye on
cars trying to overtake him. Harroun would track the competition
himself by using "a peculiar contraption" that had never been
seen on a car: a "rearview mirror."

For the first Indianapolis 500, the car that set the pace by leading the racers once around the two-and-a-half-mile oval was
driven by the man who had built the raceway, Carl Fisher. As the
race began at 10:00 A.M., Frayer was at the wheel. Eddie watched
the gauges and tires and would spell Frayer by taking over at

designated distances. It was while Eddie was behind the wheel
that a car driven by Art Grenier lost a wheel, lurched wildly, and
crashed. The impact threw Grenier's mechanic through the air
and into auto racing history as the Indy 500's first fatality. Taking
over the Red Wing from Eddie at the four-hundred-mile mark,
Frayer competed the race, placing eleventh. Ray Harroun won it
with an average speed of 74.59 miles an hour.

With the excitement of big-time racing in his blood, Eddie
found it hard to go back to selling cars and competing on dirt
tracks. When Lee Frayer declared that his own racing days were
over, the Columbus Buggy Company's Red Wing racer in the 1912
Indianapolis 500 was driven by Eddie. He was in fourth place
when a crankshaft bearing burned out. It was the end of the
race for him, and for the Red Wing. The company that built it,
Firestone-Columbus, soon went out of business, becoming, as
Eddie noted a little wistfully, "just another of the 1,600 discontin-
ued American automobile brands."

As for himself, Eddie "was tired of the constant entertaining
that was part of automobile selling." He liked racing "good cars
fast, to pit my automobile knowledge and driving skill and plain
old guts against the world's best." He enjoyed the "racing fraternity" and wanted to be part of it. But how might he break into it?
During this period he had become "increasingly interested" in
the Mason Automobile Company. A firm that had formed in Wa-
terloo, Iowa, then shifted its operations to Des Moines, it made a
two-cylinder, chain-drive auto called the Mason. The chief engineer was a brilliant young man in his twenties named Fred Duesenberg. Determined to join the Iowa company, Eddie sent a
telegram to the Columbus Buggy Company announcing that he
was resigning (again) to take a job he didn't have, then bought
a one-way train ticket to Des Moines. A surprised Duesenberg
informed him that there was no place at Mason for a driver, but
because of Eddie's other experience, offered him a job as a mechanic. It paid three dollars a day, sixty less per month than
Eddie had garnered as an auto salesman.

A year later, on the eve of a three-hundred-mile race at Sioux
City, Iowa, Duesenberg's Mason Automobile Company had three

sleek racing cars, an assortment of spare parts, and a seven-man racing team. With total liquid assets of seven silver dollars, it was on the brink of bankruptcy. To help keep the firm afloat, Eddie had poured all his savings into it while working sixteen-hour days and lunching on a chocolate milkshake fortified by two raw eggs and consumed on the job as he hand-built the racers. But an attempt to win cash and prestige at the Indianapolis 500 proved to be "a waste of time and money." By the time of the Sioux City race, the company was so broke that the cars had to be stored under the grandstand while the team slept on cots.

The surface of the Sioux City track was in such horrible condition that Eddie called it "gumbo." To protect the drivers of the three cars from rocks that flew up from the surface, Eddie fashioned some wire mesh windshields. The chief competition would be Spencer Wishart's powerful Mercer, fastest of all the entries. The only chance for Duesenberg's team to win was to follow the strategy used against Barney Oldfield at Columbus and hope that Wishart's powerful car would blow out its tires on curves.

On a bright and sunny day, with the stands packed with spectators and reporters who had come "looking for blood," the race began as Eddie and Thayer hoped. From the start it was a duel between Eddie's Mason and Wishart's Mercer, with Wishart in front on straightaways and Eddie coming even on curves, lap after lap. With five miles to go and holding a slight edge, Eddie saw to his horror that a rock from the track had struck his riding mechanic, Eddie O'Donnell, on the forehead and knocked him out. Forced to control the car's oil pressure himself, and determined not to stop and lose the prize money, Eddie finished forty seconds ahead of Wishart. A second Mason came in third, for a total purse of $12,500. Feeling rich, and with O'Donnell conscious again, Eddie took the team to celebrate solvency at the best hotel in Sioux City with hot baths and a fine dinner.

The next morning brought a rude awakening. Wishart had lodged a protest, claiming that he had been credited with one lap too few. A check of the race's time record sheets seemed to validate the protest. But after Eddie demanded that they be looked at again, Wishart conceded that he'd been mistaken. Eddie's response was ungracious. Demonstrating a character trait in the form of blunt speaking for which he would often find himself faulted throughout his life, he told an audience at a banquet in his honor, "I know for a fact that officials sent here [to Sioux City] from other cities were responsible for the trouble, and I also know that some of the officials placed bets on the final outcome of the race, and on a certain car to finish in first place."

With one newspaper headline declaring RICK MAKES UGLY CHARGE, he posed for a photograph at the railroad station as he accepted the winner's check for ten thousand dollars, wearing a strawhat and blue summer suit. Six weeks later he entered another race with Wishart and his big Mercer, but not on an oval track. This contest was a road race at Elgin, Illinois. Again driving Duesenberg's car, he alternated the lead with Wishart for 180 miles. But as he was gaining on the Mercer on a straightaway, he watched Wishart's car wobble, swerve, smash into a tree, and wrap itself around it, killing Wishart instantly. Forty-two miles and a few minutes later, a car driven by Bill Endicott cut in front of the Duesenberg, forcing Eddie to careen into a ditch and toward a telephone pole. Dodging it, he sideswiped a fence, only to see another pole, then a third. Lurching onto the road with a bent rear axle, he ended the race at the 202-mile mark.

Despite bad breaks and the constant danger, Eddie felt he was part of a "golden period." Racing was fun. He relished the rewards of recognition and money, but most of all he believed that he and his competitors were making a contribution to the automotive industry in a "clean, honest sport" with never a suspicion of a "fix." The drivers knew and respected one another, and each was prepared to sacrifice himself to save someone else's life. But neither were they averse to taking advantage of a rival's weakness. They were part of a daredevil fraternity in what was now a major sport in which drivers were lionized.

To sportswriters, Eddie Rickenbacher was "the Speedy Swiss," "the Big Teuton," "the Dutch Demon," or just "Rick." One imaginative scribe for a Los Angeles newspaper concocted a story that he was actually Baron Edward von Rickenbacher, a Prussian nobleman whose stern father, "a colonel of uhlans," had cut him off without a penny, forcing "Baron Edward" to make good on his own in the United States.

After a German racing star, Christian Lautenschlager, won the French Grand Prix and two other Germans came in second and third at the same time that Eddie had won in Sioux City, an exultant writer offered a poem in the July 9, 1914, edition of the magazine *Motor Age*:

> *All Germany is on a spree*
>   *And other lands is scorning;*
> *The Teuton clan now leads the van*
>   *While France is wearing mourning:*
> *One, two and three in the Grand Prix*
>   *First also at Sioux City—*
> *Just quaff your beer, don't shed a tear;*
>   *The Dutch ask not for pity.*

> *Great Kaiser Bill has had his fill*
>   *Of Pilsner and lager;*
> *He loudly boasts and drinks deep toasts*
>   *In praise of Lautenschlager;*
> *And across the sea a victory*
>   *Has led this peace-plan knocker*
> *To plan to knight in his delight*
>   *That Deutscher, Rickenbacher.*

Eleven days before the poem appeared, a *New York Times* headline had blared:

HEIR TO AUSTRIA'S THRONE IS SLAIN
WITH HIS WIFE BY A BOSNIAN YOUTH
TO AVENGE SEIZURE OF HIS COUNTRY

In Sarajevo, capital of Serbia, someone had thrown a bomb at an auto carrying Archduke Franz Ferdinand, heir to the Hapsburg Empire. It bounced off the side of the royal vehicle and exploded against a following auto, injuring two officers. That evening as Ferdinand and his wife were driven through the city again, seventeen-year-old Gavrilo Princip, a Bosnian Serb who had a role in the failed attempt at bombing, took advantage of the slowing of the car to step toward it with a pistol in hand. He fired two shots. One struck the archduke, who bled to death as he was being rushed to a hospital. The other killed his wife. Over the next month the nations of Europe went to war. Austrian troops attacked Belgrade, Germans marched into Luxembourg and made a demand for passage across Belgium, and Britain demanded observation of Belgian neutrality. When Kaiser Wilhelm paid no heed, Britain and France declared war. In the United States, the president, Woodrow Wilson, announced a policy of neutrality.

Among the effects of war mobilization on a French automaker, Peugeot, was a sudden need for a man to drive its entry in the Corona road race in California. Regarding the Peugeot as a superior car, and preferring the challenge and the variety of road racing to "going around and around" on a track "like a ball on a string," Eddie put in a bid and was accepted, with expenses paid and half the earnings. Although the Peugeot jumped off to an immediate lead, the engine soon weakened and that was the end of Eddie's race.

Having attained the status of racing car celebrity with his name appearing in newspapers, and deciding that "Edward Rickenbacher" looked "a little plain" in print, he decided he ought to have a middle name. After inserting several initials, he found "V" pleasing to his eye. Trying names that started with the letter, he settled on "Vernon." Other decisions made at this time were that no important decision should be made before noon, and that ideas that came to him in the night should be examined and considered in the light of day before they were put into effect. In pondering the numerous close calls with being killed that had been a hallmark of his life, he concluded that because "the Lord above had shown a special interest" in protecting him, it was "about time that I began to show some appreciation for this Divine consideration," and that the least he could do was to improve the condition of his body and mind that the Lord was obviously saving for some purpose. As a result, he began exercising for fifteen minutes every morning and night, a routine he would continue for the rest of his life, along with praying on his knees before going to bed. He also wrote out a list of rules by which to live. The first was: "Always conduct yourself as a gentleman. If you do not, you not only inflict discredit upon yourself, but also upon automobile racing, the means by which you earn your livelihood."

This Rickenbacher credo was distributed to the men who worked for him at his new job. He took it after the Corona race in order to join Barney Oldfield and another driver, Bill Carlson, in racing for the Maxwell Automobile Company, even though he knew that Maxwells were not superior cars. The Rickenbacher rules were:

> *If you don't like the way we do business, if you don't like your teammates, don't grouse and go around with a long face. Quit this job and get another one somewhere else. The trouble with a lot of people is that they are not willing to begin anywhere in order to get a fighting chance. My advice is: Throw away that false pride. No honest work is beneath you. Jump in and demonstrate your superiority. Once you get on the payroll, make up your mind to master everything about your job, and get ready for the job at the top. Your particular task is merely one end of a trail that leads to the driver's seat. That is my philosophy of success. It works. I have tried and proved it.*

The job proved short lived. Maxwell chose to get out of racing. Using $25,000 in savings, Eddie bought the company's four racers with the intention of forming his own racing team, but he recognized that if his plan were to be realized, he needed much more money to buy spare tires and parts, and to pay drivers and cover travel expenses. Seeking financial backing, he turned

to Carl Fisher and one of his three partners in the Indianapolis
Speedway, James A. Allison. The others were Frank Wheeler of
the Wheeler-Schebler Carburetor Company and Arthur Newby
of the American Chain Company. The four men had created
the Prest-O-Lite Company, which built gas tanks carried on
running boards for the gas headlights of all autos at that time.
With finances in hand, work began to prepare four Maxwells.
The plan was to enter two of them in alternating races, a
scheme that would allow participation in every major race in the
country.

Winning seven of sixteen meets in 1916, the Maxwell Special
team split $78,000, giving Eddie an income that year of $60,000.
Among the records he'd set were:

> One-mile circular track, Providence, Rhode Island:
>   45 4/5 seconds;
> 100 miles on a one-mile circular track, Providence:
>   86 minutes, 2/5 seconds;
> Two-mile dirt track, Sioux City, Iowa: 1 minute,
>   5 seconds;
> Two-mile speedway, New York: 1 minute,
>   3 4/5 seconds; and
> 300 miles on a mile-and-a-quarter track, Omaha:
>   an average of 93 mph.

Deciding to try his skills in California, he joined a team of
Duesenbergs for the Grand Prize and Vanderbilt Cup road races
to be held in Santa Monica and quickly found himself in the publicity spotlight that was shining on a new class of American
celebrities known as "movie stars" in a section of Los Angeles
called Hollywood. Five years earlier the Horsley brothers, incor-
porating themselves as the Nester Company, had leased an old
tavern and converted it into a studio to make a cowboy picture,
The Law of the Range. They were quickly followed west by Cecil
B. De Mille and other producers. Among them was a moviemaker

who made comedies that featured madcap car chase scenes in which "jalopies" dodged and weaved amid other autos and street-cars on Los Angeles streets. Visiting the Mack Sennett studio, Eddie watched the antics of Roscoe "Fatty" Arbuckle, Snub Pollard, Charlie Murray, Al St. John, beautiful Mabel Norman, and a chubby former Broadway comedienne, Marie Dressler.

A few months earlier, film actress Irene Tams had sent Eddie a telegram telling him she loved speed and admired "endeavor" and was so "interested in your welfare that, if you will cease racing," she would marry him. Eddie's night-letter reply said he was "grateful" for the offer, but that "I cannot at this time see my way clear to give up racing, for a woman is only a woman, but my soul mate is a racing car."

Several days before the first race at Santa Monica, while driving for pleasure among the orange groves surrounding the town of Riverside, he saw an airplane parked near a small hangar on a grass field. Never having seen a plane up close, he swung his car off the road and drove across the field to the hangar. As he bounded from the car, a young man stepped from the hangar and surprised him by sticking out a hand in greeting. "Hi, Eddie, I'm glad to meet you," he said. "My name is Glenn Martin. Would you like to take a ride?"

Looking anxiously at the two-seat, double-wing plane was a daredevil auto racer who had always had a fear of heights. Despite his experiment with flying a canvas-winged bicycle from a barn roof, he suffered "a galloping case of acrophobia" that left him dizzy if he simply looked down from a tall building. With a combination of pride in being known for bravery on a racetrack and a life of craving for a new adventure, he replied, "Sure."

Recalling this chance beginning of a life devoted to aviation in which he would become a hero in wartime and a legendary flier in his own time, Eddie wrote:

> *I climbed into the rear seat. Glenn spun the propeller*
> *to start the engine and jumped into the front seat. It was*
> *a smooth takeoff. Finally I worked up my nerve and*

looked over the side. I was pleasantly amazed to find that I had no feeling of dizziness. We stayed up for about thirty minutes as Glenn pointed out the sights at the top of his voice. The whole flight was fascinating. He did not put the plane through any maneuvers; just staying up was enough in those pioneering days.

Finally he brought the plane down for a landing. The way the ground came up swiftly to meet us gave me a terrifying moment. If I had been at the controls, I would have tried to level off while we were still one hundred feet in the air. We taxied back to the hangar and climbed out. I told him how much I had enjoyed flying.

"But I wish you would tell me something," I said a little sheepishly. After all, I was known as a death-defying racing driver. "Why is it that I didn't have a fear of height up there?"

Martin explained that in a plane there was "nothing to judge height by because there's no edge to look over." Eddie thanked Martin again and hurried back to the auto racing track "in order to do a little bragging to the other drivers" that he had flown in an airplane.

While out for another auto tour of the California countryside, Eddie noticed a lone, single-seat military plane parked in the middle of a cow pasture with the pilot standing next to it, forlornly poking at the engine. When Eddie stopped to ask if he could be of assistance, the pilot introduced himself as Maj. T. F. Dodd of the Army Air Service. "The engine runs," he said, "but it doesn't deliver enough power to stay aloft. Do you know anything about engines?"

Diagnosing trouble with the ignition system, Eddie found that a coupling had slipped off the magneto and quickly fixed it, then watched admiringly and longingly as the plane took off.

On November 16, 1916, in a 195-mile road race, the Duesenberg's engine failed after only 49 miles. Two days later Eddie had to drop out midway through a 403-mile course. After winning the final race of 1916 at Ascot Park, he was the country's third-ranked driver. What he and his fans and an adoring press didn't know was that he had run his last auto race.

CHAPTER 3

Taking Wing

L ATE IN THE 1916 RACING SEASON, EDDIE MET A HANDSOME, POISED Englishman named Louis Coatalen. Introducing himself as managing director of the Sunbeam Motor Works in England, he said, "There is no more racing in England because of the war. However, we would like to continue racing in this country. May I ask if you have made plans for the 1917 season?"

Eddie replied that he hadn't, but that he had raced against Sunbeam cars and had great respect for them. If Eddie were interested in joining the Sunbeam organization, said Coatalen, "I'm sure we could work out a mutually agreeable arrangement. We should like you to come to England at our expense and work with us in preparing our cars."

Never having crossed a body of water wider than the Mississippi River, Eddie was aware, along with the rest of an outraged country, that a German submarine had sunk the liner *Lusitania* on May 7, 1915, killing 1,200 passengers and ship's crew, including 128 Americans. Despite the dangers of sailing across the Atlantic Ocean in wartime, he accepted Coatalen's offer and booked onto the small American liner *St. Louis*. Arriving in Liverpool, he immediately found himself the main character in a comedy that might have been scripted by his Hollywood friend Mack Sennett.

While still on the ship, a British official who was suspicious of a passenger with a German-looking name demanded, "What is your purpose in England? Don't you know there's a war on?"

Conducted to another cabin, Eddie learned that his inquisitor had a dossier on him that included the newspaper spoof identifying him as Baron von Rickenbacher. Suspected of being a spy, he was strip-searched, detained, and forbidden to contact anyone. Finally permitted to go ashore for Christmas Day, he was accompanied by a pair of British agents. Persuaded that he was not a spy, they let him call Coatalen at his home in Wolverhampton, and then to meet with Coatalen the next day at the Savoy Hotel in London. Released to Coatalen's custody, he was ordered to report twice a day to the police station at Wolverhampton.

After working during the week at the Sunbeam factory, he returned to London, reported his presence to the constabulary, and checked into the Savoy for the weekend. From his room overlooking the Thames River, he watched Royal Flying Corps training planes and deduced that an airfield was nearby. Learning that it was close to an auto track, Brooklands Speedway, he was amazed that it was unguarded and that he could walk right in and stroll around. He admired the airplanes and envied the young men who were learning to fly them. Listening to some of the older pilots who had flown in combat and were now instructors, he thrilled to the stories of aerial warfare. When he told Coatalen that he wanted to join "those brave Englishmen and fight the Germans in the air over France," Coatalen replied, "You can serve us better behind the wheel of a Sunbeam Six."

On February 3, 1917, after Germany declared unrestricted submarine warfare on the high seas and the United States severed diplomatic relations with Berlin, the German government announced that Americans would have five days to leave England. "That was the end of the Sunbeam racing team," Eddie noted. Rushing to join a flood of his countrymen sailing for home, he managed to book an upper berth on the *St. Louis*. Again interrogated, he was allowed to go, but warned that he would be kept under surveillance. He left believing that "the Allied cause was just" and with a determination to organize an air squadron of American racing drivers and use his celebrity status to persuade the United States to get into the war. He would do so by speaking in New York, Columbus, Detroit, and Chicago, confident that "the glamor of racing" would attract large crowds and lengthy stories in newspapers.

The first to appear, on February 18, was a *New York Times* article. Headlined FLYING CORPS OF DARING DRIVERS PLAN IF WAR COMES, it reported, "There is a movement among racing drivers and their mechanics to enter the flying corps of the United States Army if this country should be drawn into the war. Eddie Rickenbacher [note: Eddie still spelled his name with an "h"; he would change it to "k" a year later], who recently returned from a two months' stay in England, where he found that aviation had enlisted the services of many men formerly connected with motoring, is the sponsor of the plan."

"If war is declared," Eddie was quoted, "I will enlist at once for aviation work."

At the time of this promise, the United States Army had been developing an aviation branch for less than nine years. Its first aircraft had been a modified version of the plane flown by Ohio bicycle makers Orville and Wilbur Wright. In raw and windy weather on December 17, 1903, at Kitty Hawk, North Carolina, their first demonstration of controlled-power flight, with Orville aboard the kitelike machine, had lasted twelve seconds and covered 120 feet. In a fourth and last demonstration of the day, Wilbur had stayed airborne for fifty-nine seconds and 852 feet. The plane they delivered to the army at Fort Myer, Virginia, was flown by Lt. Thomas E. Selfridge. Knowing more about flying than anyone in the army, he was the first army officer to have manned a powered airplane, the *White Wing*, which had been developed by the Aerial Experiment Association. The group's president was the man who was credited with inventing the telephone, Alexander Graham Bell. That test of *White Wing* had occurred on December 6, 1907, eleven days before the Wrights brought their airplane to Fort Myer. With Orville piloting and

Selfridge aboard as an observer, it crashed, seriously injuring Wright and giving Selfridge the distinction of being the first U.S. Army aviator to be killed.

Because of the accident, the army postponed delivery of the Wright brothers' plane pending a series of flight performance tests. They were conducted from July 27 to 30, 1909. As part of the Wright's contract with the army, the brothers were expected to train two officers as pilots. Instruction began on October 8. At College Park, Maryland, Lt. Frank P. Lahm and Lt. Frederic E. Humphreys trained for a little more than three hours each before making solo flights. As part of their instruction, Wilbur Wright showed them how to cut the motor and glide safely to the ground, a skill that was essential because of unpredictable engine performance.

Satisfied with the plane, the army purchased it for $30,000. On November 3, Lt. George C. Sweet of the U.S. Navy was invited to take a ride in the plane, enshrining him in navy history as the first navy officer to fly. Use of airplanes as weapons of war was first tested on August 20, 1910, when a Springfield .30-caliber rifle was fired from a plane by Lt. Jacob B. Fickel at Sheepshead Bay, New York. The pilot was another aviation pioneer, Glenn Curtiss. Dropping a bomb from a plane was demonstrated at an air meet in San Francisco on January 15, 1911, by Lt. Myron S. Crissy. He dropped it over the side of a Wright airplane piloted by P. O. Parmalee. The following day, at an altitude of 2,000 feet, Lt. G.E.M. Kelly, an infantry officer, took the first reconnaissance photo to locate troops in the San Bruno Hills, California. Two days later Eugene Ely, a Curtiss exhibition pilot, landed on the after-deck of an anchored battleship, the *Pennsylvania*, and then took off.

On March 3, 1911, Congress appropriated $125,000 for army air operations for fiscal year 1912, to be established as part of the Signal Corps. The following month the army opened its first permanent flying school at College Park. It was there on October 10 that a bombsight and dropping device designed by Riley E. Scott was tested. The next week at Beaumont, Texas, the first aerial reconnaissance using a motion picture camera was carried out by cameraman E. R. Shaw during a flight from Beaumont to New York. But what would become an enduring love affair between the army's air service and motion pictures had occurred on Long Island, New York, on September 30, 1911. After an air meet held by the Aero Club of America, a young army lieutenant, H. H. Arnold, known to his colleagues as "Hap," had been employed as a "stunt man" for the leading actor in a pioneer film about airplanes titled *The Military Air Scout.* Arnold later demonstrated how well he knew how to fly by taking a Wright plane to a record-setting altitude of 4,674 feet and maintaining it for fifty-nine minutes at the army's aviation school at Augusta, Georgia (January 25, 1912). Five years later Eddie Rickenbacker would meet Arnold, by then a captain, when Eddie was racing at San Diego, California, around the time of Eddie's first ride in an airplane.

Recalling that experience upon his return from England in February 1917, Eddie took liberties with the truth by telling the reporters who met him at the dock in New York, "I have already had some experience."

He then announced, "I leave for the West tomorrow, where I shall see many of the boys and at once put the matter up to them. I think many of them are looking at it just as I do. War would practically put a stop to racing and we have a training that our country would need in time of war. We are experts at judging speed and in motor knowledge. This is also true of the mechanicians, and I am sure we could all quickly qualify for aviation work. I expect to get up a body of not less than fifty of us who will volunteer if war is declared."

During the tour, Eddie suspected that he was still being watched. The intuition proved right in Los Angeles when a British agent sidled up to him in the lobby of his hotel. "I just want to tell you," he said, "that my government and I are now fully satisfied as to your status as a loyal and patriotic American. But I do want to thank you for the wonderful trip that I've had following you about this interesting country."

Having recruited race car drivers to join a group called the Aero Reserves of America, including Ralph De Palma, Ray Harroun, Ralph Mulford, and other famous drivers, Eddie took his proposal to the head of the Army Signal Corps. Brigadier General George D. Squier told him that the army was "not interested in racing drivers as pilots."

To Eddie's astonishment, one of Squier's aides explained, "We do not believe that it would be wise for a pilot to have any knowledge of engines and mechanics. Airplane engines are always breaking down, and a man who knew a great deal about engines would know if his engine wasn't functioning correctly and be hesitant about going into combat."

Disillusioned, Eddie decided to wait and see "what would develop." Meanwhile he had to earn a living. Consequently, he agreed to drive a German Mercedes in a five-hundred-mile race on Memorial Day in Cincinnati, Ohio. Returning to his hotel room after a day of practicing with the Mercedes, he found the phone ringing. The caller was Maj. Burgess Lewis, an old friend and racing enthusiast. "Eddie," he said, "we're organizing a secret sailing to France. We need staff drivers. Would you like to go?"

"It sounds wonderful," Eddie replied, "but I'd like to think about it overnight."

He told Lewis he would have his answer at eight in the morning, then spent the night "weighing the pros and cons." Although the United States had finally declared war on Germany in April, no troops had been sent to France. Liking the idea of being among the first, he figured that if he could get overseas, he might find a way to get into the fight as an aviator. But if he wanted to go, Lewis informed him in the morning, he would have to leave for New York right away. This meant finding a replacement to drive the Mercedes in the race. After "working like a beaver until noon turning the operation over to the crew chief," Eddie headed for New York, but with a brief stop in Columbus to visit his mother, without telling her he was en route to France. At noon the next day he was a sergeant in the U.S. Army. Less than twenty-fours later he was on a ship bound for France in the first contingent of the American Expeditionary Force under the command of Gen. John J. "Black Jack" Pershing. The headquarters commander was "a tall captain named George S. Patton." To Eddie's surprise, the aviation officer was the Army Air Service major whose engine Eddie had gotten running in a California cow pasture, T. F. Dodd, now a colonel.

After landing at Liverpool, the American Expeditionary Force went overland to a port on the English Channel. When it landed in France on June 26, Pershing recalled the French officer who had fought in the American Revolution by announcing, "Lafayette, we are here." Expecting that Pershing would have the best possible staff driver, war correspondents assumed that it was the famous Eddie Rickenbacker, but the officer to whom he was assigned was, to Eddie, an even more impressive figure. Ardent advocate of airpower, Col. William "Billy" Mitchell was the son of a wealthy Wisconsin senator. Enlisting as a private in the Spanish-American War, he was given a commission at the intervention of his father and joined the Signal Corps. An outstanding junior officer, he displayed initiative, courage, and leadership. After duty in the Philippines and Alaska, he'd been assigned to the General Staff and was its youngest member. Excited about aviation and its possibilities, he learned to fly in 1916 at the age of thirty-eight. During the month of April 1917 he was the first American army officer to fly over enemy lines in France.

Relieving Major Dodd as aviation officer on June 30, 1917, his first task was to find a location to establish an army aviation advanced training school. The place that he chose while traveling the countryside with Eddie at the wheel of "a big flashy Packard" was a wheat field at the village of Issoudun. With an appropriation by Congress of $640 million, the army's Aviation Section was authorized to expand to 9,989 officers and 87,083 enlisted men. Chief of the Army Air Service was Brig. Gen. William L. Kenly. His appointment made it the first time that control of army air activities was under a single commander. On the day that the United States declared war on the Central Powers, the Aviation Section of the Signal Corps had consisted of thirty-five pilots, 1,987 enlisted men, and fifty-five training planes. Navy and U.S. Marine Corps air units had a combined force of forty-eight officer-pilots, 239 enlisted men, fifty-four planes, one airship, three balloons, and one air station.

The U.S. 1st Aero Squadron arrived in France on August 13, 1917, commanded by Maj. Ralph Royce. Among the arrivals was twenty-year-old Quentin Roosevelt, the youngest of four sons of former president of the United States Theodore Roosevelt. Quentin surveyed the training base at Issoudun and wrote to his father that it was a "hell of a place," and that the flying equipment was "wretched." Eddie Rickenbacker would describe Quentin as "hearty" and "absolutely square in everything he said or did."

Eager to fly himself, and probably envious of the dashing, younger Roosevelt, Eddie was not above using an influential friend to help put him into a cockpit. The friend was New York banker James Miller. Unexpectedly meeting him on the Champs-Élysées in Paris, he learned that Miller was slated to command the Issoudun flying school. Just as surprised to see Eddie, Miller said, "You're just the man I'm looking for. I need an engineering officer."

"I'll be glad to do the best I can to help you," Eddie replied. "But I think an engineering officer for a flying school ought to know how to fly himself."

Miller said, "I'll see what I can do."

When Miller made a formal request to Colonel Mitchell that Eddie be transferred to the flying school, Mitchell was reluctant to lose his famous driver. He asked Eddie, "Do you really want to fly?"

"Anybody can drive your car," Eddie said. "I'd appreciate an opportunity to learn to fly."

A few days later Eddie received orders to report for a physical examination for pilot training. By chance the doctor was an old friend and racing enthusiast. Pronouncing Eddie fit, he overcame an age problem—Eddie was twenty-seven, and the army required its pilots be no older than twenty-five—by recording that Eddie's birth date was October 8, 1892, two years later than his actual one.

Operated by the French with French planes, the primary training school for pilots was at Tours, southwest of Paris. Most of the students were Red Cross drivers. Like Eddie, most had seized an opportunity to get to France before the main American force arrived. Their first planes were the three-cylinder Morane-Saulniers. Their wings were clipped to keep them from taking off. Running back and forth on the ground, they reminded Eddie of grasshoppers.

As an auto racer Eddie had steered cars by turning a wheel. Guiding a Morane-Saulnier was done with foot pedals. After receiving a brief lecture about the plane, but no demonstration, he climbed into it alone. When the sputtering little engine built up sufficient speed, he pushed the control stick forward. Comparing steering with his feet and working the stick to "the old trick of patting your head and rubbing your stomach," he made his first practice run wobbling from side to side with the tail bobbing up and down "like a frightened roadrunner" until he "had the hang of it."

With the practicing in the flightless Morane-Saulnier completed, his next challenge was flying a Caudron. It had "a tremendous wingspread" and was powered by a Le Rhone nine-cylinder engine. A propeller behind the pilot moved the plane at a top speed of eighty miles an hour. At six-foot-two, Eddie had trouble squeezing into a seat designed for smaller men. After two short flights with an instructor, he was declared ready to solo.

"Scared to death," steering with his feet and trying to anticipate the right moment to lift the plane's tail in a crosswind, he started across the grassy field. Lumbering and bumping along, the plane headed straight for a hangar. Barely missing it and scattering observers, he eased back on the stick and the plane lifted into the air. With the Caudron's broad wings assuring that he remained aloft, he followed the instructions he'd been given in lectures: to make his first turn to the right, put the right wing down and push on the left rudder. The plane curved gracefully, but after maneuvering it for several minutes, he faced the reality of an already old aviation joke: "Flying is the second greatest thrill known to man. Landing is the first."

As he prepared to bring the plane down, he remembered his fear during the flight with Glenn Martin that Martin was going to plow the plane into the ground. Now he felt that it was he who was descending too fast. "Scared stiff," he eased back on the stick to let the tail drop and waited for a bump. When he felt none, he looked over the side and found that he was still fifty feet above the ground. With plenty of landing field ahead, he worked the plane down "step by step." Over the next two weeks he clocked twenty-five hours' flying time and "went forth" from the primary training base at Tours with pilot wings pinned to his uniform, wearing the silver bar of first lieutenant in the Signal Corps, and obligated to report to Capt. Jim Miller at Issoudun as engineering officer.

Arriving in the latter part of September, he found the Precision Training School a mire of mud and buildings still under construction. With the first contingent of student pilots scheduled to arrive around the first of November, he was told that his first task was to purchase millions of dollars worth of French aircraft, spare parts, machine tools, and other equipment. He also had to bring in mechanics and get them organized. The planes were the Nieuport 28. The planes had been given to the Americans because the French had adopted the sturdier Spad XIII. Built for use in pursuit, the Nieuports came with a reputation for fragility and a propensity for shedding their wing fabric when making a dive.

Along with the Nieuports the French sent a team of instructors to show the Americans how to fly in formation, teach them dive-bombing techniques, and demonstrate skills required to survive a new kind of combat known as the "dogfight." Quentin Roosevelt wrote to his mother, "The French monitors make us do all the wild flying stunts that were considered tom fool tricks at home." Formation flying looked "fairly easy" from the ground, "but when you get up in the air," he reported, "trying to keep a hundred-and-twenty-horsepower kite in its position in a V formation with planes on either side of you, you begin to hold different ideas as to its easiness."

In these early days of American involvement in a war that was expected to "make the world safe for democracy," Roosevelt and the brash young pilots at Issoudun were unwittingly on their way to creating a romantic legend. Their exploits would enshrine them with heroes of history and fairy tales. College men who'd donned goggles, soft leather helmets, and rakish silk scarves to perform feats of daring and courage in the French skies, they would make a fascinated world believe that in the air, warfare could be as gentlemanly as the sports they had played in college. These novitiate fliers, wrote historian Hans Christian Adamson, were "neat and nifty youngsters, full of ambition." They went to France in 1917 in snug tailor-made uniforms, Sam Browne belts, handmade boots, and custom-made caps. Sons of America's wealthy, they were fresh out of Harvard, Yale, and Princeton. They arrived at Issoudun expecting to find their flying school in full operation. Instead, they saw a mud-hole and a tough Swiss-German chief engineer with a grammar-school education who gave them "grubby" chores. They also found an adjutant named Wiedenbach and officers named Tittel and Speigel. When Capt. James Miller was replaced in October by a German-named major, the would-be aviators called their officers "those five German spies."

A better banker than soldier, Miller was relieved after he'd failed to salute General Pershing. The new boss was Carl Spaatz, nicknamed "Tooey." A year younger than Eddie, he was born June 28, 1891, in Boyertown, Pennsylvania. A graduate of the United States Military Academy, class of 1914, he'd served with the 25th United States Infantry at Schofield Barracks, Hawaii, for a year, when he was detailed as a student in the aviation school at San Diego. He'd served with the 1st Aero Squadron under Gen. John J. Pershing in the punitive expedition into Mexico. Promoted to first lieutenant in 1916, he joined the 3d Aero Squadron in San Antonio, Texas, a year later and was promoted to captain. His first command post in France had been the 31st Aero Squadron. He would run the aviation school at Issoudun continuously, except for a month at the British front, until August 30, 1918. With a temporary promotion to major, he would join the 2d Pursuit Group in September 1918. As a pursuit pilot and flight leader in the 13th Squadron, he would be credited with shooting down three German Fokker planes and receive the Distinguished Service Cross. Americans would know him better in World War II as commander of the 8th and 12th Air Forces in North Africa and Europe, followed by command in the Pacific, including the strategic bombing of Japan and the two B-29 missions that dropped the atomic bombs that ended the war. In 1947, President Harry Truman would appoint him chief of staff of the new United States Air Force.

To the young fliers at Issoudun in November 1917, the new boss was "Herr Spaatz," though not to his face. He and the other "Prussian" officers in charge of building the training base, Herr Wiedenbach, Herr Tittel, Herr Speigel, and Herr Rickenbacker were "the Kaiser's Flying Carpenters." Aware of these sarcastic remarks being made behind his back, Eddie felt "some desire to get even." The opportunity that presented itself was the condition of the airfield. Strewn with rocks that often flew up and broke the wooden propellers, it was a hazard to planes and to the men who flew them. Worried about running out of props and recognizing a chance to put "the Ivy Leaguers" in their place, Eddie requisitioned a hundred buckets, handed them out, sent "the boys" out into the mud to pick up the rocks, and found "the groaning and moaning" music to his ears. Part of his resentment against the men was "the fact that they were perfecting their flying while I was working around the clock making their training possible."

The only way Eddie could improve his own skills was to "duck into lecture sessions between chores" and pick up whatever data he could. To apply what he'd learned, he would have to sneak an airplane out and take it up without benefit of an instructor. "Supervised instruction was dangerous enough," he noted, and the proof of it was "a graveyard right there on the field for those who did not apply what they had learned in class." Among the maneuvers discussed in the classes was "the tailspin." Vital to a flier in combat, the maneuver required stalling the plane and kicking the rudder control hard. This sent the nose down and the tail swinging around. The centrifugal force put the plane into a nosedive, allowing the pilot to escape attack by German planes. After several secret attempts at tailspinning, Eddie found he was able to "flutter down almost to the ground." But it was an accomplishment about which he felt he had to keep his mouth shut. Until one memorable afternoon.

Every Sunday afternoon at Issoudun, Eddie recalled, "the college boys" put on a football game that "the big brass in Paris" would make special trips to see. During one of those games, Eddie returned from a flight to Tours. Looking down on the players running up and down the field, with spectators crowding the sidelines, he discerned "an excellent opportunity to demonstrate a real tailspin." Coming down low over the field at about five hundred feet, he threw his plane into a dive. "Down it went," he wrote, "closer and closer and closer over the players. Frankly, it scared the pants off me too. Everybody beneath me, players and spectators alike, scattered for cover. Only then did I pull out of the spin—and just in time too. I sure broke up that ball game."

Called "on the carpet" by Major Spaatz, Eddie was grounded for thirty days. "But it was worth it," he noted. He was, he said, merely obeying an order from his mother. Having written to her that flying was much safer than auto racing, he'd gotten a reply containing the advice of a worried parent: "Be sure to fly slow," she said, "and close to the ground."

Upon arriving in France with the first contingent of the American Expeditionary Force, General Pershing had disappointed the French by telling them that his troops would need many months of preparation before going into battle. They did so on November 2, 1917, by taking over from French troops at Berthelemont that evening. At three in the morning one of their outposts came under artillery fire. The barrage lasted an hour. Then came a raiding party of 213 men from a Bavarian regiment. Outnumbering the Americans four to one, they killed three. One was shot, one had his throat slit, and the other had his skull crushed. Twelve Americans were captured. Informed of the first American deaths of the war, Black Jack Pershing wept.

Three days earlier, German Gotha bombers had dropped the first incendiary bombs on London, but many of the eighty-three ten-pound bombs failed to explode. Those that did killed ten civilians. In the first raid on England by Gothas on May 25, 1917, twenty-three of the planes had taken off from two airfields in Belgium. Because of clouds, only two reached their targets. Dropping only five of a capacity of thirteen bombs per plane, they killed 95 people and wounded 192. Of this new kind of warfare,

German scientist Albert Einstein wrote to a friend in Belgium, "The ancient Jehovah is still abroad. Alas he slays the innocent along with the guilty, whom he strikes so fearsomely blind that they can feel no sense of guilt."

As the untested young American pilots at Issoudun were nearing completion of their seventeen weeks of training, a Royal Flying Corps pilot was killed southwest of the town of Bourlon. Cited by *The Times* of London in its "In Memoriam" column as "an Unknown Airman, shot down on November 23rd, 1917, whilst attacking a German strongpoint," he was Lt. A. Griggs, an American volunteer with an Australian squadron.

Other Americans who had been impatient to get into the war had joined the Escadrille Americain. When the German government questioned U.S. neutrality, the name was changed to Escadrille Lafayette. Its founders were Dr. Edmund L. Gros, director of the American Ambulance Service, and Norman Prince, an American expatriate already flying with the French. Stationed at Luxeuil, they had a French commander, Capt. Georges Thénault, and Nieuport planes. Settling in luxury at the Grand Hotel, they selected an Indian head as their insignia and painted it on the fuselages of their planes. Presently the unit was based at Bar-le-Duc and assigned to escort bombers.

When a call went out for more American volunteers, fifty more enrolled. In late 1916, Spads replaced the Nieuports. By January 1917, Raoul Lufbery had shot down seven German planes to become the leading American ace. Although born in France (March 14, 1885), he had moved with his father to Connecticut. Left in the care of his grandmother until he was nineteen, he learned to speak a little English. Service in the army in the Philippines earned him American citizenship. While in Indochina in 1912 he met renowned aviator Marc Pourpe and worked for him as foreman and mechanic. The two of them moved on to Europe and Africa. In Africa in 1913, Pourpe made the first round-trip Cairo–Khartoum flight, with Lufbery along to arrange for fuel, maintenance, and spare parts. In August 1914, Lufbery had joined the French Foreign Legion as an infantryman, but was transferred to France's aviation service as Pourpe's mechanic. Within a few months Pourpe was dead and Lufbery had enrolled for pilot training at Chartres. Although not a naturally gifted flier, he was persistent. He joined Escadrille Lafayette on May 26, 1916, and savored his first victory on July 30 over Verdun. By October 12 he had knocked down three more. The seventh was in January 1917. For his subsequent victories, including seventeen over the German lines, he was hailed as "ace of aces" and seen as a role model for the trainees at Issoudun, and none more so than Eddie Rickenbacker. The Escadrille Lafayette had inspired him to propose to his auto racing colleagues that they start an aero squadron.

After completing advanced pilot training, the men of Issoudun's Class Number One would have to qualify in the use of machine guns at the School of Aerial Gunnery at Cazeaux. But when the list of those going on to the next phase of training was posted, Eddie found that his name had been omitted. Perplexed at not being included and confident that he was as good a pilot, if not better, than the others, he confronted Major Spaatz.

Was it an oversight?

No.

Had he been deleted, Eddie asked, because of the buzzing incident?

Certainly not.

Because the others didn't like his often bossy attitude? That he hadn't gotten along all that well with them?

The reason Rickenbacker wasn't going to gunnery school, Spaatz replied, was that he was an engineering officer, and there was a more pressing need for his talents as a mechanic.

Eddie proposed that his assistant was just as competent.

"You've got your orders," said Spaatz.

"But I want to get into combat!"

"You're too important to me in your present post, and that's that."

Leaving Spaatz's office, Eddie went directly to the school's surgeon. Reporting that he was sick with a cold and suffering from exhaustion, he demanded immediate hospitalization. A check of his temperature by Dr. Goldthwaite confirmed that he indeed had a fever. But in a burst of honesty, Eddie explained that he expected that during his hospitalization, his assistant would soon show Spaatz that Rickenbacker wasn't as indispensable as Spaatz thought, and the orders sending Rickenbacker to gunnery school would ensue. Released after two weeks, he rushed to Spaatz's office.

"I'm on to your game," said the major. "But if your heart's set on going to Cazeaux, you'll be no damn good to me around here. Good luck."

CHAPTER 4

Hat in the Ring

I N AN ADDRESS TO THE CONGRESS OF THE UNITED STATES ON JANU-
ary 8, 1918, Woodrow Wilson, who had labored as president to
keep the United States out of the war, presented his vision of a
peaceful postwar Europe based on "fourteen points." They ranged
from territorial concerns to free navigation of the sea, disarma-
ment, trade equality, colonialism, "autonomous development of
nations," Polish independence, "open covenants of peace openly
arrived at," and formation of a general association of nations to
preserve peace through guarantees of political independence and
territorial integrity to great and small nations alike.

President Wilson's declared enemy, ex-president Theodore
Roosevelt, whose four sons were in the war, dismissed the four-
teen points as nothing more than "fourteen scraps of paper."
Wilson's plan for peace, Roosevelt thundered, was one "without
victory." Wilson's "league of peace" was a design for surrender of
American sovereignty.

On battlefields as Wilson outlined his dream, the descriptive
word was "stalemate." In Britain, the government of Lord Balfour
was planning to send 420,000 men to join the 2 million already
under arms. The horrors of war, he said at Edinburgh, Scotland,

two days after Wilson's speech, were "nothing" compared to the idea of a negotiated "German peace."

Kaiser Wilhelm's answer to both Balfour and Wilson was that war was "a disciplinary action by God to educate mankind."

After surveying the front line at the Ypres salient, Great Britain's minister of munitions, Winston Churchill, wrote to his wife, "Nearly 800,000 of our British race have shed their blood or lost their lives here during three-and-a-half years of unceasing conflict." Death, he said, was as commonplace and as little alarming as the undertaker, quite "a natural ordinary event, which may happen to anyone at any moment, as it happened to all these scores of thousands who lie together at this vast cemetery, ennobled and rendered forever glorious by their brave memory."

Flowing toward the stalemated war in January 1918 from the United States were more than twice the number of men in the ranks of the U.S. Army when war was declared. During the war, a total of 4,791,172 men would serve in America's armed forces. More than half of them would be drafted through a mechanism that wily legislators had chosen to make more appealing-sounding by naming it Selective Service. In all, a little more than 2 million soldiers would go, in the words of George M. Cohan's wildly popular song, "Over There," to serve in forty-two divisions, each with about 27,000 enlisted men and a thousand officers. All but a small fraction of them would see combat. At war's end the casualties in the American Expeditionary Force would total 48,909 killed and 230,074 wounded. Deaths in all U.S. armed forces would total 112,432, more than half of them caused by a pandemic of influenza-pneumonia.

Of the handful of men who'd volunteered to fight the war in the skies, none was more enthusiastic and hungry for glory than Eddie Rickenbacker as he departed Issoudun for gunnery school at Cazeaux. Time and again he'd agitated for training, only to be put off by some "emergency," military technicality, or declaration that he was far too valuable as a mechanical engineer. General Pershing had been blunt. To Black Jack it was a question of age. "Look here, Eddie," he'd said. "You know you are getting on in years. War flying is for youngsters just out of school. It's not for mature men."

But at age twenty-seven, Eddie had kept up with or surpassed the "just out of school" twenty-one-year-old student fliers at Issoudun. Auto racing had taught him the essentials of coordinating the brain and body at high speeds. A lifetime of deliberate exposure to danger had shown him to be fearless. Now, at the gunnery school in southeast France, he was one step away from his goal of combat flying. But he arrived at Cazeaux with a single experience firing a gun. On a hunting trip to Tucson, Arizona, he'd fired a shotgun at a rabbit, but the kick of the gun had knocked him "head over heels."

Training at Cazeaux began with practice on the ground at fixed targets. This was followed by standing in a boat in the middle of a lake and firing at a target pulled by another moving boat. Having never imagined that he would be in "this little boat, bobbing up and down" with a 30-caliber rifle in his hands, he missed the target repeatedly. Blasting away at it day after day, with his shoulder black and blue from the recoil, he mastered the challenge. Next came the Lewis machine gun, fired from a plane at a cloth target. Ten feet long and resembling a sock, it was attached to a three-hundred-foot-long rope streaming behind an old Caudron bomber piloted by two Frenchmen. The gun with its hundred rounds of ammunition was mounted on the top of a wing of a Nieuport. The plan was to fire on the target while diving. Students who crashed because they went into a spin or swooped too close to the ground, Eddie noted, were buried under a *croix de bois* (wooden cross). Executing the dive and opening fire on the sock, Eddie riddled the towrope, cutting it in half. When he landed the Nieuport, the pilots of the Caudron rushed toward him, shouting angrily in French and gesticulating wildly. He was supposed to shoot at the target, they yelled, not at the airplane! For Eddie's next practice exercise, the Frenchmen made the towrope five hundred feet long.

One day after a wearying gunnery drill, Eddie landed and examined the blackened, cordite-pitted muzzles of the guns and noted in the diary that he'd begun keeping, "I can see that aerial warfare is nothing more than scientific murder." After three weeks of gunnery school he noted that he was "a pilot, able to fly and shoot."

Granted ten days' leave, Eddie headed to Paris to see his friend, Colonel Mitchell, to report on his progress and implore Mitchell to expedite his transfer to a combat unit at the front. He had been in Paris as an enlisted man driving for General Pershing. Now he was an officer with pilot's wings on the breast of his uniform, ample money in his pocket, and the attractions of the fabled City of Lights awaiting him. Like thousands of young Americans in Paris, he let go of the strictures of home and indulged in everything the city offered, but with only a cursory look at the treasures of the Louvre, Notre Dame Cathedral, Napoleon's tomb, and the Bois de Boulogne.

He started smoking cigarettes and left behind a life of abstaining from strong drink for one that included beer, wine, and cocktails. But he imposed on himself a rule that he would never take an alcoholic drink at any combat base to which he might be assigned. Drinking would be done only while on leave and would cease twenty-four hours before returning to duty.

His leave ended on March 4, 1918, with orders to report to a new unit, the 94th Aero Pursuit Squadron. "It had taken me almost a year to reach the front as a combat pilot," he wrote in his diary, "but I was there."

Based at Villeneuve, some twenty miles behind the lines, the 94th Aero Pursuit Squadron was the first to be composed entirely of Americans. Its commander was Maj. John Huffer. An American who had lived most of his life in France, he'd served with Escadrille Lafayette. Also at the base was the 95th Squadron under the command of Captain Miller, who had been Eddie's first commanding officer at Issoudun. The pilots were the students from Issoudun who had called Eddie "Herr Rickenbacker." They greeted him at Villeneuve with the same disdain.

In the parlance of aviation at the time, the base at Villeneuve was an "aerodrome." The public was beginning to realize that airplanes were quickly becoming more than motorized kites and

had other uses than taking some brave souls up for rides and giving places for crazy "wingwalkers" to entertain gawking crowds
whenever a "flying circus" came to town. More sophisticated
folks no doubt knew that an aerodrome was something like a
railroad station, except that there were no tracks. Airplanes arrived and departed on flat, grassy fields. They were kept in
"hangars." But while an aerodrome in the United States might
have several planes, the one in Villeneuve had "squadrons," each
with a score of pilots and three mechanics per plane. And the airplanes of war were equipped with machine guns.

Assigned to Flight One, Eddie was given a brand-new, snug,
one-seat, "baby" Nieuport. The squadron had twenty planes and
pilots and two hundred mechanics. Invited to dinner on his first
night at the base by Captain Miller, Eddie was introduced to
America's "ace of aces," Maj. Raoul Lufbery.

The most famous of Allied fliers greeted Eddie with, "So you're
Eddie Rickenbacker, eh? Miller tells me that in America you are
a wonderful racing driver. But the boys say that over here you are
a low-down slave driver."

Short, stocky, soft-spoken, sober-minded, and affable, Lufbery
learned that Eddie was also called Rick. Liking each other immediately, the two men found that they had much in common.
Like Eddie, Lufbery had started as a mechanic, but by persistence
had become a pilot. Whether Eddie could ever match Lufbery's
record in combat remained to be seen. The veteran and the initi-
ate discussed every maneuver in which Nieuports could be flown
and every type of attack. Many of his victories, Lufbery said, had
been while he was on lone patrol.

"There's a hell of a lot of difference," he went on, "in going out
alone, no matter what the odds are against you, and in going out
as a member or a leader of a group of pilots who may or may not
be as good as you are. It's a great responsibility to shepherd these
pilots out and get back home safe. I prefer to fight alone, on my
own."

Although Eddie was itching to take to the air in his new plane,
his first two days were spent on the ground because of bad
weather. When March 6 dawned clear, Lufbery announced that

he would lead a flight of three unarmed planes on a patrol over German lines. Of the twenty pilots in the squadron, only two could be chosen. As Eddie waited nervously, hoping to be one of them, there was, he recalled, "a long moment of silence as he looked us over."

Seated next to Eddie was Lt. Douglas Campbell. A Harvard graduate, he'd had ground school training in the United States but had not flown before arriving in France. While at Issoudun he had done staff work. Like Eddie, he had used his off hours to teach himself how to fly in a Nieuport that was used for advanced training.

"Rick," Lufbery said, "you and Campbell be ready to leave at 8:15."

"Yes, sir," said Eddie, trying to be nonchalant, while Campbell made a brave attempt to conceal his emotions. As the other pilots gathered around the chosen pair, they masked their disappointment with jokes and well-meaning advice. In the lingo of combat pilots created by British aviators, they warned Eddie and Campbell to "Look out for Archie." A term for antiaircraft fire, the word was inspired by the closing lyrics of a London music hall song: "Archibald! Certainly not!" Pilots used the phrase facetiously whenever an enemy shot came too close for comfort. In time, "Archibald! Certainly not!" was shortened to "Archie."

In the new lexicon of pilots, some of the terms that Eddie learned were:

Bank: Tilting a plane sideways in rounding a corner.

Boches: Germans (also called Boche, Huns, and Heinies).

Ceiling: A plane's maximum altitude.

Contact: Sparking the engine.

Coupez: Cutting off the spark.

Flying Circus: German squadron whose planes had red noses, commanded by Manfred von Richtofen, known and feared as the "Red Baron."

Jagdstaffel: German term for a fighting squadron.

Joystick: The plane's steering control.

Office: The cockpit.

Panne: Forced landing because of engine failure.

Sauce: Gasoline.

Vrille: A tailspin.

Wind up: Scared, as in having a chill, or wind, go up
the spine, causing one's hair to stand on end with
fear.

Zoom: Pitching the plane suddenly up or down at
great speed.

Eddie would be taking up a single-seat Nieuport powered by a
110-horsepower Le Rhone rotary engine. Designed for top speed,
it was capable of 107 miles an hour. Assured by his mechanic that
the airplane was the "best machine" in the hangar, Eddie lit a
cigarette and waited for Lufbery. When he arrived at eight o'clock
sharp, he gave a few instructions and one order to Eddie and
Campbell: "Stick close to me."

Wearing a fur-lined flying suit, helmet, and goggles, Eddie
watched Lufbery's plane take off. When Campbell followed, Eddie opened his throttle and cast a longing glance at the field just
as the plane's tail lifted and the wheels began to skim the sparse
grass. Pulling the plane up, he headed after Campbell. Soon the
majestic ruins of Rheims raced past below his right wing. About
half an hour later at fifteen thousand feet somewhere between
Rheims and the Argonne Forest, he looked down at what appeared to be old trenches, earthworks, and artillery shell holes
that were so close to each other they resembled a honeycomb, except that they stretched for miles in every direction. No trees. No
fences. No buildings. No sign of life. Just chaos, ruin, desolation.

Trying to keep up with Lufbery's plane at fifteen thousand feet,
Eddie's "baby" Nieuport was suddenly buffeted by a stiff wind. As
it pitched and rolled, he began to feel airsick. Feeling cold and
more nauseous, he clenched his teeth and prayed that he could
shake off the sickness. Looking straight ahead and concentrating

on Lufbery's plane, he heard an explosion behind him followed by a jolt of rushing air that bounced the Nieuport into a roll. Keeping control, he heard more thuds from behind. Worried that the buffeting had damaged the tail, he looked back and saw black smoke balls of exploding Archie shells well behind and below.

Elated that his "long dreamed and long dreaded novitiate was over," knowing that he was all right and that he could fly, he felt confident that in coming through the antiaircraft barrage he had banished fear and doubt and validated his belief that the powers within him had no bounds. Every experience in his life had been a preparation for this test. The harum-scarum years, the knack for mechanics, the excitement and perils of auto racing did not compare to what he knew must come in air combat as he pitted his experience and self-confidence against the fabled veterans of the Red Baron's Flying Circus—and beat them.

Floating along over enemy lines in ecstatic contemplation of future victories, he realized that Lufbery was leading him and Campbell homeward. Glancing at the clock on the dashboard, he saw that he'd been aloft almost two hours. Approaching base, he looked beyond the tips of the Nieuport's wings and welcomed the contrast between the beauty of the snowy, unscarred land below and the ugliness of the trenches and pitted landscape he'd left behind. After circling the field, he glided to earth. Quickening the speed of the propeller, he taxied toward a hangar and a welcoming crowd of pilots and mechanics. Basking in the envious expressions of the men who hadn't flown into a barrage of Archie shells that day, he and Campbell joked that the Huns must have "cost the Kaiser a year's income in artillery shells," with no result. Of enemy planes, they said, "None had dared to venture up against us."

Listening to the bragging, Lufbery chuckled. No enemy? Really? Obviously, Eddie hadn't noticed a formation of four German Albatros planes two miles ahead of them when they turned back, and that another enemy two-seater was even nearer, at five thousand feet above the lines. With Eddie blushing and gaping astonishment, Lufbery asked, "Rick, how much of that shrapnel did you get?"

"Not a bit," said Eddie.

"Really?" asked Lufbery, pointing to a hole in the tail of Eddie's plane, another in the outer edge of a wing, and evidence that a third fragment had passed through both wings not a foot from the cockpit.

Had the German planes that Eddie overlooked on his maiden flight over enemy lines attacked, he, Campbell, and Lufbery would have been like "sitting ducks." The Nieuports had no machine guns because the weapons hadn't been delivered. This came as a shock to a group of French pilots from neighboring fields. Eager to assist in training their American allies, they had volunteered to lead patrols over German territory. On several occasions the flights came close to enemy planes. But it wasn't until one of the Frenchmen examined one of the Americans' planes closely that they noticed the lack of armament.

"That was the end of our French escorts," Eddie noted. "It never occurred to us to tell them. We had all thought it was a big joke. The French thought we had lost our minds. We never had the opportunity to fly with the English. They would probably have enjoyed the joke as much as we. Where the French were cautious, according to their considered military policy of getting the best possible results with the least expenditure of men and planes, the British were daring, almost foolhardy, also as a matter of military principle. They started flying combat at eighteen, and a daring style came naturally to them. American pilots were more daring than the French, more wary than the English. As for the Germans, they liked to fly in close formations, hunting in packs. Americans preferred every-man-for-himself style of aerial combat."

No finer example of the American style of flying could be found than Eddie's friend, Capt. James Miller. Having left family and home and a prosperous business in New York, he had earned the respect and love of all the fresh pilots because of his desire to get into the skies and win a combat against an enemy aviator. After a frustrating delay in getting into combat because he had been put in charge of organizing the flying school at Issoudun, he'd arrived at Villeneuve a few days before Eddie to take command of the 94th Squadron only to find that he had no planes. But a few days after Eddie's first sortie above German lines, Miller announced with giddy delight that he'd been invited to fly with a French squadron into the same region that Eddie had visited.

The following evening, Eddie learned that Miller was missing. Flying from Rheims to the Argonne Forest, he had found himself alone and under attack by two German squadrons. Shot down, he died of wounds a few hours later. The lesson in this "first and most sorrowful loss" for Eddie was that he must not permit himself to cherish friendships. Their "going" would upset the work he had to do. "If one permitted constant anxiety for friends to weigh down one's spirits," he wrote, "one could not long continue work at the front."

In mid-March 1918 the Germans were preparing a massive push on the Western Front. Its objective was to drive the British from the Somme before the American troops could be in position to aid the British. By driving the French from the Aisne, the Germans would be able to threaten Paris. The offensive began on March 21 with an artillery barrage that lasted five hours, including the use of gas shells. Over the next two weeks, 2 million shells would rain on the British lines. In the air, 261 British planes were pitted against 326 German fighter planes. In the first day of aerial warfare the British would lose sixteen planes, the Germans fourteen. But the Americans were still not ready to enter the fighting.

Eighteen miles from the lines, Eddie could see observation balloons and hear the booming guns. Out of concern over the German advances, the squadrons at Villeneuve were ordered to move to an aerodrome at Epiez, thirty miles back. Arriving on March 30, the 94th still had no planes capable of joining the battle. But they did have a new, experienced pilot, Capt. James Norman Hall. A veteran of the Lafayette Escadrille, he was also the celebrated author of two books, *Kitchener's Mob* and *High Adventure.* With him was another air veteran, Capt. David McK. Peterson, of Honesdale, Pennsylvania. "We had all heard of these boys," Eddie noted, "and idolized them before we had seen them."

Hall's arrival at Epiez had been spectacular. Eddie recorded it this way:

A day or two after we had settled down in our new aerodrome we heard the buzzing of an approaching machine. All hands rushed out to see what it meant. A Nieuport bearing American colors assured us that it was a friend and probably another new member of our squadron, since he was preparing to land on our field.

He shut off his engine and glided down until his wheels skimmed the ground. The next instant her nose struck the mud and in a twinkling the machine had somersaulted over onto her back and slid along toward us tail foremost. We walked out to the wreck to secure the remains of the raw pilot who hadn't yet learned how to land a machine, and some of us made rather caustic comments about the authorities sending us such unsophisticated aviators. Imagine our stupefaction when we discovered the grinning face of Captain Hall himself looking at us upside down!

Fortunately he wasn't hurt in the slightest, and I think he would have been glad if he could know how much good it did all of us young pilots to discover that even the best airmen can sometimes come a cropper.

Based at Epiez were two squadrons, Eddie's 94th under Maj. John Huffer and the 95th under Captain Miller, both of which had been at Villeneuve. None of their pilots had been able to do any fighting because of the lack of machine guns. Nor had anyone in the 95th been given instruction in the use of airplane guns. Consequently, when the long-awaited weaponry arrived on April 3, 1918, the pilots were thrilled. With the guns came a supply of warm flight suits and crates of spare parts. The "foolish virgins of Squadron 95," to use Eddie's language, were sent back to the gunnery school at Cazeaux to learn how to use the guns, while Eddie's 94th was sent to a vacated French air base at Toul. They arrived on April 10. One of the most important railroad connections in a region of rolling hills and forests, Toul was barely eighteen miles from the front. Fifteen miles east lay Nancy. A highway connecting Nancy to Luneville ran parallel to the enemy lines and was in easy shelling distance. North and west of Toul was Verdun.

Knowing that the 94th would soon be committed to combat, the men of the squadron decided that their planes needed a distinctive emblem.

"Since all squadrons were known by a certain type of insignia as well as numbers," Eddie recalled, "we naturally tried to find a design appropriate for our squadron. During many of our discussions, someone in our squadron suggested using Uncle Sam's hat in colors. Someone else asked, 'Why not Uncle Sam's hat in the ring?' "

The expression "hat-in-the-ring," Eddie remembered, had been coined by Theodore Roosevelt during one of his campaign speeches when running for president. "Because it was so significant, and realizing that we were the first American fighting squadron on the front," Eddie noted, "it was a logical tie-in for the insignia as it was designed." One of the pilots, Lt. Johnny Wentworth, happened to be an architect, so it fell to him to design it. Taking the design to a Paris jeweler, Eddie had a little insignia made of silver. It was worn by all the pilots of the 94th above the wings on the left side of their tunics and eventually became recognized as the 94th's official insignia. (Later, because the hat in the ring was used on a commercial product, the adjutant general instructed the 94th to discontinue its use. An Indian head would be substituted as the squadron insignia.)

On the evening of April 13, 1918, Eddie found himself among "a happy lot of fliers." In their hands were the first war flight orders given by an "All-American squadron commander to All-American pilots." At six o'clock the next morning there would be a two-hour patrol at an altitude of sixteen thousand feet from Pont-à-Mousson to St. Mihiel by flight leader Capt. David Peterson, Lt. Reed Chambers, and Lt. E. V. Rickenbacker.

CHAPTER 5

First Blood

T OO EXCITED TO SLEEP, EDDIE REVIEWED EVERYTHING HE'D EVER read or heard about airplane fighting and envisioned the coming day. Boches were zooming toward him from every direction. Skillfully averting them, he sent each tumbling earthward in flames and trailing smoke. When an orderly came in to rouse him from bed at five o'clock, the field was shrouded in mist. During a "merry breakfast," Captain Peterson told him and Lieutenant Chambers that if something were to go amiss with his plane and force him down, the mission would continue with Eddie in the lead. But first, Eddie and Chambers were to go up and check the flying conditions at fifteen hundred feet. After circling the field several times, Eddie saw Peterson take off and climb to join them. After a few minutes Peterson broke away and headed back to the field.

Assuming that Peterson was having engine trouble, Eddie thought, "It's my show now." He signaled Chambers to follow him.

Flying northwest from Toul above the valley of the Meuse River to St. Mihiel, they turned east on a course that took them over the towns of Apremont, Xvray, and Flirey toward Pont-à-Mousson on the Moselle River. With confidence rooted in innocence, he felt as though he could continue all the way to the Rhine and into Germany itself. Reality burst upon him with a blast of antiaircraft fire. Exploding harmlessly below the tail of Chambers's plane, the greeting from Archie so unnerved Chambers that he swerved his airplane so close to Eddie's that they nearly collided.

Reaching Pont-à-Mousson, they reversed course to St. Mihiel and repeated the round-trip four times, with intermittent Archie fire but encountering no German planes. After the last trip, and mindful that the mission was to last only two hours, Eddie signaled Chambers to head for Toul. As they winged southwest, Eddie discovered to his horror that the route was blanketed with dense fog. With fuel running low and unable to see the ground, he realized that Captain Peterson had not landed because of engine trouble. He had wisely chosen not to chance flying in such conditions.

Recognizing that there "was nothing for it" but to dive through thick fog clouds, Eddie nosed down into them and immediately lost sight of Chambers. Steering by compass with the needle of the altimeter dropping rapidly, he flattened out at a thousand feet and saw a railroad near Commercy that he knew would guide him to back Toul. To keep it in sight, he maintained an altitude of one hundred feet. But the relief of a safe landing vanished as Captain Peterson greeted him with a torrent of declarations that he'd been a bloody fool for flying in fog. Certain that he would soon be informed that Chambers had crashed and been killed, Eddie got out of his flying clothes and walked to headquarters to make out his report. When a telephone rang, he expected to hear that Chambers had cracked up.

Braced to be told that Chambers was dead, Eddie heard the operations officer shout, "Boche planes spotted over Foug. Sound the alert!"

At that moment someone yelled, "A German plane has crashed in flames on the field."

Rushing toward the crash, Eddie saw a second German slam nose down five hundred yards away. The first had been shot down by 94th pilot Alan Winslow. The second had crashed after

being forced down by Douglas Campbell. Amazingly, the first enemy planes brought down by American fliers had met their doom
on the very field from which the 94th had launched its first day of
operations. Equally amazing, the German pilots had survived.
Questioned as to why they'd been flying in fog, they reported that
they were sent up to attack two patrol planes that had flown between Pont-à-Mousson and St. Mihiel. They'd followed two American planes until they lost them in the fog. In making their way
back to their base at Metz, they had mistaken the American field
at Toul for their own.

Feeling that he had played an indirect part in the downing of
the German planes, Eddie also learned that Chambers had made
a safe landing on a nearby field and would be back at Toul that
evening. Noting in his diary that the first American victory had
occurred on April 14, 1918, Eddie wrote, "The episode put great
confidence into all of us and we felt we were a match for the
whole German air force."

News of the double victory resulted in a cascade of congratulatory messages from all over the United States, along with praise
from British and French aviators. But following up on the
achievement was impossible because of inclement weather. "War
to us," Eddie remembered about those heady first days, "was very
much like a plunge into an unknown planet. We knew something
of the wiles of the enemy and were familiar enough with the dangers that every pilot was so fond of describing. But there remained always that inner fear of a new menace. Ever constant
was the impression that luck might for an instant desert us and
that instant would end the war for us. We often wondered just
what new danger would be thwarted by pure luck each time we
went for a patrol into enemy territory."

Eager and impatient to find out on April 23, Eddie brightened
with a telephoned report that an enemy plane had been sighted
flying west to east in the familiar area between St. Mihiel and
Pont-à-Mousson, a town now firmly in the hands of the Germans.
Because no one else on the base at Toul was ready, Major Huffer
sent Eddie to find the Boche. Taking his Nieuport up as steeply as

it could climb, he set course for Pont-à-Mousson. At eight thousand feet above the town he saw the knifelike edge of an airplane heading toward him, but as he flew into shooting distance he saw that the Spad was French. Disappointed at finding no "game" in the air over the town, Eddie returned to Toul and found himself greeted as if he were a hero. He learned that in the sector where he'd been flying, an American artillery battery had seen a Boche fall from the sky in flames. The assumption among the pilots at Toul was that Eddie had shot it down. "It was a pity to have to tell them the truth," Eddie noted, "but it had to be done." (How the German plane had been brought down was never discovered.)

The next day Eddie was airborne again to check out a report of a German flying over St. Mihiel. Determined to get his first victory, he flew through low-hanging clouds directly over enemy lines at three thousand feet, making him a splendid target for Archie. Passing over the town to the north, he sighted what appeared to be an enemy plane just ahead. Having been told by Major Lufbery that Germans were fond of leading Allied planes into traps, he decided to be wary. Approaching the plane with a finger lightly touching the machine gun trigger, he glanced up and saw a black Albatros above him. Pulling on the joystick, he zoomed up to attack. But as he was ready to fire his first hostile shots in the war, he spotted a pair of fighters five hundred yards away and coming toward him head-on. Feeling "an intense desire to get home as quickly as possible," he climbed, dived, executed tailspins, and circled only to find the planes matching each maneuver until escape presented itself in the welcome billows of a cloud.

Emerging from the overcast half an hour later, Eddie headed for base. When he landed, he was met by Douglas Campbell. "Hello, Rick," Campbell said. "Why the devil didn't you wait for us?"

A second puzzled-looking pilot, Charles Chapman, blurted, "Where did you go after we lost you in the clouds? We've been home almost half an hour."

Too embarrassed to confess that he had taken them for two

Germans, Eddie replied, "I thought I remembered seeing a Boche and went back to make sure. I guess I was wrong."

At noon on April 29, 1918, after five rainy days of no flying, the sun broke through at the Toul aerodrome. Listed to be on alert for action, Eddie waited at a hangar for word that an enemy plane had been sighted. The call came at five o'clock. A French outpost reported that a German two-seater had been observed at Beaumont. Taking off with Capt. James Hall, he was soon in sight of a plane that turned out to be a three-seat French aircraft. Looking for Hall, he found him "cavorting about amid a thick barrage of black shell bursts across the German lines." Evidently waiting for Eddie to overtake him, Hall appeared to be having a delightful time, doing loops, barrel rolls, sideslips, and spins. When Eddie caught up, Hall wiggled the plane's wings and turned back toward Pont-à-Mousson. As Hall suddenly changed direction and curved up into the sun, Eddie saw a German plane. Recognizing it as a new Pfalz, he followed Hall in a way that kept them between the unsuspecting German and the glare of the sun.

While Hall positioned for an attack, Eddie kept at an altitude on the other side of the Pfalz, hoping to cut off any attempt at its retreat. When the German suddenly began a climb, Eddie realized that the German had seen him. As the Pfalz zoomed past Eddie's Nieuport, Hall opened up with his guns. The German banked to the right, with Eddie on his tail and Hall not far behind. Gaining on the Pfalz, Eddie fired at 150 yards and watched tracers cut into the tail. By raising the nose of his plane, he directed bullets along the fuselage of the Pfalz until they raked the cockpit. At two thousand feet above the enemy lines, he pulled out of his dive as the Pfalz curved slightly to the left, circled a little to the south, and plunged into the ground at the edge of a woods a mile inside the German lines.

Many years later, Eddie wrote:

> *Though pilots were lionized during the Great War,*
> *though news of my first victory went out all over the*
> *world and communications of congratulation came in*

by the hundreds, the true gratification of an aerial victory comes from your fellow pilots. They know how easily it could have gone the other way, and their acclaim means more than all the applause from the outside world. There never has been a closer fraternity than the one that existed among the pilots of a squadron fighting together high in the sky, and no group of fighters had a greater spirit than those of the 94th Squadron. There on the muddy French airfield, surrounded by my fellow pilots of the Hat-in-the-Ring Squadron, I experienced the greatest elation of my life.

I had no regrets over killing a fellow human being, I do not believe that at that moment I even considered the matter. Like nearly all air fighters, I was an automaton behind the gun barrels of my plane. I never thought of killing an individual but of shooting down an enemy plane.

As for the method, that was how we fought. All pilots, German and Allied alike, strove to gain an advantage over the adversary. The advantage could have been in superior flying ability and marksmanship, in equipment, in numbers. When the skies were even and neither could gain the advantage, there was no battle. Frequently two pilots of equal skill would spend an hour or more fencing in the sky, each seeking to obtain the superior position over the other. When one or both ran low on gas, they would simply give each other a wave and fly back to their respective aerodromes.

Though we were out to shoot down planes and the best way to shoot down a plane was to put a burst of bullets in the pilot's back, there was never, at least in my case, any personal animosity. I would have been delighted to learn that the pilot of the Pfalz or any other pilot I shot down had escaped with his life.

The day after his victory, Eddie was notified that the commanding officer of the 6th French Army intended to award him and Hall the country's highest award for valor, the Croix de Guerre with Palm. While American newspaper headlines attributed the victory to the man who had been one of the nation's most celebrated auto racers, Eddie insisted that James Hall's presence, if not his bullets, had won the victory and given Eddie "that wonderful feeling of self-confidence" that made it possible for him to return to battle in the expectation that he would handle similar situations successfully.

Flying with his hero, Major Lufbery, on May 1, to look for a German plane that had been sighted over Montsec, near St. Mihiel, Eddie eagerly anticipated joining America's ace of aces in aerial battle. He found after half an hour over their destination that there was no sign of the reported Boche. But as they passed over Pont-à-Mousson at six thousand feet, Lufbery went into a steep dive. In hot pursuit, thinking that Lufbery had spotted an enemy below and was about to open an attack, he realized that Lufbery was experiencing trouble. His propeller had stopped turning and Lufbery was circling in search of a place to glide into a landing. When he settled gently onto a muddy field, Eddie thought he was all right. But then Lufbery's Nieuport flipped over onto its back. Swooping down to a hundred feet, fearing that Lufbery had been killed, he was relieved to see him crawl from under the plane on hands and knees. He was fine, but he was down less than three miles from enemy lines.

Unable to attempt a landing to rescue him, Eddie flew back to base to show the spot of the crash landing on a map, hoping that men would be sent there overland. To his amazement, the squadron's commander, Major Huffer, jumped into a car and raced to the downed hero's rescue himself. When he arrived, he found Lufbery with only a slightly scratched nose. While awaiting help, Lufbery found that the cause of his plane's trouble was a burned out cylinder.

The incident resulted in a lively discussion between Eddie and Lufbery on the worst fear of pilots: being in a burning plane as it hurtled toward the ground. Built of wood with fabric wings covered in a highly flammable strengthener called "dope," a hit plane could quickly turn into a flaming coffin. Because American pilots had no parachutes, the question was whether to burn to death or jump. "I'd stay with the machine," said Lufbery. "If you jump you haven't got a chance. If you stay, you may be able to slideslip your plane down so that you can fan the flames away from yourself. Perhaps you can even put out the fire before you reach the ground."

Vulnerability of fabric wings was driven home to Eddie the following day, although not directly. Around noon, Lt. James A. Meissner and a Lieutenant Davis were ordered to protect a French photographic reconnaissance plane near Pont-à-Mousson. As it flew between seven and eight thousand feet, Meissner and Davis circled about a mile above in Nieuports to look out for German planes. When two Albatroses suddenly swooped from out of the sun, they attacked Meissner and Davis. By deft maneuvering, Meissner rose above the first Albatros and immediately dived, firing long bursts from his machine gun. As the German spun downward, Meissner wondered if the pilot was "playing possum" by deliberately going into a spin to lure his attacker closer. A puff of black smoke and a sheet of flames proved otherwise. But the thrill of Meissner's first victory was fleeting. From the ground arose a storm of machine gun fire and shrapnel from exploding Archie shells that stripped away the fabric of the Nieuport's left upper wing and peppered the leading edge of the other, leaving it flapping and tearing in the wind.

Knowing that without those supporting surfaces the Nieuport was doomed, Meissner decided that since he was going to die, he was entitled to a splendid military funeral. Such a grand send-off would be a certainty only if he crashed on Allied territory. By easing up on his speed, he reckoned that his chances of getting away from German-held ground were good. Whether the tattered, limping Nieuport could clear the no-man's-land between the lines was doubtful. If he managed to do so, the prospects of crashing on American territory were excellent. If he hit the ground in a slow, controlled crash, he figured he might even survive.

With all but a few wildly flapping shreds of the wing fabric gone, he skimmed slowly over the cratered, tree-stripped, lifeless earth between the barbed-wire barriers on each side of no-man's-land and sputtered above the American trenches. Below, the troops affectionately known at home as "doughboys" gazed with wide-eyed wonder at the crippled airplane and its fuselage painted with a top hat in a ring. Moments later the plane's bicycle-style wheels struck muddy ground, sending the Nieuport into a cartwheel that ended with the plane flat on its back.

Struggling from under it, Meissner assured himself that he was in one piece, then turned his thoughts to the Albatros that he'd shot down. It was his first victory. That is, if anyone but he had witnessed it. Without such a confirmation, he could not be credited. Still wondering when he returned to base by car, he found that word of his adventure had preceded him. With a flock of war reporters and photographers crowding him, he was told that his victory–the fourth by a 94th pilot–had indeed been observed by the crew of the French photoreconnaissance plane.

Later that afternoon Captain Peterson returned from a mission with a confirmed fifth victory for the squadron, but at a terrible cost. Out of four planes that had gone on patrol that morning, one would never return. During an attack by four Pfalz fighters, Charles Chapman's plane had gone down in flames. "It was our first defeat in combat," Eddie noted, "and sadly did we feel that loss."

On Monday, May 6, 1918, the pilots of the 95th Squadron returned from gunnery school at Cazeaux. Among them, Eddie noted, were the squadron's captain, John Mitchell, "an old boy from Fay School, St. Mark's, and Harvard," and former president Teddy Roosevelt's youngest son, Quentin. Three of his brothers–Theodore Roosevelt, Jr. (called Ted), Archibald, and Kermit–were also in the war in France, but serving in the infantry. The last to be sent overseas, Quentin had taken flight training at Mineola, Long Island, New York. Because he was Teddy's son, his first commanding officer named him flight commander. Protesting that he had no experience and that he might jeopardize the lives of his men, Quentin declined the honor, but then was directed by other superior officers to obey orders. How he would perform on his first mission remained to be seen. That Quentin was popular with the men of the 95th was not in doubt. On the day he'd finished training at Issoudun, all the mechanics had lined up outside a hangar to say good-bye. "Let us know if you're captured," said a sergeant, "and we'll come get you."

Roosevelt brothers' biographer Edward J. Renahan, Jr. noted that Quentin's men not only liked him, they were worried about him. "Unlike his colleague, the precise and pragmatic Eddie Rickenbacker," he wrote in *The Lion's Pride: Theodore Roosevelt and His Family in Peace and War*, "Quentin was a daredevil who courted risk and glory. His men at Issoudun knew him well enough to understand that once he got into combat, he would be both selfless and voracious in his search for victory."

Assigned to the 1st Pursuit Squadron of the 95th Squadron, named the "Kicking Mule" and with such an emblem, Quentin was so eager to get into the air in a combat plane that on his first day at Toul he took up a plane "for a half hour ride" in order to "get used to it."

He wrote to his mother, "When I first got over here I wondered why every flier was not killed within the first three months of his flying. Now I have changed so far the other way that I feel as though a man could hardly drive one of these machines into an accident, short of completely losing his head."

Two days after Quentin Roosevelt and his companions in the 95th arrived, Eddie and the pilots of the 94th were alerted that four enemy planes had been sighted and were heading south from Pont-à-Mousson. Because Eddie's Flight One was on standby, he, Jimmy Hall, and Edward Green took off to intercept the Germans. When they arrived at an altitude of twelve thousand feet, Eddie observed a moving shadow two or three miles inside American lines. A two-seater, the German plane was directing artillery fire against an American position near Beaumont. The three American planes began a direct dive together. As they neared their unsuspecting prey, the sky filled with puffs of black smoke from exploding artillery shells, signaling a warning to the German plane, an Albatros, that it was about to be attacked. Then Eddie saw four Pfalz scout planes moving toward him in a diagonal direction.

Pulling ahead of Hall's plane, Eddie wigwagged his wings to alert Hall to the oncoming Germans. As Hall resumed the lead, the trio of Nieuports were in a position to dive to attack when they chose and remain out of reach of the Germans, so long as they stayed above them. Selecting the rear Pfalz, Eddie set his sights, with the distance rapidly narrowing. Opening fire at two hundred yards, he watched tracers rip into the German's wings. He continued shooting to within fifty yards. As the Pfalz went into a spin, Eddie pulled up and looked around to see if he was being targeted by another plane.

Finding none, he witnessed a display of aerial acrobatics by either Hall or Green. Less than a hundred yards away, a Nieuport was in a steep dive with a Pfalz close on his tail, pouring fire into the Nieuport's fuselage and cockpit. Suddenly the tables turned. Zooming up into a loop, the Nieuport was now above the Pfalz and riddling it with bullets at a rate of 650 a minute. As the Pfalz spun down in flames, Eddie swooped next to the Nieuport. Expecting to see Hall, he found Green grinning back at him. Hall was nowhere in sight.

Winging back toward base through a furious storm of Archie, Eddie and Green crossed a maze of trenches with still no sign of Hall's plane. When they landed, Eddie rushed to Green to ask about Hall. Green exclaimed, "I saw him dive into a Boche just as I began my attack. The next I saw of him, he was going in a spin and the Boche was still firing at him as he was falling. He must have struck just back of those woods behind Montsec."

What Eddie and Green had no way of knowing was that Hall had overtaxed his Nieuport by diving too fast. A wing gave way, but Hall had nursed the plane along with the engine at half speed and crashed in an open field and gotten only a broken ankle. Captured by Germans, he dined that night as the guest of German aviators, then was taken to a hospital in Metz and then to prison. He would remain there until the town was occupied by French forces on November 19, 1918–eight days after an armistice ended the war.

Eddie later learned that after the Germans had fled Metz, Hall had limped to Paris to rest and celebrate his freedom at the Inn of Monsieur de Crillon, the favorite rendezvous and oasis for aviators in Paris. Eddie would also learn that on the day Hall had crashed, Hall had watched Eddie shoot down a German plane, confirming a victory that Eddie had not been able to prove, and therefore would otherwise never be officially credited to him.

On the day that Hall had failed to return to base, the world believed that America's ace of aces and author of two bestselling novels was dead. "Every pilot who had the privilege of his acquaintance," Eddie recalled, "burned with a desire for revenge."

Within fifteen minutes after landing, Eddie encountered Major Lufbery "walking with a set look of determination on his usually merry features that presaged no mercy to the enemy." Seeing Lufbery's approach, his mechanics began pushing his plane from its hangar. Without a word Lufbery pulled on his flying suit, climbed into the plane, and headed toward Germany. After flying for an hour and a half without seeing an enemy plane and running low on fuel, he spotted three German planes north of St. Mihiel. Attacking them alone, he shot down one and watched the others flee.

The next day, May 8, 1918, Eddie was named to replace Hall as commander of Number One flight. "While very much gratified by this promotion," he wrote, "I could not help realizing that before the day was over some other man in my Flight might be taking over the command in my place just as I was taking it from Captain Hall."

CHAPTER 6

Lucky Eddie

ONE WEEK BEFORE EDDIE RICKENBACKER ASSUMED COMMAND OF Squadron 94's number one flight at Toul, the Supreme War Council of Allied leaders had convened in Abbeville, near the Channel coast, to map war strategy. Present were the commander in chief of Allied forces on the Western Front, French general Ferdinand Foch; Premier Georges Clemenceau of France; British prime minister David Lloyd George; and the commander of the American Expeditionary Force, John J. Pershing. To a prediction by Foch that unless troops of the United States were committed to the line at once all would be lost, the flinty American general known as Black Jack said, "I do not suppose that the American army is to be entirely at the disposal of the French and British commands." Rather, he declared, "We must look forward to the time when we have our own army."

That was fine in principal, said Lloyd George. "At the present time, however," he went on, "we are engaged in what is perhaps the decisive battle of the war. If we lose the battle, we shall need tonnage [ships] to take home what there is left of the British and American armies."

Bristling with anger, Foch glared across the table at Pershing.

"You are willing," he said incredulously, "to risk being driven back to the Loire?"

"Yes, I am willing to take the risk," Pershing replied calmly. "Morever, the time may come when the American army will have to stand the brunt of this war, and it is not wise to fritter away our resources in this manner."

"Can't you see," said Lloyd George in frustration, "that the war will be lost unless we get this support?"

"Gentlemen," Pershing replied, "I have thought this program over very deliberately and I will not be coerced."

With the issue unresolved, the council met again on May 2. It did so with Lloyd George noting that since March 21, Britain had suffered 280,000 casualties and the French more than 340,000. "If the United States does not come to our aid," he continued, "then perhaps the enemy's calculations will be correct. If France and Great Britain should have to yield, their defeat will be honorable, for they would have fought to their last man, while the United States would have to stop without having put into the line more than little Belgium."

Pointing out that the United States had declared war "independently," Pershing stressed that the morale of America's soldiers "depends upon their fighting under our own flag." But he would allow 130,000 infantrymen and machine gunners on their way to France in May, along with 150,000 more scheduled to arrive in June, to join the Allied line. All others would remain and act under American command.

Compelled to accept Pershing's terms, Lloyd George complained by letter to the British ambassador in Washington. "It is maddening to think that though the men [Americans] are there, the issue may be endangered because of the short-sightedness of one General and the failure of his Government to order him to carry out their undertakings."

While Pershing was standing fast in France, the United States government was taking steps to remove the Army Air Service from the Signal Corps by creating two air departments, the Bureau of Aircraft Production, and the Bureau of Military Aeronautics with Maj. Gen. William L. Kenly as its director in the United

States. On May 29, Brig. Gen. Mason M. Patrick was appointed chief of air service for the American Expeditionary Force. Like the AEF ground troops under Pershing, U.S. airmen would retain their independence in choosing when and where to fight.

On May 11, 1918, Eddie decided to patrol across German lines in the company of Reed Chambers. Considered by Eddie to be a "daredevil by all appearances," Chambers was an eager flier who tempered his bravado with "a rare caution." Scouting the skies over Thiaucourt, they discovered four "splendid" Albatros planes in "good formation" four miles inside German lines. Eddie signaled Reed with wigwagging wings and the two Nieuports turned toward the Albatros group. Flying parallel, they arrived within "fair shooting range," only to see the lead Albatros bank over and run. When the other three followed, Eddie and Chambers were left with "a vacant sky over Thiaucourt." Through "sheer impudence," Eddie recorded, they had bluffed a superior force into turning tail.

Four days later the commander of the 6th French Army, General Gerard, arrived at Toul to present medals recognizing the valor and courage of men of the 94th Squadron, including the Croix de Guerre to Eddie, Jimmy Meissner, and David Peterson, with crosses given posthumously to Lt. Charles Chapman and Capt. James Norman Hall, then believed to have been shot down and killed. While dressing for the formal ceremony, Eddie was advised by his "gallant messmates" to be sure to shave closely and use plenty of talcum powder on the cheeks that Gerard would certainly kiss in the French fashion of giving medals. The ceremony began shortly after three o'clock in the afternoon with a march by three companies of French troops and a military band. Also present was a large contingent of the American 26th Infantry Division and its band. Lined up on the field were all the 94th Squadron's Nieuports. They shone brightly as the sun glinted off their red, white, and blue markings. Mechanics and enlisted men stood in ranks beside the planes. Suddenly, to the blare of horns from both bands, General Gerard and his retinue strode from behind a hangar.

Eddie's first thoughts were of how proud his mother would be of him, then turned to how he would attempt to stretch his face to such a height that no general would ever be able to plant a kiss on each of his cheeks. The 26th Division band struck up "The Star-Spangled Banner." Next, a brief, congratulatory speech by Gen. Billy Mitchell. Then, with Eddie and Jimmy Meissner "shaking in well-polished boots," came the French general. A "kindly looking man," he had "a businesslike military efficiency in his features and movements" as he approached the three recipients with the medals and the citations.

The Croix de Guerre, Eddie noted, was "a beautiful medal in bronze, artistically designed and executed" suspended from a ribbon of striped red and green on which were fastened a palm leaf or star, depending on whether the award was presented by a division (star) or army (palm), one for each citation. Eddie's bore a single palm. To his great relief, Gerard made no attempt to present it with an accompanying kiss. Ceremony over, the 94th airmen took off in their planes to put on an exhibition of stunts. When that was done, Meissner sidled up to Eddie and said, "What do you say to going up and getting a Boche?"

Shortly after they were airborne they spotted a two-man German Rumpler, capable of the highest ceiling of any German two-seater. Climbing at top speed to overtake the Rumpler, Eddie was disappointed to see the plane turn and dash safely away toward Germany.

While Eddie had enthusiastically accepted Meissner's invitation to get a Boche, Eddie's closest friend in the squadron was Reed Chambers. They enjoyed discussing "new tricks and wiles" for outsmarting and outflying "the crafty Hun." The game of war aviation, Eddie noted, "was so new that any day some newcomer may happen upon a clever trick that none of us has before thought of." As in his racing days, when he and Lee Frayer had devised winning strategies for the track, he and Chambers often sat up late at night thinking of ways to get the better of the enemy, then rose early in the morning to test in daylight the plan that had enraptured them the previous evening.

During a scheming session on the night of May 16, 1918, Eddie and Chambers decided to test the old adage of the early bird

catching the worm. By taking off well before dawn, they sur-
mised, they could "climb clear out of sight and out of hearing
long before the Huns were out of bed." By "hanging around their
front yard," they calculated, they just might pick up a stray German photoreconnaissance plane alone over Allied lines. Putting
the plan into action at four o'clock on the morning of May 17, they
were soon at eighteen thousand feet with unlimited visibility and
confident that they surely would enjoy the upper hand of any
two-seater German that might wander below. As Eddie laid in
wait with no result, he began to feel indignant at the thought of
having crawled from bed so early to find perfect weather, only "to
be nullified by the refusal of the fish to bite."

Deciding that he'd picked the wrong fishing hole, he headed for
Metz. Twenty-five miles behind German lines, it had one of the
best German aerodromes. Also there was a famous old fortress set
deep in the valley of the Moselle River. Sheer thousand-foot bluffs
flanked the river before it made a sudden turn a mile below the
"queen city of Lorraine." But as Eddie flew over the aerodrome,
expecting to find quarry, no Germans presented themselves. Regretting that he had no bombs to drop on the hangars below, he
turned toward a German base at Thiaucourt.

When he neared the aerodrome, he descended to eight thousand feet, slowed the engine in order to glide as silently as possible over the German airfield outside the city, and watched three
Albatros planes take off one after the other. When the last Albatros had its back toward him, he began to narrow the distance.
Over Montsec, north of St. Mihiel, he estimated that he was three
thousand feet from his target. Spotted by antiaircraft gunners below, he was met by Archie blasts that were intended to alert the
German planes of his presence. Duly warned, the German airmen looked around and saw his Nieuport diving. As the last Albatros in the formation swerved, Eddie was less than two
hundred yards away, diving at a furious pace and heedless of
everything but the target. Closing to fifty yards, with the Albatros
darting steeply, he opened fire and watched tracers rip into the
back of the pilot's seat.

As the German plane fell away and began to flutter, Eddie

pulled back sharply on the stick and started a climb. Severely stressed by the maneuver, the Nieuport's top right wing tore and blew away. This caused the plane to turn on its right side and the tail to swing up, putting the plane into an uncontrollable downward spiral. As the remaining Albatros planes opened fire, Eddie wondered why they were wasting ammunition on a plane that was obviously going to crash. Wondering where he would hit the ground, he fastened his eyes on the woods of Montsec and envisioned his mother opening a cablegram informing her of his death.

Looking over the side of the plane, he saw a line of trucks and a group of men, waiting, he supposed, to gather souvenirs from a smashed American airplane and probably from the body of the dead pilot. Desperately pulling open the throttle with a disregard for the consequences, he found that the Nieuport leveled out. With the landscape whizzing below, he saw that he was making headway faster than he was descending. If he could keep the battered ship aloft for five minutes, he calculated, he would cross Allied lines, only two miles ahead. Talking to the plane as if it were a horse, he promised that if they both survived he would give her a good rubdown when they reached the stable.

Crossing the Allied line at a thousand feet, he saw the number 94 on a hangar and knew he was home. Barely missing the hangar, the plane pancaked onto the field. Startled visiting French fliers who rushed to the spot exclaimed that his Nieuport had resembled a bird with a broken wing. Never mind that, Eddie answered. Where was Reed Chambers?

No one knew. But a few minutes later Chambers's plane set down. He had been back in Germany, he explained, and in coming out had seen two Albatros planes returning to their base. This indicated to Eddie that the one he'd attacked had gone down. Unfortunately, Chambers had not seen the engagement, so Eddie had no one to confirm his victory. But early the following day, observers of the French 8th Army reported unofficially that at 6:24 the previous morning they had seen Eddie's crippled plane staggering homeward and that an Albatros had crashed a few hundred yards inside their line. Official confirmation of Eddie's solo victory was made on May 27, 1918. (His first credit, on April 29, had been shared with Captain Hall.)

Looking back on a brush with death, Eddie was philosophical as he wrote, "I had passed through rather a harrowing experience. Yet I do not recall that I felt anything unusual had happened, as I slid over the edge of my cockpit and inquired for Reed Chambers. This is one of the curious results of flying in wartime: A kind of fatalism soon possesses a pilot to such an extent that he learns to take everything as a matter of course."

Fatalism would serve him well.

Regardless of how much natural flying talent a new pilot might have shown in training elsewhere, Eddie's duty was to accompany him during his first experience over enemy lines. One of these novices, a lieutenant named Kurtz, arrived at Toul about a month after the 94th Squadron began operations. He'd trained with Eddie at Issoudun, but while Eddie had gone on to gunnery school at Cazeaux and then to Toul, Kurtz had been sent to England to teach gunnery to thousands of young Americans who'd been drafted into the Air Service. Eager to experience combat, Kurtz had wangled his way out of teaching and been sent to the 94th Squadron. As second in command at the time, Eddie accompanied him on his first sortie, called a "voluntary patrol" because it hadn't been ordered up, to check a report that German planes were airborne. The third pilot on the patrol was Reed Chambers. As they got into their Nieuports, Eddie was not surprised to see that Kurtz looked a little nervous.

Taking off in perfect weather, the planes flew in a V formation with Chambers to the left of Eddie's plane and Kurtz on the right. A hundred meters behind and a little higher, he was instructed to maintain that position, consider himself a spectator, and test his guns en route with a few short bursts, so long as his plane was pointed toward Germany. If the formation became scattered and he was unable to find Eddie and Chambers, he was to fly south until sure of being over French territory, and land. At 14,500 feet and safely above Allied antiaircraft gunners who might think the three planes were German, Eddie looked forward to "the hazard and adventure" of flying over enemy lines.

Catching the shimmer of what he believed was a German photo plane at 19,000 feet, he decided the Boche was out of reach. Suddenly white puffs appeared ahead and above, meaning that "more Huns were abroad" in the vicinity. Spotting three single-seat Albatroses about half a mile forward, he wagged his wings to alert Chambers and Kurtz. Analyzing the situation, Eddie saw that the Germans had the advantage of higher altitude. Taking advantage of it, they swooped down with guns blazing. Maneuvering in response, Eddie and Chambers were now at an equal altitude. As the Germans broke off combat, Eddie succeeded in separating one Albatros from the others. In a running fight in which it was his life or the German's, they were over the German-held city of Thiaucourt.

As both pilots sparred like prizefighters in a ring, the German fired incendiary explosive bullets that cracked all around Eddie's plane. Should one strike his fuel tank, the fight would be over with the German the victor. Executing a half turn, Eddie suddenly was on the German's tail. "In those few critical moments which constitute the turning point of a fight," Eddie wrote, "the aviator usually has all thoughts of self drive away."

With the German in a position in which he was unable to turn his guns, giving Eddie a chance that would probably be lost in a second, Eddie fired both his guns. Raked by bullets, the Albatros went into a spiral that seemed certain to end in a crash—unless the pilot was able to pull it out. In such a "giddy dive," Eddie well knew, the hands of an "artful pilot" were "the only highway to safety." Should that happen, he was prepared to resume the battle, but at a lower altitude over enemy ground. Not knowing if other Germans were lurking above, Eddie chose not to follow the Albatros down. Unable to witness the plane's fate, the issue of whether he had scored a victory would be left in doubt.

Regaining altitude, Eddie discovered two planes speeding toward him. He assumed they were Germans out for revenge. With speed his only recourse, he pulled hard on the throttle and turned the nose of the Nieuport down and raced as he had never done in a car on a track. But in this case the prize was not a trophy; it was his life. Deciding that the best tactic was to turn and fight, he soon had one of the advancing planes within firing range. As he sighted on the plane, it abruptly swung up, revealing a wing with the concentric red, white, and blue insignia of the U.S. Air Service. In an instant of realization that the pilot was Reed Chambers and that the second plane was that of Kurtz, Eddie turned to show them his colors.

"It is not often that a man rises to the degree of joy I felt as we headed for home, the flight over, and all three safe," Eddie recalled. "I had every reason to believe my German was down, possibly Chambers had got another, and Kurtz for his first time over [German lines] had deported himself wonderfully."

Winging toward home base and looking around for Kurtz, he couldn't find him. But as he approached Toul, he saw Kurtz's plane circling another nearby airfield. In the next instant, he watched Kurtz's plane drop into a tailspin. Slamming into the ground, it exploded in flames in a patch of barbed-wire entanglements that made a landing to rescue Kurtz impossible.

After landing his own plane at home base, Eddie sped on a motorcycle to the crash site "with a vague hope" that he might yet be able to do some good. He found the horror of charred remains of the man who'd been his companion at flying school and only one brief hour before had set out with him "full of life and hope."

Mystified by the cause of the tragedy, Eddie learned from a mutual friend that Kurtz had confided that he had been subject to fainting spells at high altitudes and feared blacking out in the air during a mission. Eddie assumed that it had been Kurtz's apprehension that had caused his apparent nervousness at the beginning of the flight.

Following Kurtz's funeral the next morning, a French outpost in no-man's-land reported that a sentry had seen Eddie's battle with the Albatros and that the plane had indeed crashed.

"I had got my Boche," Eddie recorded, "but I had lost a friend, and he had perished in the manner dreaded by all aviators, for he had gone down in flames."

A few days after confirmation of Eddie's success during Kurtz's first and last patrol, Lt. Walter Smyth sauntered up to Eddie and asked, "Rick, where do you find all these Boches of yours?" Shaking his head, Smyth continued ruefully, "I've been over the lines two or three times and I haven't had a single look at an enemy machine. I would like to go across with someone like you who always gets some fun. Will you take me with you on a voluntary patrol?"

Liking Smyth's spirit, and with his regular patrol scheduled for late afternoon, Eddie told him to be ready at nine o'clock. Their destination was the vicinity of St. Mihiel. Flying at seventeen thousand feet, they found no enemy and set out for a run from Pont-à-Mousson to Verdun. As they crossed the small town of Mars-la-Tour, Eddie glimpsed an Albatros two-seater making toward Verdun. With the German several thousand feet below and two miles ahead, the Americans enjoyed the advantages of being two against one, altitude, surprise, and the sun at their backs.

Diving and firing, Eddie flew past the startled German. A moment later he found the obviously experienced pilot of the Albatros suddenly above him. Recognizing that his opponent was an old hand at dogfighting, Eddie reversed their positions, coming out on top, but in no position to fire. Instead, he found himself looking into the business ends of the adroit German's brace of machine guns.

In an attempt to bank sharply right, Eddie went into a tailspin. Recovering, he watched the Albatros making a fast spurt for home. Meanwhile, Smyth was "composedly sailing" above and "appearing to be quite enchanted with the entertainment." Realizing they were twenty-five miles into enemy skies, Eddie chose to "retreat while retreating was good," fully satisfied that he'd given Smyth his "money's worth." When he looked for Smyth, he was not to be seen.

Fearing that Smyth had run into Germans and in the unequal combat had crash-landed, Eddie flew toward base feeling responsible for whatever had happened. As he neared Toul, he saw a large crowd gathered at the center of the field. When he landed and hurried to ask if anyone knew what had happened to Smyth, he was stunned to hear them talking not of Smyth, but about Maj. Raoul Lufbery.

The beloved "Luf," America's "ace of aces," the most revered American aviator in France, had been shot down in flames min-utes earlier not six miles from Toul.

About an hour after Eddie and Smyth had taken off, a report came in that a German photo plane was at that moment directly overhead. The only pilot on the field ready for flight, a lieutenant named Gude, who had never flown in combat, immediately took off. As the men on the ground watched, Gude appeared to score a hit, but the Albatros remained aloft. As it turned to retreat, Gude attacked again. Antiaircraft guns also opened up. But the German sailed away through the barrage, dodged Gude, climbed, and headed toward Nancy.

Observing the engagement with increasing impatience was Lufbery. Depsite his many victories, he had yet to down a German plane over Allied territory, and therefore had never seen the wreckage of a plane that he'd shot down. Seizing the opportunity to go after a Boche above Allied territory, he commandeered a ready Nieuport and took off in pursuit of the Albatros. Less than five minutes later he came within range of the plane at two thou-sand feet. Everyone on the ground watched breathlessly. After a burst of machine gun fire, Lufbery swerved away and appeared to struggle with jammed guns. With the weapons evidently cleared and beginning a second attack, his plane burst into flames.

A moment later the observers below saw Lufbery standing in the cockpit. As the flames licked around it and thick black smoke formed long plumes along the fuselage, they watched in horror as their hero jumped. He hit the ground just north of Nancy, in the garden of a woman's house with a small nearby stream. Be-lieving that death on the ground was always preferable to a fiery one, he had leapt from a flaming plane that was going 120 miles an hour, two hundred feet up. A tracer bullet that had hit the plane's gas tank had also sheared off the thumb of his left hand as it gripped the joystick. He'd apparently jumped in the hope that he would fall into the stream.

The next day, May 20, 1918, he was buried in a plot that the men of the 94th Squadron called "airman's cemetery." Attending the funeral were the top brass of the French 6th Army, the commander of the U.S. 26th Division, chief of the air force of America, Gen. William "Billy" Mitchell, and hundreds of officers from all branches of the Allied services. With other pilots of Flight One, Eddie flew over the cemetery in formation at fifty feet and dropped flowers.

"Returning then to our vacant aerodrome," Eddie wrote, "we sorrowfully realized that America's greatest aviator and Ace of Aces had been laid away for his last rest."

In an attempt at avenging Lufbery's death, a French pilot had pursued the Albatros and was shot through the heart. His plane crashed about a mile from the place where Lufbery had plummeted to his death. When Douglas Campbell tried to down the German plane, he'd found it too far ahead to catch. Spotting a two-seat Rumpler, he engaged it in a brisk battle, killed the rear gunner, and wounded the pilot. The plane crashed with both wings torn off within Allied lines. Later in the day Eddie accompanied Douglas to the site so Douglas could get a souvenir.

The elusive Albatros that had cost Lufbery's life was finally shot down by a French pilot, and both German aviators were captured.

On May 28, nine days after Lufbery's death, Eddie and Douglas Campbell went on a voluntary patrol to see if they could "bag a few Hun machines." If Eddie succeeded, it would be his fourth win, one short of the number needed to be designated an ace. In beautiful weather, they headed toward Pont-à-Mousson, careful to conceal their presence from the Germans by keeping inside Allied lines. After several patrols between Pont-à-Mousson and St. Mihiel, they turned for home and noticed an enemy formation coming from Mars-la-Tour. Climbing to eighteen thousand feet, Eddie made out a pair of two-seat Albatroses and four single-seat Pfalz fighters below. Waiting for them to cross into Allied airspace, he had the advantages of altitude, the sun, and surprise. As he began his attack dive, the two Albatroses and their quartet of protectors turned back. Although the range was hopelessly long, he and Campbell fired occasional bursts and soon found themselves above Thiaucourt and engaged in an aerial game of catch-me-if-you-can with four fighters that tried again and again to lure the Americans into the trap of going after a decoy Pfalz.

The challenge for Eddie and Campbell was to "get down at the bait and dispose of him and then regain our altitude before the superior enemy formation could descend upon us." In this high-flying game of cat and mouse, Eddie was confident that his and Campbell's judgment was as good as that of the Germans, that he and Campbell had the better position, and that they could rely on their Nieuports to outpace the fighters in a race to reach the temporarily unprotected pair of Albatroses. Diving side by side with throttles wide open, they left the four Pfalz planes hopelessly behind by a mile and went after the first of their quarry. Riddled with more than a hundred bullets from each Nieuport, the Albatros spun down and crashed in the Ratta Woods at the edge of the town of Flirey.

Expecting an attack by the four German fighters, Eddie watched them rush toward the second Albatros, surround it, and escort it northward toward their base. Reflecting on what he called "the surprise of the day," and on later retreats that he saw as "this craven characteristic of the enemy air fighters," Eddie wrote, "No matter what their superiority in numbers or position, if we succeeded in bringing down one of their number the others almost immediately abandoned the combat and gave us the field. It may be military efficiency but it always appeared to me to be pure yellowness."

On May 30, 1918, known as Decoration Day, a holiday of remembrance for the dead of the American Civil War that in the future would be Memorial Day for the fallen in the Great War, and an occasion for a five-hundred-mile automobile race at a brick-paved speedway in Indianapolis that would be another chapter in the life of Eddie Rickenbacker, the American aviators at Toul were alerted that the British were planning an air raid on a German railroad at Conflans. The notification included a request that the Americans provide protection for the British planes on their way back. The attack was scheduled to begin at eight in the morning.

The American plan provided for Lt. Jimmy Meissner to lead six Nieuports of the 94th Squadron and Lt. John Mitchell to command six planes of the 95th Squadron. They were to rendezvous over Thiaucort, about halfway to Conflans. Not a part of the mission, but thinking "the chances were good for a little private scrap," Eddie took off on a voluntary patrol a few minutes after the two squadrons were airborne. When he reached Flirey at fifteen thousand feet, he was "in a splendid position to witness the whole show." He wrote of it:

There were the British squadrons returning from this expedition against the supply depots on Conflans. They had evidently dropped all their bombs and had aroused a hornets' nest in so doing. A large formation of enemy planes were following them hot-foot and our fighting machines were climbing up to intercept them. Ahead of the British airplanes a furious storm of shrapnel indicated that Archie was not caught napping. The German shells burst below and ahead of the bombing squadron but ceased as soon as the pursuing Hun machines approached that area. Those German batteries were putting up a beautiful performance but they were lacking one essential. They couldn't hit the target.

My own formations were at that moment passing over Thiaucourt and were dashing forward with all speed to the rescue of the approaching Englishmen. It looked like a regular dogfight was being set up. The Americans should reach the R.A.F. boys at about the same time that the Huns [in Fokker fighters] overtook them from the rear.

Suddenly I noticed something going wrong with the American formation below me. Evidently another enemy flight had come up from the west and had started a free-for-all to prevent the Nieuports from giving aid to

> *the bombers. As I watched this encounter I noticed one*
> *of our Nieuports, some three thousand feet below me*
> *and a little to the west, first flutter and then begin to fall*
> *out of control. Ever since the beginning of the stage set-*
> *ting I had been edging my way toward the center of the*
> *field where the opposing forces must meet. Now they*
> *were practically under me.*

As the stricken Nieuport went into its tailspin, Eddie saw two Al-batroses going after it and decided to jump into the fray. De-scending "pell mell" after one of the German planes, he fired at long range and continued blasting until he saw the Albatros falling away "quite beyond control" while the other Albatros veered off.

Continuing down after the Nieuport that appeared to have been hit, Eddie watched it pull out of its spin and with one long bank begin to climb. Its pilot had engaged in a ruse and "was coming back to fight." Climbing above him, Eddie flew into the continuing battle between the Nieuports and Fokkers. Darting from one battle to another with a "savage sort of elation," he had a "glorious feeling" at downing an enemy and "the sweetness of such a victory," knowing that he had saved "a comrade" who was now following him in searching the sky from place to place for "a favorable opening."

Observing a running fight that had broken off from the main battle about five kilometers in the direction of Pont-à-Mousson, Eddie followed the little Nieuport he'd saved to join five other American planes in a battle with five Albatroses. As the "show" drifted toward the Moselle River, he increased altitude and pre-pared to select a target. While looking for the most favorable door into the dogfight, he saw the same little Nieuport that had been in trouble over Thiaucourt diving on the tail of an Albatros while another Albatros was on his. A moment later both the Germans had maneuvered above the Nieuport.

In position for a second time to help the pilot of the Nieuport, Eddie fired a long burst into the nearest Albatros and saw at once that it was finished. Trailing smoke, it continued straight until it crashed into trees on the east bank of the Moselle. While Eddie's diving attack was going on, the pilot of the besieged Nieuport turned hard to let the remaining pursuer pass. But the stress of the abrupt maneuver caused his right wing's fabric to rip off.

Recalling that the loss of wing fabric had nearly claimed Jimmy Meissner's life just two weeks earlier and that the same difficulty had caused Captain Hall to crash, Eddie marveled that the pilot of the damaged Nieuport was somehow keeping the plane under control. As the plane staggered toward Allied lines, Eddie drew next to it to see who had pulled the ruse that had led to the demise of one Albatros, outpiloted two others, and was now "certainly something of an artist" in keeping his crippled plane aloft.

Twenty feet away from the battered plane, Eddie looked into the cockpit and saw that its pilot was Jimmy Meissner. "Turning a cheery grin" and "taking his ease," he waved a hand in greeting. With Eddie staying close all the way back to Toul, Meissner set the plane down "in a little crash" and bounded out of the wreckage "as blithe and merry as ever."

"Thanks, old boy, for shooting down those Boches on my tail," said Meissner. "I'm beginning to like coming home without any wings on my machine."

"I got two Huns through you today, and I thank you for them," Eddie replied, "but you must really stop this sort of thing. It's getting on my nerves."

CHAPTER 7

Enjoyable Game

"F ROM THE FREQUENCY OF THESE ACCIDENTS TO OUR NIEUPORTS IT may be wondered why we continued to fly them," Eddie Rickenbacker wrote in an account of his exploits in the Great War that he titled *Fighting the Flying Circus.* "The answer is simple– we had no others we could use. The American Air Force was in dire need of machines of all kinds. We were thankful to get any kind that would fly."

Noting that the French had discarded the Nieuport for the sturdier, stronger Spad and that the United States had to take the out-of-date Nieuports or go without, he complained that American pilots found themselves "compelled to venture out in Nieuports against far more experienced pilots in more modern machines."

A product of the Societe Anonyme des Etablissements Nieuport, formed in 1909, the single-seat biplane flown by Eddie and his compatriots had been originally designed for racing. The fighter version, Nieuport 28, appeared in 1914. The Spad (an acronym for Societe pour Aviation et ses Derives) had also been made for racing. A single-seat fighter, it was powered by a 140-horsepower Hispano-Suiza liquid-cooled engine and armed with a forward-firing machine gun that was synchronized to fire through its propeller arc. A later model, introduced in mid-1917, had a 220-horsepower engine and two forward-firing guns.

The first American-made plane, called the DH-4, built by Dayton Wright Company on an English design and fitted with a Liberty engine, had arrived in France on May 1, 1918. It made its first flight on May 17. It would not go out on patrol until August 2, along with eighteen planes of the 135th Corps Observation Squadron from a base at Ourches, France. A consignment of U.S. flying boats, six HS-1s, arrived at Paulliac, France, on April 24. Not until August 17 would an American-made bomber, a Martin MB-1, make its maiden flight in the United States. The first standard bomber of the Air Service, it would never see combat. Later modifications of it would be used by the Post Office Department.

Venting frustration with the sorry condition of the U.S. Air Service on April 21, 1918, Theodore Roosevelt wrote to his son Quentin, "I think that we really are somewhat aroused . . . that we are of so little weight in the terrible battle now going on . . . For example, a layman like myself is utterly unable to make out what our airplane situation is. We all know that you have no bombing planes (I am doubtless using the wrong terms), but we cannot tell you how soon you will have them, and in what proportion you will get them from the French or be utilized by the French fliers. Therefore I have no idea whether there is any possibility of you getting to the front—whether you are fighting, or raging because you can't get into the fighting line."

While Theodore Roosevelt's concern was the condition of American aircraft, the vast majority of Americans were fascinated by accounts in their newspapers of the daring and bravery of the dashing young men who operated them. To quench their thirst for stories and for heroes, men and a few women of the Fourth Estate who had rushed to Europe as "war correspondents" were often flamboyant, colorful, energetic news-seekers who had a disdain for military regulations that got in the way of their reporting. Among them were Floyd Gibbons of the *Chicago Tribune*, Jimmy Hopper of *Collier's Weekly*, Peggy Hull of the *El Paso Tribune* (she paid her own way to get there), Irvin Cobb for the *Saturday Evening Post*, Harry Hansen of the *Chicago Daily*

News, Westbrook Pegler and Fred Ferguson of United Press, Alexander Woollcott (abandoning his job as theater critic of the *New York Times*), and a chubby scribe for the *New York Tribune* named Heywood Broun. So disheveled and unkempt was he that General Pershing took one look at him and asked, "What happened to you? Did you fall down?" For all of these reporters and others, no story proved of more interest to their readers than exploits of aviators, especially those that dealt with young men who'd earned the title "Ace."

Inevitably, reporters who had earned a living keeping score in the form of election returns, baseball and football games, prizefights, and other sports competitions were drawn to keeping track on behalf of an avid public of how many enemy planes had been shot down and by whom. It was American reporters who decided that to be an ace a man had to shoot down five planes. For the British the official RAF magic number was three. Learning that the famous race car driver Eddie Rickenbacker had qualified as an ace, the American correspondents knew they had a good story and that it could only get better—assuming that Rickenbacker didn't get shot down and killed, which would certainly be a sensational headline-maker itself.

In Eddie the reporters found a man to match their concept of how an ace should look. "In his racing days," noted Eddie's friend and biographer Hans Christian Adamson, "Eddie's appearance was almost clerically austere; now, he had large patch pockets on his tunic which fitted his tall, slim, well-set figure as a shell fits its egg. He wore a strictly irregular British Royal Flying Corps cap with United States insignia. His riding breeches had an arrogant flare and were of the finest whipcord. He sported French high-laced boots and swung a colorado-claro Malacca cane on the field and off."

Acutely aware of his fame, Eddie was reticent about being called a hero. "When I was racing," he pointed out, "I learned that you can't set stock in public adoration or your press clippings. I heard crowds of a hundred thousand screaming my name but a week later they couldn't remember who I was. You're a hero today and a bum tomorrow—hero to zero."

"More to the point than his appearance," wrote aviation historian Robert J. Serling, "was his perfection of flying techniques. He was not really a skilled pilot but his combat effectiveness was deadly. He checked out his own guns before every patrol. He developed a technique of cruising just above stall speed to save fuel and be assured of maximum engine performance when needed. His years on the race track had given him judgment of distance and speed that few pilots possessed, and he made sure that he and not the enemy had the advantage of position and altitude before he attacked like a striking hawk."

Also attributing Eddie's prowess in the air to his racing experience, biographer Finis Farr wrote, "He had achieved self-control on the racetrack by a similar method of running ahead of the nervous breaking point just as he tried to run ahead of the other cars. The surroundings at airdromes were similar to racing pits and set familiar nervous reactions going. There were the same crews of mechanics, the roaring of engines, the note of chivalry, the feeling of squires preparing a knight errant for the quest when the ground crews helped Rick to his place at the controls before wheeling out car or aircraft. Flying clothes were the same as racing clothes. In each case he was setting out, gloved and helmeted, to face dangers from which he might not return."

In all his close calls, Eddie said, he experienced fear only after it was over. "Fighting," he explained, "requires a different kind of bravery from that involved in flying. The combat pilot must be mentally prepared to shoot and kill and to be shot in return. Some pilots have sufficient motivation and bravery to learn to fly, but going out to kill or be killed over the lines required a different type of courage. Some did not have it."

After he became a pilot, events followed at such a whirlwind that it never occurred to him to review what had gone before. He looked back over the five victories that made him an ace and recalled every maneuver he'd made in every combat and compared it with the one made by his adversary. He also recalled how many mistakes he'd made and recognized that his survival had "happened too many times to be luck." Caution was important, yes, but never timidity. Aware that he had a reputation for getting close enough to an adversary to "hit him with a baseball bat," he believed that he had to be bold, "but only at the right moment."

On the day before Eddie became an ace, the German army had swept into Soissons, taken 50,000 French prisoners, and captured 650 artillery pieces and 2,000 machine guns. On May 30, 1918, as Eddie was shooting down two Albatroses, the Kaiser's troops were at the river Marne near Château-Thierry. On June 1 they were forty miles from Paris.

That morning Eddie had "an interesting little fracas" with a two-seat Rumpler within the German lines. Disappointed that its pilot declined his invitation to fight, he flew back to base and arranged to take "a little joyride" by car to Nancy. A city of about 30,000, it prided itself on the title "Little Paris of the East." He found its shops almost empty and its glory considerably dimmed. The talk of the inhabitants was rife with worry about the Germans' "big push" on Paris.

At a restaurant called Walter's on Stanislas Place, Eddie learned that it was named after a Frenchman who had emigrated to the United States. He had been the chef at New York's Hotel Knickerbocker. On a nostalgic visit to France, Walter had been caught by the war and enlisted in the French army. Wounded a few months later, he retired and opened the restaurant. Offering a mostly American menu, it quickly became a favorite of American aviators. Gossip among the pilots was that their squadrons were about to be moved to another sector to help in thwarting the German advance.

Without immediate American assistance, warned General Foch to General Pershing at a meeting of the Supreme War Council at Versailles, the defensive line would crumble. But with an immediate commitment of 250,000 U.S. forces under temporary French command, the attack could be halted. "The battle, the battle," Foch exclaimed, "nothing else matters."

Pershing's reply was chilling. The United States had no such number of troops available. He had at his command 170,000 troops, with 140,000 more to disembark in France in July.

"This," said Premier Clemenceau, "is a great disappointment."

In the meantime the Americans on hand were available, under American command, to go into the line at Château-Thierry to form a bulwark against the German advance toward Paris. On June 3, under severe pressure by the Germans at Belleau Wood, Sgt. Dan Daly of the U.S. Marines was asked if the Americans intended to withdraw.

"Retreat hell," Daly snapped. "We just got here."

The next day Eddie Rickenbacker was in the air again with Lieutenant Smyth "to take a look" at the enemy near Pont-à-Mousson. Having become an ace by downing Germans in their territory, he longed to claim one over Allied ground and "having the satisfaction of seeing what sort of prize I had bagged." Noticing the smoke puffs of American antiaircraft fire that meant German planes were in the vicinity of Toul, he wagged wings to signal Smyth to follow him in search of them. Sighting a two-seater Rumpler photoreconnaissance plane over "our very front lawn," he calculated that he had just the right altitude for a leisurely direct attack that would drop the Rumpler a few miles from a hangar of the Toul aerodrome.

Nearing the Rumpler, he saw the number "16" and an insignia in the form of a rising sun painted on its fuselage. Envisioning hanging the 16 and the emblem as trophies on the wall over his cot, he aimed his machine gun at the pilot of the Rumpler and squeezed the trigger. But after the first burst of fire, the gun jammed. Unscathed by the bullets, the German turned to run. With the machine gun unjammed, Eddie chased the Rumpler toward Thiaucourt with all hopes of a victory in Allied territory lost. As German ground fire crackled and sparkled around him "like a dozen popcorn kernels," he watched with anger and frustration as the Rumpler descended safely to the ground.

Back at base, he restrained his seething anger at the armorers and mildly suggested that thereafter they make a more careful preflight examination of the gun. When he arrived at the hangar the next morning expecting to go on another voluntary patrol, he found the mechanics with the machine gun disassembled. A defect had been found in its mechanism. Without the gun, there could be no mission in Eddie's Nieuport. Looking around for a substitute, he settled on a plane that carried two machine guns. It was Smyth's. Agreeing to be grounded, Smyth watched Eddie wing toward German territory.

For a time no enemy appeared, but then a two-seater photo plane presented itself from the direction of Metz, accompanied by a pair of escort scout planes. Lurking high with the sun at his back, Eddie waited until the formation crossed the Allied line. As the photography plane passed below, he could not believe his luck. It was the Rumpler that had eluded him yesterday. Again picturing the 16 and rising sun adorning the walls of his sleeping quarters, he let the plane go deeper into the territory of its enemy.

As No. 16 left Commercy behind, Eddie darted down. It was to be a straightforward fight in the open. With mind racing as fast as the Nieuport, he anticipated the German's moves. At the first burst of gunfire from his rear he could be expected to dive. Then the combat would start.

As Eddie swooped down toward the Rumpler's tail, he saw the man in the rear seat rise and look back. Evidently the pilot had seen Eddie's plane in his rearview mirror and yelled an alert. The man in the rear "office" opened fire. But instead of diving, the pilot zoomed up. This forced Eddie to go under the Rumpler. As he did so, he was shocked to discover that he was under fire from a gun in the Rumpler's belly. This was a revelation; "an unheard-of method of defense." To make matters worse, he found both his guns had jammed. Circling away and out of range, he managed to clear only one. The German was now heading homeward in the direction of St. Mihiel.

Engaged in a forty-minute shooting match with the German rear gunner ("the nimblest airman" he had ever seen), Eddie found himself well behind German lines. As he hoped to get in a killing burst, his gun jammed again. The German departed. The show was over. But the day's adventure wasn't. As Eddie turned homeward, the Nieuport's engine froze. Having been up for more than two and a half hours, the motor's oil supply had been exhausted. Powerless, Eddie looked for a landing spot, but every field was laced with barbed-wire barriers. With no choice but to set down, he barely cleared the top of a wire fence and landed without crashing.

With Smyth's plane left to be recovered by mechanics and an "airplane ambulance," Eddie returned by car to Toul to learn that Douglas Campbell had been wounded that morning, but had managed to return to base. A fragment of an exploding bullet had slammed into his back, barely missing his spine. Although Douglas had scored a sixth official victory, he would never fly in combat again.

"Had it not been for that unfortunate accident," Eddie wrote, "Lieutenant Douglas Campbell would undoubtedly have one of the highest scores claimed by an air fighter, for he was just entering upon his full stride."

Grateful that Douglas survived, the airmen of the 94th Squadron found great amusement in Eddie's frustrated duels with Rising Sun No. 16. Knowing that he could never rest until he'd gotten the elusive quarry, they bet one another, not as to the outcome, but on how long it would take Eddie to collect the plane's insignia for his wall. Lying awake at night, he made plans to build a house someday "suitably designed to set off those works of art to the best advantage."

Obsessed like a mythical knight on a quest for the Holy Grail, he was up early the next morning with "just one resolve." Seeing nothing else in the sky and searching for nothing else, he was in his own Nieuport, now fitted with a pair of Vickers guns that added weight to the plane. He flew in the direction of what he now knew was No. 16's favorite path. Suddenly, as though they'd made an appointment, the German appeared.

Unable to reach his preferred altitude because of the extra weight of the new guns, Eddie met the Rumpler at twenty thousand feet, but the German was still climbing, its two-man crew confident that they could ascend higher than any Nieuport. With Eddie two thousand feet below, they appeared to pay no attention to their neighbor as they headed for Nancy and Toul to snap photos of railroad depots. Occasionally the rear-seat observer-gunner fired at Eddie and was met with return bursts, each with no effect.

"So we continued along all over the northeast of France," Eddie would note in his diary. "I suppose most of the films they developed that afternoon showed the details of my Nieuport below them."

With the realization that he'd been defeated again, Eddie looked homeward, imagining his two adversaries laughing at him as he gave up the chase. Undaunted, he was in the air the following morning in a borrowed plane that its pilot promised could attain 20,000 feet. But with all of Eddie's coaxing, it reached only 19,000 as, "prompt and businesslike," No. 16 appeared with an escort, but two thousand feet higher and beyond Eddie's reach.

"With rare magnanimity," Eddie noted, "my old friends kindly came down a few hundred feet to keep me company. I joined the procession as of yore and the two machines made another grand tour of the northeasterly cities of France where we photographed all the railroad lines and canals, took a turn over several aerodromes, French, British, and American, surveyed the charming landscape in all directions and finally decided to call it a day and go home."

Accompanying them to their base, "sedulously maintaining the proper distance" between them and "mindful of their most delightful courtesy," Eddie turned about and made for home.

That night, as Eddie looked forward to another encounter with No. 16 in the morning, he came down with a fever and was ordered by a doctor to take a forty-eight-hour leave in Paris. When he stepped off a train at Gare de l'Est on June 6, 1918, the Germans were only forty miles away along the river Marne, preparing for a new assault. Hoping to blunt it, a thousand British and French aircraft attacked railway yards at Metz and Thionville. Not for a quarter of a century would the skies of France be clouded with such air armadas, but on June 6, 1944, American and British bombers flew to support the greatest invasion from sea in history on the fortified beaches of Normandy.

Two days before Eddie arrived in the City of Lights, Premier Georges Clemenceau had vowed to the French Chamber of Deputies, "I shall fight before Paris, I shall fight in Paris, I shall fight behind Paris."

Studying the faces of Parisians and a flood of refugees fleeing the Germans, Eddie saw terror gripping young and old alike. On the streets he found dazed and wandering people who had hastily departed their homes east of Paris. Most of them clutched whatever they had been able to carry. "They had all been walking for many miles," he noted. "Their clothing was dusty, worn, and crumpled. Their faces were pinched and wretched and an indescribable look of misery and suffering filled every countenance." Recording that a few old men accompanying women hobbled along empty-handed "with the utmost patience and abandon, leaving the whole care of the migration to the energetic women of France," he saw a demoralized Paris overflowing with refugees who had "no money, no food, no idea of where they wanted to go."

After "a good night's sleep away from the customary roar of artillery," Eddie ventured from his room like a tourist to take in the sights on the kind of fine, bright morning that romantic American songwriters of New York's Tin Pan Alley, who probably had never been to Paris, extolled in dreamy love ballads. After breakfast, strolling along the Champs-Élysées, under the Arc de Triomphe, and through the gardens of Bois de Boulogne, he saw fear in faces of Parisians who had been unable to flee their city. Or perhaps they had been so moved by Clemenceau's defiant rhetoric that they were unwilling to simply hand the city over to the Germans.

During his forty-eight hours, Eddie tried to "fancy the exulting German officers" walking the same beautiful avenues, driving their cars through the splendid woods, and occupying the city's magnificent palaces. What came to mind was a poster that had appeared all over the United States urging contributions to a French liberty loan campaign. It had depicted a French soldier with fixed bayonet above the vow, *"Ils ne Passeront Pas!"* When the United States declared war on Germany, millions of Frenchmen had taken to heart the words of George M. Cohan's musical pledge that "the Yanks are coming" and "we won't come back till its over Over There."

The Americans had come, but many fewer than the French had expected, and under the command of a general who seemed not only unwilling to throw them into battle, but downright contemptuous of his French allies. But American aviators had come, flying first as the Escadrille Lafayette, then in French hand-me-down planes–and had done very well; very well, indeed.

Feeling rested and refreshed after two days, Eddie set out for Toul by way of AEF headquarters at Chaumont, where he'd started in the war as a chauffeur. Now he was a certified ace, and the news that greeted him was heartening. Having heard American complaints about the narrow escapes experienced by Americans in their secondhand Nieuports, Gen. Benjamin Foulois had promised to see that American squadrons got the new, powerful Spad.

Few aviators in France did not know all about Foulois. Having enlisted in the U.S. Army at the time of the Spanish-American War, he'd served with the engineers in 1898–99 and in the Infantry from 1899 to 1901. That year he received his commission as second lieutenant. When he graduated from the Army Signal School on June 19, 1908, he was detailed to aeronautical duty. Appointed to an aeronautical board of Signal Corps officers for conducting airship and airplane trials, he was one of three officers to fly Dirigible No. 1 in August 1908. During the 1909 Wright Flyer speed qualification test by Orville Wright, he had been the passenger. With Lt. Frank P. Lahm he was taught to fly the army's first airplane, then was sent to France as the U.S. delegate to the International Congress of Aeronautics. Returning from Europe in October 1909, he was given flight training on the army's first plane, but on November 5 the craft was damaged, leaving him without a plane. He was then ordered to take it and a group of enlisted men to Fort Sam Houston, San Antonio, Texas, and teach himself to operate it. With inadequate funds and support, he began his self-instruction aided by letters from the Wright Brothers, which corrected his piloting errors. In 1911 he'd designed the first airplane radio receiver and carried out the first airplane reconnaissance flights. Relieved from flying in July of that year, he returned to aviation duty with the Signal Corps Aviation School at North Island, San Diego, California, in December 1913. He later commanded the 1st Aero Squadron in Mexico during the campaign led by Black Jack Pershing in 1916 to arrest Pancho Villa, and then was appointed chief of air service, AEF. If anyone could deliver the coveted Spads, Eddie believed as he returned to Toul, it was General Foulois.

Awaiting Eddie's arrival at Toul was a batch of cablegrams from the United States. They congratulated him on becoming an ace. He also learned that Jimmy Meissner, Alan Winslow, and Thorn Taylor had downed a Hanover two-seater during a ten-minute battle just north of Thiaucourt. But more exciting than all of this was notification that the 94th Squadron should expect to be moved to a busier sector of the front, probably the Château-Thierry region. After two months at Toul, Eddie noted, all "the boys" were restless and eager "to get into the thick of the battle down on the Marne where the 'Big Push' was now taking place."

Evidently part of German strategy was a change in air tactics. Their planes, Eddie noted, were now flying in formations. By taking to the sky in groups, he supposed, they hoped to scare away the more cautious of their adversaries. Although he was famous as a "lone wolf" in the air, Eddie recognized that to contend with this innovation, the 94th had to practice formation flying. Consequently, Nieuports took to the air day after day, met at a designated altitude, and formed a small fleet to explore offensive and defensive maneuvers as a group.

The first test came on June 18, 1918. Informed that the British would be mounting a raid on rail yards at Thionville, a town west of Metz that was a favorite German gateway to the front, Eddie asked for volunteers to accompany him. Six raised hands. Among them was a visitor.

Hamilton Coolidge of New York, a close friend of Quentin Roosevelt, had come over from the 95th Squadron. Having no experience in combat, "Ham" grabbed the opportunity to learn combat from the 94th's newest ace. The plan was for the 94th planes to meet at two thousand feet, circle until everyone was present, and proceed in close formation. Then they would rendezvous with the British bombers at 7:30 P.M. at sixteen thousand feet over Thionville.

Unknown to Eddie as the planes took off, a group of Ham Coolidge's former buddies in the 95th Squadron had heard about the British raid, and some of its planes were also departing to

lend them a hand. Aghast at the possibility of midair collisions
when he realized this, Eddie signaled his pilots to break away
and follow him. Time was pressing. But only three of his formation followed him while the others slipped into the 95th formation. Apparently unsure what to do, Ham Coolidge flew on alone.

When Eddie arrived over the Moselle at Pont-à-Mousson and
saw heavy Archie fire in the direction of Metz, he knew that the
British bombers were the attraction. Flying toward the smoke
puffs, he noticed that an American plane was evidently in
trouble. As it spun down, he raced toward it, but the plane leveled
off at four thousand feet and turned toward home. After escorting
it back over Allied lines, Eddie returned his attention to aiding the
British. Near St. Mihiel he rejoined his formation and found that
Ham Coolidge had attached himself to it. But as they cruised the
skies, the British were not to be found.

With dusk rapidly overtaking the land below, but the sun still
shining at fifteen thousand feet, Coolidge and another pilot broke
from formation and started home. Figuring they were having engine trouble, Eddie assessed the situation and decided that if he
were to have sufficient light to land at base, it was time to turn to
leave. Approaching Toul almost at dark, he saw a Nieuport flash
past in the opposite direction. Because no veteran aviator would
invite disaster by continuing to fly in such failing light, and certainly not be heading toward enemy lines alone, Eddie banked
over and started in pursuit of what had to be a new pilot. Overtaking the plane, he swerved ahead and wagged his wings. When
he circled back, he was relieved to see the Nieuport follow. Safely
down, the errant, embarrassed, profusely apologetic, and grateful
flier was Ham Coolidge.

Going to bed that night, Eddie looked back on that first day of
formation flying and judged it a "confused mess." A few hours
later he found himself in formation again, winging northward
before dawn and convinced that the distant thundering of a
tremendous artillery barrage from the German lines meant that
something big was on. Ahead, the blasts of the guns between Pont-
à-Mousson and St. Mihiel lit the sky like lightning flashes and
turned the trenches below his plane into a maze of inky shadows

visible through a thin veil of fog. Assuming that the shelling was a prelude to German troops going "over the top," he came in low, strafing the ground, but found no masses of soldiers. After several passes that left him out of ammunition, he returned to base.

Reloaded and refueled, he was soon back, making ground-skimming attacks in the region of Seichprey at daybreak. But now he saw Germans in the trenches. Raking them was "a very enjoyable game." Watching the troops flee in terror, he found himself chuckling with delight at single-handedly spreading consternation. Imagining the helplessness he'd inspired among the enemy, he was, he would recall, "having the time of my life."

Of an attack on an artillery emplacement he wrote:

> *One particular battery of 77s lay a mile back of the lines and seemed to be having a particularly jolly party. Their flashes almost doubled the other batteries in rapidity. I determined to fly over and pay them a visit, since none of the infantry seemed to care to stick up their heads in the trenches. Accordingly I turned a bit to the rear and came upon the battery from behind and at about one hundred feet above the ground.*
>
> *As I neared them I saw six or eight three-inch guns standing side by side in a little clearing, the line of gunners all rushing swiftly to and fro, picking up and passing forward the fifteen-pound shells. The guns were firing at the rate of almost one shot each second. A continuous flash could be seen from the little battery, so rapidly did the gunners work. In a twinkling after my first shot the whole battery became silent.*
>
> *Pointing my nose directly at the end of the line, I pressed my triggers and raked the whole line before straightening out my airplane. Then with a quick bank I came about and repeated the performance. Before I had started back every man had fled for shelter and not a gun was firing. I circled back again and again, chasing the scattered groups of gunners to their respective*

> *dugouts and firing short bursts at their heels as they*
> *fled. It was the most amusing party I had ever attended.*
> *I couldn't help wondering what kind of reception I*
> *would get if a sudden* panne *(forced landing) dropped*
> *me within their clutches.*

Out of ammunition again, Eddie departed happily.

Still mystified by the enormous German artillery demonstration when he had seen no sign of the makings of either an Allied or German land assault, he was given an explanation by a war correspondent. Visiting the 94th Squadron with the idea of filing a story about the aviators, Frank Taylor of the United Press news syndicate ventured his opinion that the Germans had been sparked into action by an experiment with gas warfare. It had been conducted during the night by the American Gas Organization over German trenches in retaliation for a German gas attack. Taylor theorized that the artillerymen behind the lines must have smelled the fumes, decided that an Allied offensive had begun, and had gone into action with their guns.

Satisfied that this was the reason for the bombardment that had gotten him out of bed, Eddie basked in knowing that he had put to flight hundreds of enemy soldiers while enjoying the "choicest hour of hunting" he'd ever known.

CHAPTER 8

Balloonatical Fakers

O N JUNE 17, 1918, MARSHAL FOCH TOLD GENERAL PERSHING
that the people of France were asking, "Where are the
Americans, and what are they doing?"

At that moment some were battling Germans at Belleau Wood.
On June 11 two U.S. divisions had participated with four French
divisions in a counterattack. Other Americans were taking off
from aerodromes daily to battle Germans in the skies with increasing skill. The day after Foch's meeting with Pershing, the
U.S. 96th Aero Squadron hit the Dommary-Baroncourt railway
yards in the first AEF daytime bombing raid.

At its base at Toul, the 94th "Hat-in-the-Ring" Squadron was
anticipating orders to shift operations to a field closer to the action at Château-Thierry. But much on the mind of its newly
minted ace, who had enhanced his reputation as a bold lone wolf
by strafing a German artillery battery, was a tempting form of a
prize that the Germans called *Drachen*. Observation balloons that
hung a mile or two behind the lines at about two thousand feet,
tethered to a truck, they allowed an observer with a telescope
to scan the ground for a radius of ten miles. Resembling giant,
elongated sausages but not equipped to fight back effectively with

machine guns because they could not maneuver, they were al-
luring bait for fighter pilots. The real danger came from gunners
on the ground firing explosive bullets called "flaming onions."

The pilot who had scored more victories against balloons than
anyone in any air service was Belgian ace Maj. Willy Coppens.
He'd shot down more than twenty *Drachens* with flaming rockets
and never been wounded. He succeeded by attacking from a low
level, then swooping up. But he attacked only in the morning or
late in the evening when the visibility of the men in the balloon
was limited. Thinking about the best way to go after a balloon
himself, Eddie liked the idea of an early morning attack, but envisioned a quick burst of hot tracer bullets while diving, then doing it again and again until the huge gasbag was set on fire.
But he would not go it alone. Hoping to gain a reputation for the
94th as a balloon-killing squadron, he laid out the plan for Reed
Chambers, Jimmy Meissner, Thorn Taylor, and a Lieutenant
Loomis. He got an enthusiastic response, followed by approval of
the plan by the squadron's commander.

With information on *Drachen* locations provided by a French
observation squadron, they scouted their targets and planned
strategy for a June 25 attack. Taking off at half past four in the
morning, they went their separate ways. Over the village of Goin
half an hour later, Eddie saw his balloon in the distance and
switched off the plane's engine for a silent glide to a point where
he would turn it on and catch the enemy by surprise. If the engine didn't restart, he would be either a sitting duck for Archie or
a crash-landed prisoner of war, assuming he wasn't killed in the
crack-up of the Nieuport.

Looking down, he watched the balloon's ground crew preparing for their day and felt grateful they were upholding the reputation of Germans as conscientious and reliable workers.
Because his approach depended on stealth, he flattened his glide
to minimize the sounds of singing wires between top and bottom
wings. With the earth appearing closer and closer, he began a
wide circle with the plane's nose down, then banked and saw the
balloon catching the first rays of the rising sun.

Facing him was the emblem of Boche aviation, a huge Maltese

cross. With a shift of rudder he was able to sight his machine guns at its center. Snapping on the switch to start the engine with his left hand, he squeezed both triggers with the right. White-hot tracers streaked into the balloon.

The observer in the balloon was so surprised that he dropped his spyglass and went over the side of the basket dangling below the balloon and parachuted away with a look of terror.

Flames appeared on the balloon.

And went out.

Then Eddie's guns jammed.

Up from the ground flashed flaming onions.

Swerving to the right of the balloon, Eddie passed close enough to reach out and touch it. Yet, with the largest target in the world before him, after all the risks he'd taken, he'd failed to set it ablaze. He knew his burst of bullets had hit home, but there was the *Drachen*, intact. And now he was on the receiving end of gunfire.

Why the balloon hadn't exploded was a mystery. Had it been wet with nighttime dew? Did it have a special protective coating? Was Willy Coppens just a better man than he?

Back at base at 5:45, Eddie found that he was the last of the balloon-hunters to land. None had claimed a *Drachen*. Shaking his head, he said, "I think that we are the rottenest lot of balloonatical fakers that ever got up at two-thirty in the morning."

Two days later all the squadrons at Toul were ordered to move. The new base was to be a former French aerodrome at Touquin, a small village about twenty-five miles south of Château-Thierry and the river Marne. The airfield was large and smooth. Quarters for the 94th officers were in an abandoned chateau a few miles south of the base. Gorgeously furnished, it was the finest habitation the pilots had known. But for most of Eddie's first week at Touquin he found himself laid up in a hospital with a serious fever and bouts of chills.

While doctors pondered the cause and nurses kept watch for signs of him developing pneumonia, he passed time writing letters to his mother and family members, old friends, and acquaintances. He'd been doing so regularly since he'd arrived in France.

When one longtime friend noted that the "h" in Rickenbacher
had become "k," the friend had shown the letter to a reporter for
a news service. The result was a nationally distributed story to
the effect that Eddie Rickenbacker had taken "the Hun" out of his
name. A letter to members of Elks Lodge 99 in Los Angeles that
enclosed a photo of himself and related a few of his combat experiences had been printed on page one of every Los Angeles
newspaper.

    Forced by boredom into the kind of introspection that engages
everyone who is confined to a hospital, he recalled episodes in
which boldness during combat had been the most intelligent
course, but always with caution, and pondered why aviation was
a mystery as well as a delight. He'd learned that the rush of an
airplane through the sky stirred the instinct of sportsmanship
that had marked his years as a race car driver. In aerial combat
as on racetracks he had found a great difference among his opponents. Some were better than he. Most were poorer. From all of
the auto drivers he'd picked up tricks and techniques to make
him a smarter racer. In combat flying he'd been haunted by
doubts about his ability to play a significant part in the life-and-
death contest that had been going on in the air all over France.
Did he possess the gladiatorial characteristics that made the
German, British, and French aviators successful? He had started
flying with misgivings and a sense of inexperience and incompe-
tence, yet he had survived incidents similar to ones that had
ended the lives of veteran pilots. Did that mean that he was actually their better? Was he one of that exceptional class of men who,
once they'd mastered the powers of planes and guns, found they
were superior to their antagonists? Or was he just lucky?

    Lying on his hospital cot, he reviewed his combats, looking for
mistakes, analyzing every maneuver, pondering, cursing the machine guns that had jammed and the armorers who'd failed to
spot potential problems, and resenting having to go up in Nieuports instead of the Spads that were constantly promised but
never delivered. He remembered the brazen insolence of the pilot in Number 16 of the Rising Sun Squadron and knew that if he
had been in a better plane than a Nieuport, he could have flown

faster, climbed higher, outdived, and outmaneuvered them–and any other Boche machine. He had also learned that the Germans were not supermen. He'd seen enough of them to recognize in them the merely human qualities of the pilots of the Hat-in-the-Ring Squadron. He had seen enough of Boche tactics to understand that there was no mystery about them. All that was required for him to beat them was caution. The result of this self-study as he lay in the hospital waiting for doctors to free him was a determination to "begin afresh my career in the air."

CHAPTER 9

Losses and Gains

O N JULY 4, 1918, AMERICANS IN PARIS WERE DETERMINED TO CEL-
ebrate the 142nd anniversary of the Declaration of Independence in the spirit of the hope expressed by one of the Founding
Fathers in a letter written on that historic day in Philadelphia to his
wife in Boston. "It ought to be commemorated," wrote John Adams
to Abigail, "as the Day of Deliverance by solemn acts of Devotion to
God Almighty. It ought to be solemnized with pomp and parade,
with shows, games, sports, guns, bells, bonfires, and illuminations
from one end of this continent to the other from this time forward
ever more."

For American flying ace Lt. Edward V. Rickenbacker, second
in command, 94th Aero Squadron of the Allied Expeditionary
Force, also known as the Hat-in-the-Ring gang, July Fourth was
a day of personal liberation. He was given permission to go into
Paris for a day that his compatriots intended to spend in celebration. On his last visit the City of Lights had been a place of terror
and despair, with thousands of refugees pouring in from the
countryside and many Parisians packing their belongings because the Germans were advancing toward the city. But the Huns
had been stopped at the Marne with American help, and now

Paris was its old self again. The French who'd asked "Where are the Americans?" were embracing doughboys in the streets and eager to join them in saluting the birthday of the United States.

While Eddie was watching a huge parade in Paris, American troops were in action on the Somme. Along with Australians, they gained a mile of ground, took the village of Hamel, and captured 1,472 Germans. During the attack, Royal Air Force planes dropped 100,000 rounds of ammunition in history's first airborne delivery of supplies to men in battle. In the United States, ninety-five ships were launched, seventeen in San Francisco alone, in the culmination of a crusade to build transports. In French ports, supplies were coming in at a rate of twenty thousand tons a day. The purpose of the 1 million American troops and military personnel in France, declared President Woodrow Wilson in an Independence Day speech at George Washington's home at Mount Vernon, Virginia, was the realization of world peace and international morality through his Fourteen Points.

Impatient to get back into the fight and tantalized by the prospect of Spads for the 94th, Eddie stretched the bounds of his temporary release from the hospital. Rather than returning on July 5, he hitched a ride from Paris to the American Experimental Aerodrome in the suburb of Orly to inquire into the status of the long-deferred planes. Finding the major in charge of the supply depot, he was told that three Spads were on the field and earmarked for the Hat-in-the-Ring Squadron, with more expected in a few days.

Was there any reason, Eddie asked, why he couldn't have a look at one of them now?

The major saw no reason whatsoever.

Attracted to a Spad with the number "1" painted on its sides, Eddie asked a mechanic, "Is this one of the machines belonging to the 94th Squadron?"

It was indeed.

"Well, I am down here from 94th Squadron," Eddie said. "Is there any reason why this machine should not go to the squadron today?"

"None that I know of, sir."

Minutes later, with a fleeting picture of himself hauled to a court-martial, Eddie was strapped into the Spad's snug office and signaling the mechanic to pull away the chock from each wheel. Feeling "tremendous satisfaction," he taxied for takeoff with no regard for either the enormity of the offense of stealing a plane or the abandonment of his possessions at the hospital. All that mattered was getting himself to Touquin. Less than an hour after he landed, the Spad was being fitted with machine guns.

While that was being done, he climbed into his "old-time mount" and took the Nieuport up for a final, nostalgic flight. With luck and God's grace, he thought as the plane climbed, he might attain fame in the skies and join the great aces of the war–Lufbery, René Fonck, Billy Mitchell, and even the great "Red Baron" himself.

Born in Breslau, Germany, on May 2, 1892, Manfred von Richthofen was a member of the minor nobility. Commissioned in a cavalry regiment in 1912 for a war of trenches that had no place for soldiers on horseback, he transferred to the air service as an observer in the summer of 1915 and served with the *Fliegerabteilung* on the Eastern Front. After switching to *Brieftauben Abteilung Ostende* (Ostend Carrier Pigeon Unit, but in reality a bomber squadron), he took pilot training in October 1915 and was posted to the Western Front.

Over Verdun on October 26, 1916, he won his first victory, shooting down a Nieuport scout, but the score was not officially confirmed. That achievement occurred on September 17. Flying with the Jasta 2 fighter squadron, he downed a Royal Flying Corps FE2b. By the end of the year he had fifteen enemy planes to his credit. Given his own squadron early in 1917, the Jasta 11, he led his pilots in Albatros scouts to inflict so many casualties in one month that it was called Bloody April. By then he had shot down fifty-seven planes. Two months later he was given command of Jagdgeschwader 1. Consisting of four Jastas, it soon became known and feared as "the Flying Circus." He led it until April 21, 1918, when he was attacked by Sopwith Camels of No. 209 Squadron of the Royal Flying Corps and shot down with a bullet through his heart. The highest scoring pilot of any nation in the war, he had eighty confirmed kills. His successor as leader of the Flying Circus would eventually be a twenty-five-year-old ace with twenty-one victories named Hermann Goering.

Based at Coincy, a large field north of Château-Thierry, the Flying Circus's Fokkers were distinguishable by scarlet-painted noses that gave the "Red Baron" von Richthofen his colorful nickname. Another dangerous group at Coincy, Jagdstaffel No. 2, commanded by Capt. Bruno Loerzer, also flew Fokkers, but with their fuselage bellies painted bright yellow. A third famous German squadron, Jagdstaffel No. 3, was stationed near Saint-Quentin and was led by a Captain Bettenge, an ace with twenty-five victories.

While Eddie was hospitalized, planes of these groups had inflicted two losses on the Hat-in-the-Ring Squadron. In that time the 94th had three victories. But the airfield at Touquin was so far from the battle line that the pilots of the 94th found themselves limited to short patrols. The base south of Paris was roughly twenty miles from the action at Château-Thierry. When orders came for the 94th to shift from Toul to Touquin, German squadrons had already left the Verdun–St. Mihiel–Pont-à-Mousson region that had become so familiar to Eddie. He was one of seventeen pilots in a squadron with twenty-four planes. Also at Touquin were the 27th, 145th, and 95th American Fighter Squadrons.

Stationed nearby were French squadrons manned by many individuals who had preferred to serve in the infantry, cavalry, or artillery, but had been pressed into aviation. This resulted, Eddie observed, in an air force of France that did not measure up to its former prestige when its pilots had been eager volunteers. The difference between French and American pilots, noted a report of the German Intelligence Office, was that the Americans "fought more like Indians than soldiers." It complained that "they upset all our training by dashing in single-handed against our formations."

One of the American aviators at Touquin who fit this description was Lt. Quentin Roosevelt of the 95th "Kicking Mule" Squadron. As President Roosevelt's son, Eddie observed, he had at first a rather difficult time fitting in with "the intimate life of an aviation camp." All who met him for the first time expected him to have the airs and superciliousness of a spoiled boy. But

Quentin proved to be "absolutely square in everything he said or did" and became "one of the most popular fellows in the group," and loved "purely for his own natural self."

Reckless as an aviator to such a degree that his commanding officers had to caution him repeatedly, Quentin was such a notoriously brave figure that everyone expected him to achieve some great spectacular success or be killed in the attempt. Quentin's reply was a laugh. Though he had been assigned to combat flying since mid-June, he did not engage in his first dogfight until two days after Eddie returned to Touquin from Paris. It happened while pursuing a flight of German photo planes.

Five days later (July 11, 1918), returning from a patrol, he became separated from his group when a surge of wind swept him up and away from the other planes. Coming down out of clouds just north of Château-Thierry, he noticed three planes that he thought were American, until he saw otherwise. In a letter to the woman he intended to marry after the war he wrote, "I was perfectly green, but then I thought to myself that I was so near I might as well take a crack at them, so I pulled a little nearer, got a line on the end man, and pulled the trigger. . . . My tracers were shooting all around him but I guess he was so surprised that for a bit he couldn't think what to do."

When Theodore Roosevelt learned that his youngest son had shot down a German plane, he wrote to his oldest son, Ted, serving with the army in France, "The press dispatches have just carried the account of Quentin's fight with three German planes, of which he downed one and escaped from the other two. The last of the lion's brood has been blooded."

The hero of the Spanish-American War, who called leading a gallant charge by the Rough Riders up Kettle Hill in the San Juan Heights his "crowded hour," wrote to his sister Ethel, "Whatever now befalls Quentin he has now had his crowded hour, and his day of honor and triumph."

To Eddie Rickenbacker the victory scored by Quentin Roosevelt was further proof that Indian warfare left the Germans "hopeless against the Americans' recklessness." Germany's formation flying was "admirable until an American joined it and maneuvered in concert with it for fifteen minutes before shooting it up."

On July 10, 1918, Eddie awoke with a pain in his right ear so severe that he decided he'd better have a doctor take a look at it. Finding an abscess, the doctor decreed surgery at a hospital in Paris. The timing couldn't have been worse. Lying in bed four days later, Eddie heard the boom of artillery. French and American guns were pounding the German lines. The Allies had been told by German prisoners of war that a new offensive was about to begin. In response to the half hour bombardment, the Germans unleashed artillery, including nearly eighteen thousand rounds of gas shells on the Château-Thierry sector held by the U.S. 42nd "Rainbow" Division. Its leader was a swashbuckling brigadier general named Douglas MacArthur. His flamboyant style and unconventional uniform had earned him the nicknames "Beau Brummel of the AEF" and "the fighting Dude."

Forced to "fret and turn" in a hospital bed, Eddie worried about his squadron "going through with the most severe trials in its short experience." With himself laid up and Douglas Campbell away, the leadership of the 94th was in the hands of Jimmy Meissner, Reed Chambers, Alan Winslow, and Thorn Taylor.

On the French calendar, July 14 was Bastille Day, the anniversary of the storming of the Paris prison in 1787 that commenced the French Revolution. The skies over Touquin were cloudy. At Fère-en-Tardenois, ten miles behind the German lines, they were also crowded with the red-nosed Fokker planes of the Flying Circus. Led by Hermann Goering, seven of them had gone up to challenge five Nieuports of the 95th "Kicking Mule" Squadron.

Among them was Quentin Roosevelt. Brimming with customary daring and knowing that his first victory was confirmed and duly recorded in the history of the squadron, he broke from the formation and flew ahead, climbing as he went, to greet the Germans and deflect them from the squadron. Diving into the Fokkers, he opened fire, swept past the red-nosed planes with no hits, rose, and repeated his attacks. As the Germans broke formation, a lone Fokker turned to do battle. The dogfight was brisk, but Sgt. K.

Thom of the Flying Circus had more experience. Taking aim at his brave but obviously novice opponent, he fired into the rear of the Nieuport and directed a stream of bullets forward like a man using a garden hose. Two of them struck Quentin Roosevelt in the back of his head. Spinning down, the plane crashed into a field near Chamery, just west of Rheims.

On July 17, Theodore Roosevelt issued a statement: "Quentin's mother and I are very glad that he got to the front and had a chance to render some service to his country, and show the stuff that was in him before his fate befell him."

He would learn that Quentin's body had been buried by German aviators on the spot with full military honors, and that they had marked the grave with ROOSEVELT scratched into the propeller of Quentin's plane. His belongings, the German government promised, would be sent to his parents through neutral parties.

Proposals for various kinds of monuments to Quentin in the United States were turned down by Roosevelt. But one form of remembrance pleased him. The airfield at Mineola, Long Island, where Quentin learned to fly, was named Roosevelt Field. From there on May 20, 1927, Charles A. Lindbergh would take off on an unprecedented solo flight to Paris that would make "Lucky Lindy" America's most honored civilian aviator.

But on Bastille Day 1918, the pilot who would be hailed as the country's greatest military aviator and "ace of aces" was stuck in a Paris hospital with an earache, and itching to get back into action in his spanking-new Spad against the vaunted legatees of the Red Baron.

CHAPTER 10

Fighting the Flying Circus

O N JULY 24, 1918, JOHN SINGER SARGENT CLIMBED INTO A British tank for what he thought would be "a joy ride up and down slopes, over trenches and looping the loop generally" in the area of the towns of Ypres (also spelled Ieper), Arras, and Péronne. The sixty-two-year-old American-born artist whose lavish portraits of English aristocracy had made him wealthy and famous had been asked by the British minister of information, Lord Beaverbrook, to go to France to portray in oils on canvas morale-boosting scenes of troops of Britain and the United States in action side by side. At one point Sargent looked at a line of tanks that seemed to his artist's eyes like "ships before Troy."

"We go on our warpath in several motors," he inscribed in his diary. "It is very hard to see anything significant in warfare."

Had he been in a plane of the Royal Air Force the next day, he would have seen three hundred tons of explosives rain on German lines in the Amiens sector. If he could have been in the air above retreating German forces on July 26, he might have witnessed the death of the British Empire's greatest ace. Prior to that day Maj. Edward "Mick" Mannock had a record of seventy-two kills. Flying with him on July 26 was a young New Zealander, Lt.

Donald Inglis. After downing his seventy-third German, Mannock decided to strafe the enemy lines that day. Hit by rifle fire, his plane crashed and exploded, killing him and Inglis.

On July 28, on ground where Lt. Quentin Roosevelt had been killed two weeks before, American troops entered Fère-en-Tardenois. At nightfall, battles to take two villages, Seringes and Sergy, would be recorded as the bloodiest day the Americans had experienced. A war correspondent reported, "A great day in history indeed." With the area firmly in American hands, an old friend from Quentin Roosevelt's years at the Groton School, Bill Preston, went looking for Quentin's grave. Accompanying him were another Roosevelt family friend, Colonel McCoy, and the Roman Catholic chaplain of New York's illustrious "Fighting 69th" Division, Father Francis Duffy. To mark the grave, Preston had brought a cross inscribed with Quentin's name and the dates of his birth and death. Father Duffy offered a prayer.

"The grave is an ordinary soldier's grave," Preston wrote to the young woman Quentin would have married, "similar to hundreds of others that cover this part of the battlefield."

Among the Germans in their retreat in the closing days of July was a Corporal Hitler. For "personal bravery and general merit," on a recommendation of his regimental adjutant, he would be awarded the Iron Cross, First Class.

Also at the front lines after having conferred with the Allied high commands in London and Paris was the American assistant secretary of the navy, Franklin Delano Roosevelt. He was a distant cousin of Quentin Roosevelt. With such a distinguished visitor, the men of an American artillery battery let Mr. Roosevelt fire one of their guns at a railway junction at Bazoches, eight miles away. A spotter plane reported a hit. How many, if any, "Huns" he had killed, Roosevelt noted, he would "never know."

On July 31, 1918, Eddie Rickenbacker was out of the hospital and "able to mount my Spad and again take my place in fighting formations." He did so despite doctors having told him that because of the condition of his ear he would never be able to fly again. To put the prognosis to a test, he ran his Spad through several maneuvers and landed it with the "satisfaction of knowing that I had fooled the doctors and was good as new, in spite of my punctured ear." But July 31 was also a day of terrible loss for the squadrons at Touquin. Each lost heavily, but the severest was that of the 27th Squadron. Of six planes that went up to engage the Flying Circus, one returned. Among the missing was Lt. John McArthur of Buffalo, New York.

Eddie valued McArthur for his caution and as a quick, clever pilot and a fine shot. He learned later, and wrote, that McArthur had led an attack "like Horatius of old, [and] embraced all the spears in his own breast." But the sacrifice was in vain. Except for one plane, the entire squadron ran out of gas and dropped to earth. Some landed safely. Others crashed in shell holes. All were taken as prisoners of war.

Late in the evening of July 31, Alan Winslow, who had scored the Hat-in-the-Ring's first victory, was also shot down. He survived the crash and was captured, but his left arm had been shattered by a bullet, requiring amputation. Winslow would never fly again.

On the first of August, as much with a desire to avenge Winslow as a need to test his punctured eardrum in combat conditions, Eddie joined a formation of escorts for three French photo planes. Designed as a combination bomber/reconnaissance plane, the Breguet model Bre14 was a two-seat biplane produced by the Societe des Avions Louis Breguet. The firm's founder's first venture into aviation (1906) had been a helicopter called the *gyroplan*. It flew, but it would be decades before the helicopter would prove itself as a war machine. The Breguet photo plane, introduced in 1916, had shown itself to be one of the most successful of the planes available to French and American squadrons.

Because the leader of the escorts for the three Breguet photo planes was Lieutenant Loomis, and in deference to the punctured ear, Eddie's purpose was to "tag along and see what happened." By flying at fifteen thousand feet (five thousand feet higher than the squadron), he would be in the "front row in the gallery" with a "wonderful view" of what he expected to be "an amazingly interesting little scrap." That is, if the men of the Flying Circus in a formation of Fokkers chose to come up to challenge the American Nieuports.

Seven enemy aircraft appeared, but they did not seem to be in any hurry to forge through the convoy of Nieuports to get at the three Breguets. The objective of the French photographers was the city of Fismes and its cluster of railways and roads, along with any artillery batteries in the area. If the Germans declined to attack the escorts, Loomis had orders not to engage them. Looking around the skies, Eddie noted plenty of other planes, hostiles and a mixture of American, French, and British. Watching the distant enemy planes, he was ready to fly in and give warning should any of them appear to menace Loomis's escorts. "Only a little rumpus was needed," he noted, "to start one of the choicest dogfights that ever was seen."

Then, the Fokker leader dipped his wings, began a headlong dive at the Breguets, and the fight was on. Eddie observed:

The Americans had the advantage from the first, for Loomis had kept his Nieuports at a good altitude above the Breguets and the Fokkers had tried to attack [the Breguets] from below. Loomis dived steadily at the tail of the nearest Fokker. This latter had no recourse open but to try and outdive him. Another Fokker got on Loomis's tail and another Nieuport followed on his tail. Soon the whole menagerie was streaming along in this fashion, every machine pouring streams of tracer bullets into the machine ahead of him. It was a splendid spectacle to witness, but I knew it would be of short duration.

One Fokker had already dropped toward earth and two of our bright-colored Nieuports were streaking it for home in the wake of the disappearing Breguets. Either these two pilots had wounds or engine trouble or else considered the wisest policy was to get out of this hurricane of flaming bullets. I looked for Loomis. There he was, way down below, with three Fokkers on his tail.

*He was vainly attempting to re-form his scattered for-
mation and but two of his machines remained. Even as
I watched them I saw several other enemy machines
drawing nearer from the north. It was high time to get
down to their aid.*

Dropping down to their vicinity, Eddie saw Loomis fire bursts,
then swerve away to the south. Putting on "the sauce," Loomis
rapidly drew away with Fokkers in hot pursuit. At this point the
Germans may have spotted Eddie's Spad and suspected they were
being led into an ambush. As they broke off and sped away, Eddie was "glad to let them go." After three weeks of no flying, he
"felt little inclined to take on anything against odds."

As Eddie turned back to join the Nieuports, he saw Loomis's
plane sinking toward earth. The propeller was turning slowly,
suggesting that Loomis's engine had been hit. Judging the distance to the ground, Eddie observed Loomis nursing his powerless plane and sailing along on as flat a glide path as the damaged
Nieuport could maintain. As Eddie flew above Loomis, unable to
lend assistance, German antiaircraft guns opened up. Watching
Loomis holding on to every inch of his altitude "with the skill of a
Cape Cod skipper," and seeing the ground draw closer and closer,
Eddie was tempted to strafe the Germans. But Rickenbacker caution ruled. He envisioned gunfire from a thousand soldiers aimed
at him from concealed positions and realized he could do nothing
as Loomis's "dainty little bird neatly skimmed over them" with no
hope of avoiding a crash right into the German lines.

Braced for the worst, Eddie watched Loomis's plane hit the
ground but miraculously bound up, then touch down again thirty
feet farther, bounce once more, cross the German line into no-
man's-land by thirty or forty yards, and land. With the plane still
rolling, Loomis leapt from the cockpit, dashed for the American
line amid a hail of German bullets, and plunged into the nearest
trench.

Deciding the day's entertainment was over, Eddie put on the
gas and headed home. An hour later Loomis made a phone call
from the front to report that he was all right.

Eight days later, with the front lines having moved from the Château-Thierry region to the river Vesle between Soissons and Rheims, the Hat-in-the-Ring Squadron at Touquin now had an abandoned Flying Circus base at Coincy to use as a refueling base just eight miles south of the German trenches. The 94th would use it fitted out with the Spads they'd long been promised.

At three o'clock in the afternoon on August 8, 1918, Eddie was ordered to lead eleven Spads to Coincy for a rendezvous with two French photoreconnaissance Spads. Although he had constant pain in his ear, he'd chosen not to report it to the squadron's doctor and risk being grounded, hospitalized, probably operated on again, and possibly banned from flying combat at a time when the Allies appeared to have finally routed the Hun from the Château-Thierry salient. Despite a German counterattack on August 6 at Molancourt on the Somme, there was a strong feeling among the Allies that the balance had shifted in their favor, perhaps not yet decisively, but encouragingly. Two days after Gen. Douglas Haig launched what was now being called "the Somme offensive," Americans engaged in the fight were members of a newly organized 1st U.S. Army, commanded by General Pershing, who remained commander of the AEF.

During refueling at Coincy, three of Eddie's Spads evidenced engine trouble. This left him eight Spads to escort the French. Encircling the pair of photo planes, with Eddie positioned a thousand yards above and on the lookout for Germans, the Americans crossed the lines in the area of Vailly. Looking around for the enemy, Eddie spotted five Fokkers to the west with the sun behind them.

Certain that the Germans had seen the Allied formation, he anticipated an attack coming out of the sun's glare. Keeping them in view, he climbed higher as his formation continued on toward Vailly. With the French busily snapping photographs, three Fokkers began an assault.

Admiring the bravery of the three German pilots in going after a formation of ten Allied planes, Eddie nosed down to intercept them, confident that it would be impossible for the trio of Fokkers to reach the photo planes without running a gauntlet of machine gun fire. But while his Spad raced toward the three Germans, he understood why the three Germans had surged into an attack. Coming on fast from the rear of the Allied formation were five more Fokkers. Realizing that the "three knights had come a-tilting" to lay a trap, he decided they must be destroyed fast.

In the right position to go after the first of the daring threesome as it swept down to fire on the photo planes, Eddie pulled up on the German's tail and began firing along the line of the German's dive. The bullets ripped the Fokker from stem to stern. As the plane fell away without bursting into flames, Eddie saw Reed Chambers "having a merry set-to" with a second Fokker as the last of the trio hastened to rejoin the original flight, now reduced from five to three.

In attacking the first Fokker, Eddie had deliberately stalled his engine. Now he found himself drifting with a dead propeller as the five Fokkers of the second formation advanced. To avoid becoming an easy victim, he turned his Spad into an almost vertical dive in expectation that the force of the wind in a fifteen-hundred-foot dive would spin the propeller as he switched on the engine. Powered again, he climbed and raced to catch up with his formation. They were already in a dash to cross the Allied line and in a hurry to get back to Coincy.

Puzzled but grateful that the five Fokkers hadn't come after him during his powerless dive, Eddie landed along with the French photo planes. Their pilots and cameramen reported that despite the German attack they'd taken thirty-five pictures. When Eddie looked over one of the French Spads, he found that the German pilot who'd attacked was not only brave, but a good shot. The French Spad's tail was riddled with bullet holes.

Although Eddie and Chambers had each scored a victory, they could not be confirmed. "One can hardly expect to get confirmations for all one's victories," Eddie noted resignedly, "since nine-tenths of our combats were necessarily fought on the German side of the lines."

Because Eddie's idea to organize a squadron of aviators from the ranks of auto racers had come to him in the spring of 1917 in

London while observing planes of the Royal Flying Corps from the windows of his room in the Savoy Hotel, he had retained a keen interest in British aviation. After arriving in France and becoming a pilot in the American Air Service, he admired the daring and the aerial tactics of the English, Canadians, Australians, and New Zealanders in what was then called the Royal Air Force. On June 5, 1918, the RAF had formed the British Independent Air Force. Commanded by Maj. Gen. Sir Hugh Trenchard, it was given the mission of carrying out strategic bombing of German cities, including Cologne, Mannheim, Coblenz, and Stuttgart. To enhance air support of ground troops in the Allied offensive of early August 1918, British pilots and observers of a new Army Co-operation Service flew over the rear of German lines to report the state of enemy defenses. Among the aviators on such a mission on the third day of the Allied offensive (August 10, 1918) were Capt. Frederick West, the pilot, and observer Lt. Alec Haslam. Both demonstrated the kind of valor that always earned the admiration and respect of Eddie Rickenbacker, even in his German adversaries.

While flying inside Germany, West and Haslam were attacked by three German planes. Haslam was hit in the ankle by a machine gun bullet while three explosive rounds ripped into West's leg. Blown off, it fell onto the controls. Lifting it off, West managed to keep the plane going and fly it back to base. A portion of his written report to his commander read, "My leg was blown off but [I] managed to do a good landing. . . . Haslam wounded in ankle. I lost my left leg. Was operated on. Luck to everybody."

On the day that West lost the leg, Eddie Rickenbacker was also in the air with orders to "form an aerial barrier" in front of a small piece of woods just back of the Allied lines northwest of Fère-en-Tardenois. Although the Allied activity in the area was not explained, Eddie supposed that the Allies were filling the area with troops and guns and wanted Eddie's planes to conceal this from enemy espionage. Landing at Coincy for refueling, he found his surmise correct. He saw long convoys of camouflaged trucks and masses of soldiers on the roads, evidently readying for a push the next day against Fismes. As the Spads were being gassed up, a lieutenant of the 1st Aero Squadron informed Eddie that he needed a few of Eddie's planes to escort him on a photographic mission. Eddie asked for and got five volunteers.

Determined that his men understand the nature of the flight of five Spads and a Salmson photo plane of the 1st Aero Squadron, Eddie explained that the region to be photographed was a large one, covering several towns between the Vesle and Aisne Rivers, that it would take some time to cover the territory, and that they were certain to be attacked before completing the job. Telling them that it would be senseless "to attempt to parley" with overwhelming numbers of the enemy, he said he would wag his wings to signal to break off without delay, photographs or no photographs. The flight took off at 5:30 P.M.

As Eddie had predicted, the formation was met over Fismes by eight red-nosed Fokkers. Certain that the Germans hoped to get behind the intruders at a superior altitude and come in from the rear with the sun at their backs, he decided to let the Germans think they hadn't been seen and go ahead with the photography until he felt the Germans were ready to attack. As the Salmson began a second circuit of the area, five Fokkers darted down while the others continued to cruise between Eddie's planes and home. Accepting the invitation to skirmish, Eddie wagged his wings to tell his planes to break off the mission, then climbed directly toward the Germans.

Thrilled by the sight of a Fokker biplane descending toward him, he began firing from a long range and watched to see which side of his Spad the Fokker intended to pass. Expecting it to swerve to the right at the last instant in an effort to get between him and the other Spads, and then attack the photo plane, Eddie was lying back with the earth under his tail and the sun under the engine (to keep the sun from shining in his eyes). As the planes whizzed past each other, he stopped firing and flattened out his dive. This left him above the Germans. Looking down in the expectation that his Spads had gotten away, he found "a regular dogfight" in progress. But he saw more Spads than should have been there. They also had different colors. They were French who had evidently been watching the Fokkers forming to attack the Americans and had decided to join the fray. Eddie's Spads and the Salmson photo plane were well below him, making for home as ordered, and were well out of the melee.

Chagrined over his lack of caution and thanking his "lucky stars" that the French had shown up, Eddie turned his Spad and waded into the combat. When a Fokker zoomed ahead of a French plane, he fired on the German and watched it go out of control and fall to earth.

Satisfied with the victory, he vowed to never again venture into hostile skies without twisting his neck in all directions at every moment of the flight to see who might be sneaking up on him, and "cleaved the air for home."

Back at base he examined three bullet holes in one wing of his Spad and called for a mechanic. "Patch these up," he said, "and find someone to paint a Maltese cross on each one. These little souvenirs will remind me to be more careful."

CHAPTER 11

Extraordinary Things

"ONE OF THE EXTRAORDINARY THINGS ABOUT LIFE AT THE FRONT," Eddie Rickenbacker mused, "is the commonplace way in which extraordinary things happen."

He remembered a moment before he was about to go into his first air combat. While his heart pounded with excitement, the image of a Liberty Bond poster popped into his head. On it was pictured a beautiful girl with outstretched arms. Below her were big black letters: FIGHT OR BUY BONDS.

After getting a cable from the Automobile Club of Columbus, Ohio, that informed him he'd been elected its first and only life member, he noted it in his diary and added, "Ha. Ha."

One day during a lull in action he'd gone to lunch at Luneville with a correspondent of the United Press. On the way back to base they saw a family of wild boar. Intending to catch a young one to be a mascot for the squadron, he gave chase on foot until the mother boar charged from a thicket and headed straight for him like a Hun on the attack. All thoughts of obtaining a mascot were immediately abandoned in favor of retreat.

After a Sunday in Paris with Lt. Cedric Fauntleroy of the 94th Squadron and two young French women, one of whom played the piano wonderfully, he wrote in his diary, "Had dinner in the Café Bois de Boulogne, went riding later taking the girls home. It was a most perfect day."

Put in charge of making arrangements for a dance for Allied officers and Red Cross nurses, he'd hung a sign on the door of the ladies' room that warned NO MAN'S LAND.

One of Eddie's most extraordinary experiences occurred a couple of days after he had been caught off guard by the second flight of Fokkers near Fismes. While refilling his Spad's gas tank at Coincy in preparation for another "flip over the lines," he was informed that his brother was in a nearby army camp. He knew that William had been at the front with a Signal Corps outfit for four months, but repeated attempts to locate him had failed. Borrowing a car from a general, he set out to find the camp in the vicinity of Fère-en-Tardenois. As he passed a group of soldiers who mistook him for a general and offered salutes, one of the men yelled, "Hullo, Rick!"

Stopping the car and looking around, Eddie saw an "undersized Doughboy" run toward the car. Eddie recognized him as a friend from Columbus. After a few minutes of chatting about old times, he drove on, finding it hard to believe that he'd once had another life. Within a couple of hours he'd been drawn back into that life by news of his brother and a chance encounter with the man from Columbus. But he knew that in a little while they would be immersed again in the war and that any of them, or all, might soon be counted among the dead, wounded, or missing.

After the reunion with William, he drove back to base over the same road. Two weeks earlier it had been enemy territory. Pockmarked with holes of artillery shells that had rained on the German retreat, it was in the process of being repaired for use by Americans. Huge road rollers were smoothing crushed gravel so that the road could be repaved. "When people want a good road built," noted a famous prewar expert on roadways, "they can finish it in an incredibly short space of time."

Along both sides of the battered highway were piles of abandoned war material that had been collected by American salvage squads from adjoining fields and woods. Other groups of soldiers

had picked up corpses, searched them for identification and useful documents, and laid them out in neat rows of numbered bodies for burial squads. Of this busy and macabre scene he would
write:

> *Rows upon rows of three-inch shells were stacked up*
> *within convenient reach of army trucks. Their willow*
> *and straw baskets, each containing a single German*
> *shell, formed a regular row six feet high and fifty feet*
> *long. Then came a space filled with huge twelve-inch*
> *shells all standing upright upon their bases. Next were*
> *stacked boxes of machine gun ammunition, hundreds*
> *and hundreds of them, occasionally interspersed with*
> *boxes of rockets, signal flares, and huge piles of rifles, of*
> *machine guns and of empty brass shells of various sizes.*
> *The value of an average German city lay spread along*
> *that road—all worthless to the former owners—all con-*
> *structed for the purpose of killing their fellow men!*

Around the time of Eddie's road trip, an unlikely looking
American war correspondent was in the same area. Formerly the
drama critic for the *New York Times* and now a reporter for the
new U.S. Army newspaper for soldiers called *Stars and Stripes*,
obese, bespectacled, and owlish Alexander Woollcott wrote:

> *I am becoming week by week, a passionate enthusi-*
> *ast on the subject of America, something I never was be-*
> *fore. I was ever so much more interested in the total*
> *cause, and not so very deep in my heart, there were*
> *doubts about the record America would make. I used to*
> *listen to the boys on the boat and in camp prattling*
> *away their easy optimism to the effect that the Ameri-*
> *can would make the best soldier in the world, that an*
> *American could beat the life out of any German, that*
> *there was something essentially strong and brave about*
> *an American. And I used to shudder because it seemed*

*provincial, because I thought it would sound offensive
in the ears of the French and English. Well, I have been
at the front with the infantry, getting to know the American under fire, getting to know whole rafts of men
from all corners of America as I never knew them before, and I do believe with all my heart, there never were
braver, gentler, finer, more chivalrous soldiers since the
world began. I think I first came to know mine own people in the woods near Château-Thierry.*

The German plan had contemplated a decisive spring offensive
against weakened French forces before General Pershing decided
that the full force of his Americans was ready for battle. On May
31, 1918, the Germans held a forty-mile front at the Marne, about
fifty miles from Paris. At this critical moment the U.S. 3d and 2d
Divisions had entered the fight and blocked the German advance
at Château-Thierry. A week later Americans had recaptured Con-
tigny, Vaux, Bouresches, and Belleau Wood. With eight American
divisions committed to battle in August and mostly under Pershing's command, the German offensive had been thwarted, turned
into a rout, and the war's momentum had shifted to the Allies all
along the Western Front.

During much of the German offensive that had begun at the
Somme in March, Eddie's desire to see combat had been frustrated. In March and most of April there had been no guns for his
plane. His first victory came on April 29. He scored four in May,
but had none in June. Then he was hospitalized with fever. When
he did get into the air, he was in the cockpit of an almost obsolete
Nieuport going against Germans in highly maneuverable,
speedy, and tough Albatroses and Fokkers. Another source of
frustration was the American Air Service policy on parachutes
for fighter pilots. Chutes were given only to balloon observers,
but they were too large and heavy for the tight confines of fighter
cockpits. Yet Eddie had seen German fighter pilots bail out of
cockpits no larger than his, and felt pleased as he sometimes
watched the man he'd been shooting at float safely to the ground.

"I never wanted to kill men," he wrote, "only to destroy machines."

Angry because it seemed that the enemy cared more about its pilots than the U.S. Air Service top brass cared about theirs, he confronted a major at Air Service headquarters in Paris.

"If all of you pilots had parachutes," said the major, "then you'd be inclined to use them on the slightest pretext, and the Air Service would lose planes that might otherwise have been brought down safely."

Remembering Raoul Lufbery and other men dying when parachutes would have saved them, Eddie exploded with shouted words of such anger and disgust that other officers rushed into the office to keep him from assaulting the major.

On days when bad weather made flying impossible, and Eddie believed that the life of a pilot had to be the most trying of any in the war, he remembered that thousands of men were living in muddy, vermin-infested trenches with no hope of enjoying the amenities available to aviators who had comfortable quarters, warm beds, a clean mess hall, and hot food. No doughboy could ever expect that being killed in action would result in his name appearing in newspapers all over the United States along with a story about his heroism and the glory he'd earned in combat. If Eddie Rickenbacker's airplane went down in flames, the people of America would find a photo of him on the front page. There he'd be in his jauntily tilted English flying corps cap, the Paris-tailored tunic with patch pockets, perhaps holding his fancy riding crop, and beaming with the big grin they'd seen so often in photos after a win during his auto racing days. If a soldier in a trench killed a German, no one kept score. And were he to kill five, nobody called him ace.

An airman's life might be short, but in the meantime it offered plenty of compensations.

CHAPTER 12

Regular Free-for-All

T HE DAY AFTER EDDIE'S BRIEF VISIT WITH HIS BROTHER, HE WAS IN the air with six other Spads of the 94th Squadron. Sailing along on patrol over enemy lines near Rheims, he spotted a number of planes far above his formation. Leading his planes higher, he saw the others darting about and exchanging shots in "a regular free-for-all." Reaching a slightly higher altitude east of the melee, he observed one group of planes in compact formation while the others were scattered and in a retreat with each man for himself. Flying closer, he saw that the winners of the free-for-all were German. In Fokkers, they were climbing and apparently trying to keep Eddie's planes below as they decided on their next move. If a fight were to take place, it would be seven against seven on a lovely morning with unrestricted visibility.

Seeing no reason not to take on the Germans on any terms they might demand, Eddie was certain that his Spad was a better climber than a Fokker, so he set a course a little steeper and headed toward them. Suddenly the last four of the Germans broke formation and began to draw away, but still climbing, in the direction of Soissons. Moments later the remaining three did the same. Because following them was an obvious choice, Eddie decided upon caution. Pondering the situation, he reckoned that the three closest Germans would wait for their pursuers to dive, then attempt to get behind the Spads. At seventeen thousand feet with the three Fokkers below, Eddie saw them disappear well back into Germany. This left the other four to deal with.

Over Fismes, Eddie led his planes a thousand feet higher in the direction of Soissons and at the same level as the four Fokkers. Wigwagging wings to signal his Spads to attack, Eddie sheared slightly to the north in order to cut off a German retreat. With the Fokkers coming on "like a flock of silly geese," he opened fire at the German flight leader's plane. But the target nosed down. The other three followed. At that instant one of Eddie's guns jammed. Then the second froze. With both guns useless, he considered withdrawing. But if he did so, he thought, his men might follow him and a golden opportunity would be lost.

Making up his mind to go through with the fracas without guns and trust the outcome to luck, he darted in and out of a furious "revolving circus that went tumbling across the heavens," always dropping lower and deeper into German lines. At some point in the battle two of his Spads broke away and turned homeward, either with jammed guns or engine trouble. Down to three thousand feet and four miles into enemy territory, Eddie noticed two flights of Germans coming up from the rear to join in the fight. So far, no one on either side had scored a victory.

With the odds now in Germany's favor and feeling "a great longing for home," Eddie signaled his men to break off the fight. Winging homeward, he struggled with his jammed guns with no result. He also gave some thought to what he'd done. He'd waded into a nerve-racking scrap with no guns and counted on the Germans not realizing it. As the flight leader he'd felt that he had no choice but to stay with his men. Thinking about this responsibility caused him to question aspirations that had been stirring in him to become the leader of an entire squadron.

Furious at being left without guns when he'd been in a position to score victories, he landed at home base and went looking for the sergeant in charge of maintaining the guns. A likable nineteen-year-old from Brooklyn named Abe Karp, he assured

Eddie that the guns had been in perfect condition. The problem could have arisen, he suggested, because the low temperature at high altitudes made the guns' lubricating oil gummy, causing sliding parts of the guns to stick. Or maybe it was the ammunition. Discerning that shell casings were not uniform in size, Abe made a template calibrated to the size of the chambers of Eddie's guns. Thereafter, if a cartridge was too large, it was discarded.

On Sunday, August 18, 1918, Eddie awoke with an ache in his right ear so agonizing he was unable to get out of bed. The squadron's doctor explained that constant twisting of his neck as he turned his head from side to side in flight combined with the cold air that buffeted him in an open cockpit at high altitudes had exacerbated his mastoiditis. He would need an immediate operation.

This meant turning over command of that day's mission by Flight One to Eddie Green, flying with Walter Smyth and a new man, Alexander Bruce.

"I regretted not making that mission," Eddie noted, "because I liked to fly with Walter. He was about twenty years old, honest, wholesome, with a grand sense of humor. He was brave, but he carried with him an atmosphere of melancholy; he seemed to sense that he was not going to live out the war. I was closer to Walter than to any other man in the squadron, and I tried to jolly him out of his black moods."

When the three planes took off for the mission, Eddie was semicomatose and awaiting transportation to the Paris hospital. Recalling that morning in his autobiography, he wrote:

> *I suddenly saw, as in a dream, Walter's plane collide with Bruce's. It seemed to happen in a cloud, yet I saw it clearly. Their wings touched and fell off, and I saw both planes plummeting to earth.*
>
> *When I next opened my eyes, I saw Kenneth Marr standing by the bed. "I have terrible news for you," he said.*
>
> *"I know," I said. "Smyth and Bruce were killed."*

*Marr's eyes opened wide. "How did you know?" he
asked. "We just got the telephone message a minute ago."
"I saw it," I said.*

Eddie learned later that the crash had happened just the way
he'd dreamed it. Bitterly writing about the accident half a century
later, he noted that if Smyth and Bruce had been allowed to have
parachutes, they probably would have lived.

"It was absolutely criminal," he declared in his autobiography,
"for our higher command to withhold parachutes from us."

As Eddie was undergoing his second ear surgery, General Pershing's newly created American 1st Army was placed under operational control of France's Marshal Henri Pétain, commander
of French forces in Lorraine. They were to take part in an offensive against the St. Mihiel salient. A bulge in French lines fifty to
sixty miles deep and ranging fifteen to twenty-six miles south of
Verdun, it had existed since September 1914 and withstood numerous assaults. Commitment of U.S. forces to the new offensive
was seen as a "christening" of the American forces and a symbol
to both the French and American people that the AEF would no
longer be on the sidelines. But the St. Mihiel action was planned
as a limited attack prior to a much larger offensive planned for
two weeks later in the Meuse–Argonne region.

Frustrated at not being able to join in the aerial portion of the
offensive, Eddie was an impatient patient. Although the surgery
corrected the ear problem (it would never bother him again), he
was left so tired and weak that he was unable to join in dancing
to the music of an army orchestra that came to the hospital to entertain patients and staff. The orchestra had been formed by Lt.
James Europe. Before the war he had been conductor for the famous dance team of Vernon and Irene Castle. Unfortunately the
graceful combination would never be seen again. British-born
Vernon Castle had joined the Canadian army, then transferred to
the U.S. Air Service. While training cadets in Texas, he'd died in
a crack-up.

Although Eddie wasn't able to dance, he was fit enough to accept an invitation from a nurse, a Miss Wilson, to sit with her on

a balcony overlooking the dance floor and listen to the music. When the evening ended, she brought him ice cream. Miss Wilson, he noted in his diary, had stirred his emotions more than any woman he'd met in France.

As he convalesced in the hospital, he learned how famous Edward V. Rickenbacker had become in the United States. An agent for a New York book publisher paid him a visit. He said that his firm was interested in Eddie writing a book about his wartime exploits. Eddie promised to think it over. In doing so he found a good deal of irony that a man who had quit school in the eighth grade and had often been ridiculed for frequently fractured language was being asked to write a book. Appreciating that he'd been approached because he'd become a famous aviator, he knew that fame was as tenuous as life. He'd learned the nature of celebrity as a race driver who was hailed as a hero in a week when he'd won and called a bum when he lost the next race. As a combat pilot he knew how quickly he could go from "hero to zero." And he was familiar with the joke among newspapermen that today's front page wrapped tomorrow's garbage. But a book was made to last. Books went onto library shelves and would be there years after its author was dead and buried, so that one day someone who'd never heard of Eddie Rickenbacker could discover who he was and what he'd done to garner fame in a long-ago war. In reading about him and the victories he'd scored to become an ace, someone in the future could realize that no man should ever again be called on to shoot another man out of the sky. Embracing the idea that the story of his life might prove worth reading, he resolved to keep a more detailed record of his exploits "with religious regularity." Should he come out of the war alive, he decided, he'd give book writing a try.

When Lieutenant Fauntleroy visited, Eddie was allowed to leave the hospital to go to lunch with him and have a pleasant meal while hearing about preparations for the offensive. His condition was also deemed improved enough for him to leave the hospital for a dinner with Miss Wilson at her apartment on the Avenue Henri Martin.

An invitation that really stirred his enthusiasm came from Capt.

Billy Mitchell. He phoned from his headquarters in Chaumont to ask if Eddie felt well enough to pick up a brand-new Mercedes automobile from a garage in Paris and bring it to Chaumont. Knowing that one of their powerful cars with a double-chain drive had won first place in the grand prix race in 1914, Eddie was eager to drive one. He found that Mitchell's had been converted from a racer to a sports car with four deep leather-lined bucket seats, but it was still capable of high speeds.

Thrilled to be at the wheel, Eddie was soon racing at sixty miles an hour on a smooth military highway between Paris and Chaumont. But as he went into a turn, he lost control and the Mercedes veered into a ditch. With the help of a group of French mechanics who happened to be passing by, he fixed a damaged chain guard, got the car running again, and arrived at the headquarters at Chaumont two hours late. As Eddie explained what happened, Mitchell glared at him but said nothing. Returning to Mitchell's office, they found a French general waiting. To Eddie's amazement, Mitchell suddenly unleashed an angry tirade that seemed to Eddie to be a show for the Frenchman, meant to demonstrate that Mitchell was a tough officer. It was a scene that Eddie believed was unwarranted and humiliating. Attributing the outburst to the pressure Mitchell was feeling as commander of the U.S. Air Service at the start of a crucial offensive in which American planes were playing a major role, he let it pass.

Having been out of action for weeks, and eager to hear how the 94th Squadron was doing in the battle, Eddie welcomed a visit from several of the 94th's pilots. They glumly reported that the squadron had not been scoring victories. Morale was low. The men needed a boost, they said, that could only come if Eddie came back. But not as a flight leader. What they desired, said the pilots, was his return as their commanding officer. And they were prepared to go to Mitchell and formally request it.

"If I'm ordered to command the 94th, I'll be proud to do so," Eddie replied. But as he spoke, he knew that it was not a good time to discuss a personnel change with a man who at that moment was planning the first great combined air-and-ground assault in the history of warfare. Mitchell was responsible for building the largest air force ever known—400 observation planes and 400 bombers, plus fleets of fighter escorts, in support of half a million infantry. The air mission involved attacks on the St. Mihiel salient to contain all German planes within their own lines, keep them from disrupting Allied supply lines, and cut off the German supply routes and means of reinforcement. To join in this fray, Eddie was told, the Hat-in-the-Ring Squadron had been ordered to move to the Verdun sector.

Unwilling to be left out of the largest air battle of the war, Eddie demanded that he be declared cured and returned to action. Released from the hospital on September 3, 1918, he left immediately by car. But when he was on the outskirts of Bar-le-Duc, he was stopped by military police and questioned as to his character and identity. Spies were abroad, an MP explained, and everyone was being stopped, no matter what uniform they wore.

The new base at Erize-la-Petite was a former German aerodrome that also had been used by French escadrilles. It lay fifteen miles south of Verdun, with the enemy lines extending from there along the Meuse to St. Mihiel, about a dozen miles to the east. The U.S. squadrons at the base were the 94th, 95th, 147th commanded by Jimmy Meissner, and the 27th led by Al Grant of Austin, Texas, who'd replaced Major Hartney when Hartney was promoted to lead the entire group of squadrons at the base.

At dinner that night, word came that "the big show" was to commence at five the next morning. Awakened at that hour by the thundering of thousands of guns, Eddie knew that the St. Mihiel drive was on.

CHAPTER 13

Ace of Aces

"IT WAS AN EXCITING MOMENT IN MY LIFE," WROTE EDDIE RICKEN-backer of the fateful day of September 12, 1918, "as I realized that the great American attack upon which so many hopes had been fastened was actually on. I suppose every American in the world wanted to be in that great action. The very sound of the guns thrilled one and filled one with excitement. The good reputation of America seemed bound up in the outcome of that great battle."

Unfortunately, when he stuck his head outside his tent, he found rain. Running through it, he reached the mess hall and found groups of pilots as impatient as he to get away. At noon the rain continued, but visibility seemed better. Judging the cloud level at about a thousand feet, he drew Reed Chambers aside and suggested they "try a short flip over the lines."

While the other pilots ate lunch, Eddie and Chambers took off and flew east at six hundred feet toward St. Mihiel. Crossing the Meuse and turning down its valley in the direction of Verdun, they saw numerous fires on the German side of the river. The withdrawing enemy had torched villages, haystacks, ammunition dumps, supply caches, and anything else that might prove to be of value to the Americans in their advance on the town of Vigneulles in a pincer movement. The main highway running north to Metz, Eddie observed, was clogged with hurrying men and vehicles carrying guns, ammunition, and supplies. Continuing south, he and Chambers flew low through the heart of the St. Mihiel salient, observing the similarly thronged main road between Vigneulles and the city of St. Mihiel. Finding a battery of 3-inch guns a tempting target, they swept down and sprayed men and horses with machine gun fire, sending the whole column into wild confusion. Terrfied horses broke away. Others were hit and fell in their tracks. The wagon drivers headed for the shelter of the woods, but one unlucky racer got only halfway across the road before running into the path of Eddie's bullets.

Breaking off the withering strafing, Eddie and Chambers headed back to base to report what they'd seen and the location of enemy forces in full retreat. The result was a commencing of devastating American field artillery fire on the road. That night Eddie learned that the German air base at Thiaucourt had been taken and that U.S. Infantry and the Tank Corps were attacking the strategic city of Montsec.

Airborne over the same road the next day, the duo of Rickenbacker and Chambers saw the U.S. advance "in full swing," but the retreating Germans were out of reach of American artillery. The morning was cloudy with occasional rain, preventing the high altitude observation planes from getting up to direct barrages. But rain did not keep the infantry from moving ahead. Looking down, Eddie saw them "fighting along like Indians," scurrying from cover to cover, crouching as they ran, throwing themselves flat, shooting at the German rearguard troops, then lurching up for another dash forward in what Eddie called "the most spectacular free show that ever a man gazed upon."

A high flying rooter for the doughboys in his Spad, Eddie heard the *rat-a-tat-tatting* of a machine gun below and felt a few bullets hit his plane. Spotting the gunners, he nosed down the Spad and swooped at the Germans with his own guns blazing, dropping one German where he'd stood and sending two others diving for cover. Recovering altitude, he found that in the fracas he'd lost track of Chambers. With fuel running low, there was no time to search for him.

About two hours after Eddie returned to base, Chambers landed to report that he had stopped at their former base at Toul and learned from the men at Toul that America's leading ace, David Putnam, had been shot down. After the death of Raoul Lufbery, the title of ace of aces devolved to Lt. Paul Frank Baer. From Fort Wayne, Indiana, and a former pilot with the Escadrille Lafayette, he had scored nine victories and never been wounded. But two days after inheriting the distinction, Baer was shot down, slightly wounded, behind German lines. His successor was Lt. Frank Bayles of New Bedford, Massachusetts, with thirteen victories, until he was killed in action on June 12, 1918. Since then, David Putnam had led all American pilots in victories. He'd scored twelve, including four kills on one engagement. On his last flight he'd encountered a formation of eight Fokkers and attacked them alone. He'd been hit almost immediately and went down in flames.

"Thus died a glorious American boy," Eddie noted sadly, "and a brilliant fighter."

With Putnam's death, the American ace of aces was Lt. Edgar Tobin of San Antonio, Texas. A member of the 3d Pursuit Group, he had six official victories—one more than Eddie.

The morning after Eddie learned of Putnam's death was clear and fine for flying. Off to look for Germans at eight o'clock, he expected to find the sky over Thiaucourt full of them. It was a place that had often given him a shudder and that he'd always approached with great caution, coming in high. But on this bright morning he crossed its abandoned airfield with "indifference" and a desire to take a close look at it. He skimmed the empty hangars with a feeling of nostalgia that was short-lived. Attracted by antiaircraft bursts about four miles north of Pont-à-Mousson, he sped toward Metz, climbing higher and scanning the horizon for enemy planes. Instead of Germans, he saw a large flotilla of the new American Liberty planes that their pilots were already calling "flying coffins." But just behind them were four fast-moving Fokkers.

Nosing up, he climbed for the sun, proceeding eastward until he was about a thousand feet over the Germans. Turning about, he flew west in the direction of Three-Fingered Lake with an "unusually brilliant" sun at his back. In a gradual dive with the engine at half throttle, he came to within a hundred yards of the last Fokker in a diamond formation. Certain that he'd not been seen, he closed to fifty yards and opened fire.

Raked by bullets, the German flipped over and began its last long fall to earth. But as Eddie turned his guns on the leader of the pack, the Germans began climbing in a maneuver that revealed the scarlet noses of planes of the famous Richthofen Flying Circus. Believing that the squadron had evacuated its aerodrome in that sector, Eddie could hardly believe that he had blundered single-handed into the Richthofen crowd. Deciding that "this was no place for me to be," he did his best "to get away in a dignified manner."

A sudden burst of fire past the nose of his Spad left him with the chilling realization that no matter where he turned there would be at least two Germans ahead of him. As they whipped their planes "with incredible cleverness," Eddie looked for an opening for a quick getaway. In an effort to outrun them, he went to full throttle and nosed straight down. When he looked back, he was relieved to see them fading away in his rear. Winging back to base he had the satisfaction of not only having outmaneuvered some of the finest aviators in the war, but was elated knowing that he had scored his first victory against the vaunted Flying Circus.

If the kill could be confirmed, he would be credited with six and tie Lieutenant Tobin. One more, and Eddie Rickenbacker would be America's new ace of aces, assuming that Tobin did not surge ahead or that another aviator didn't have an exceptional day in the skies and bypass both of them.

Finding September 15's weather ideal for hunting, Eddie left base on a voluntary patrol at half past eight in the morning and took the nearest route to where the action would be. Over the trenches at sixteen thousand feet in splendid conditions, he glimpsed six Fokkers at about his level and coming toward him from the direction of Conflans. Turning into the sun, he watched the Fokkers change direction in a climb toward the Moselle. Half a mile away, he was certain they must have seen him, but they made no move to launch an attack. At that moment he saw four Spads far below the Germans. He assumed they had come from the American 2d Fighting Group, based at Souilly. They appeared to be bombing roads and strafing enemy infantry. Seeing these Spads at the same time, the Fokkers began a dive.

Deciding to tag along as if he were part of the German formation, Eddie found himself rapidly overtaking them. At five thousand feet and unnoticed, he opened fire on the rear Fokker. Its fuel tank exploded. Evidently discouraged by the hit, the remaining five Germans broke off and headed for Germany.

Satisfied with the morning's outcome, Eddie returned to base with "some little interest and concern" to try to find ground witnesses of his last two battles above St. Mihiel. Mingled with this natural desire to become the leading fighting ace of America was a haunting dread that "the possession of this title—ace of aces—brought with it the unavoidable doom" that had overtaken all its previous holders. He wanted it, but he feared to learn that it was his. Confirmation of the sixth and seventh scores, if there were to be proof, would be found at the Balloon Section. No matter how many pilots might have witnessed the kills, official confirmation was required from ground observers. Borrowing a car, he sped to the balloon base north of Thiaucourt. He found the road closed because it was pitted with shell holes. Forced to detour, he got lost for two hours in the wooded region between St. Mihiel and Vigneulles. About a mile from American trenches he stopped to study a map and saw a flare of flames to his right. Running around the trees, he saw an American balloon enveloped in fire and its observer floating to the ground by parachute. Not far away, a second balloon had met the same fate. After a half hour of searching, he located the balloonists preparing to send up another.

When he asked if any of them had witnessed his victory that

morning, he was answered with smiles. Indeed they had watched a Fokker shot out of the sky. Not only had they seen it, they said, they'd filled out a confirmation report. Might they have seen his victory the previous day? No. But perhaps, a balloonist ventured, someone at the 3d Balloon Company had. It was located north of Pont-à-Mousson.

After watching the new balloon launched, Eddie headed for the site. Stopping again to ask directions from a group of infantry officers, he explained his purpose. To his astonishment, the officers said that they'd all seen his fight the day before, and that the plane he'd shot down had crashed nearby. To be certain they were witnesses, Eddie questioned them as to the time they'd seen the German go down. With it verified, he produced a confirmation report for them to complete and sign. As they did so, he thought, "Eddie, you are the American Ace of Aces!"

He held the title for two weeks. The man who surpassed him was Frank Luke. A member of Squadron 27, he had shot down two German observation balloons in less than four minutes. In a period of eight days he accumulated additional scores and received delayed confirmation of others that brought his total to fourteen. Not even Baron von Richthofen had scored fourteen victories in a single fortnight at the front. With admiration for Luke's accomplishment, Eddie wrote, "The history of aviation, I believe, has not a similar record. In my estimation there has never during the four years of war been an aviator at the front who possessed the confidence, ability and courage that Frank Luke had shown during that remarkable two weeks."

Called upon to make a speech at a dinner given in his honor by all the squadrons at the air base, Luke laughed as he rose and said, "I'm having a bully time!" With that, he sat down. His reward from Squadron Commander Hartney was the highest gift at the disposal of commanding officers at the front—seven days' leave in Paris.

By going to Paris, Luke missed out on a treat. A few nights after he left, a troupe of American entertainers under the auspices of the YMCA arrived to put on a show. Beginning in March 1917, the Christian service organization's National Work Council operated hundreds of canteens, known as "Y huts." At hundreds of training bases in the United States, they offered shower facilities, pool tables, reading and game rooms, phonographs, movies, sports, and other amenities, including secretaries to assist lonesome doughboys in writing letters to the folks at home. When troops were sent overseas, the YMCA followed them to provide the same kind of support with the blessing of the AEF, and in expectation that the people of the Y, most of them women, would help to maintain "contentment, camp spirit and morale."

Among the Y's offerings in France were "leave areas" in nearby towns and cities that were viewed as a means of diverting soldiers on passes from patronizing the red-light districts.

Soon after the Y began its work, American entertainers enlisted in the effort in the form of "soldier shows," at first in training camps in the U.S. and then overseas. It was at one of these training camps, at Yaphank, Long Island, that an enlistee/songwriter named Irving Berlin wrote a ditty that became the anthem of millions of doughboys. It lamented "Oh how I hate to get up in the morning" and expressed a common recruit desire to someday murder the bugler and then spend the rest of their lives in bed. (A song that Berlin wrote for "Yip, Yip Yaphank" but cut from the show would lie in Berlin's files for twenty years before being resurrected on the eve of World War II as "God Bless America.")

The YMCA troupe that arrived to entertain Eddie and the men of the squadron was led by Broadway songwriter Margaret Mayo. The roster of musical stars included Elizabeth Brice, Lois Meredith, Will Morrisey, Tommy Gray, and George Walker. The show was staged in one of the hangars. A dressing room was arranged by hanging a curtain over a truck and trailer. After a "merry dinner" in the 94th's mess hall, Eddie noted, everybody crowded into the "theater."

The show was, Eddie thought, the best he'd ever seen at the front—except one evening when the entertainment had been provided by Elsie Janis. A Broadway star who had earned the name "sweetheart of the doughboys," she was described by Alexander

Woollcott as a "lank, lovely lady." Born on March 16, 1889, in Eddie Rickenbacker's hometown, Columbus, Ohio, she had been a performer since age two. She worked in theatrical stock companies at five. At age ten she'd presented a special Christmas performance for President William McKinley at the White House. A vaudeville headliner at fourteen, she was a Broadway star at seventeen in a smash hit titled *The Vanderbilt Cup* and at twenty-two wrote and played the leading role in *A Star for a Night.* An all-around review artist, Elsie had a gift for comedy, dancing, and singing. The first woman that the AEF had allowed to go to bases near the front, she flitted from post to post and often did nine forty-minute shows a day. At the end of each appearance she led the men in singing tunes that were turned out by the songsmiths of Tin Pan Alley and London music halls. They caught and encouraged the mixed feelings of men at war, from "Goodbye Broadway, Hello France" to "Pack Up Your Troubles in Your Old Kit Bag," "It's a Long Way to Tipperary," "There's a Long, Long Trail Awinding," "Over There," a love song about a soldier who stuttered entitled "K-K-K-Katy," and "Mademoiselle from Armentieres." Also known as "Hinky, Dinky, Parley Voo," it had alternative lyrics composed by soldiers, including:

> *She's the hardest working girl in town, but she makes*
> *her living upside down.*
> *She'll do it for wine, she'll do it for rum,*
> *And sometimes for chocolate or chewing gum.*

Eddie's favorite entertainer, partly because she was from Columbus, Elsie Janis was made an honorary member of the 94th Squadron. Of the Mayo troupe's show, Eddie wrote that "the way the boys laughed and shouted during the performance must have sounded hysterical to the actors, but to my mind this hysteria was only an outlet for the pent-up emotion and an indication of the tension and strain under which we had so long been living."

.   .   .

At midnight on September 21, 1918, with the American 1st Army headquarters moved to Souilly, Gen. John J. Pershing accepted responsibility for an area that had been held by the French 2d Army. It covered the entire sector from the Moselle west to the Argonne Forest. Pershing's plan was to attack on a wide front with nine divisions, supported by nearly 3,000 artillery pieces and 821 aircraft, 604 of which were American.

Two nights later the commander of the 94th Squadron, Major Marr, returned from Paris and announced that he had orders to assume a new post in the United States. The result of this unexpected development was Eddie's appointment to succeed him, with promotion to captain. With "pride and pleasure at receiving this great honor," Eddie recalled that he had been with the 94th since its first day at the front and that the 94th had been the first American squadron to go over enemy lines. Many of his old friends had disappeared and been replaced by other pilots, some of whom had also been lost, leaving three original members— Reed Chambers, Thorn Taylor, and himself. With Raoul Lufbery, Jimmy Hall, and Dave Peterson—all now gone—the 94th led all other squadrons in victories.

"But did it?" Eddie asked himself. Suspecting that Frank Luke's "wonderful run of the past few days" might have put Squadron 27 ahead of the 94th, he walked over to the operations office to look at the records. He found that "this presumptuous young 27 had suddenly taken a spurt, thanks to their brilliant Luke, and now led the Hat-in-the-Ring Squadron by six victories."

Hurrying back to 94's quarters, Eddie convened all his pilots. In the next half hour the men "fixed a resolve" that no American squadron "would ever again be permitted to approach our margin of supremacy."

This meeting with the pilots and another with ground crews was followed by a "serious conference" with himself. Convinced that he had been chosen squadron commander because of his successes in combat and his record as a flight leader, he decided that as squadron leader he would never ask a pilot to go on a mission that he wouldn't undertake himself. He would lead by "example as well as by precept." He would accompany all new pilots, watch their errors, and help them feel more confident by sharing their dangers. He would work harder than ever. His days of "loafing" were over.

Brimming with enthusiasm in the morning, he went up alone "to see how much I had changed for the better or worse."

It would be a memorable day.

CHAPTER 14

Captain Eddie

Flying alone near Verdun on September 25, 1918, Eddie observed two German photo planes heading for the American lines escorted by five Fokkers. After climbing for the sun and confident that he hadn't been seen, he shut down his engine, put down the nose, and headed for the nearest enemy. Bursts from both his guns sent the plane spiraling down to crash just south of Étain. Intending to zoom upward and protect himself against an attack from the four remaining Fokkers, he was surprised that they did not respond. Evidently caught off guard at finding an American Spad in their midst and one of their comrades going down in flames, the four banked right and left. This cleared enough space for Eddie to slip through and dive.

As the escort planes maneuvered to regroup and the two photo planes began to draw apart with their rear-seat observers firing at him, Eddie plunged more steeply and went under the nearest German, out of sight of the gunner. Deciding to make one bold attack, he found an opening between the photo planes as they flew parallel, fifty yards apart. Cutting between them, he leveled out and began shooting. A moment later one of the Germans burst into flames and started a blazing path to the ground. At the same time the Fokker escorts streaked into view. Eddie "put on the gas" and headed for American lines.

Having scored a "double-header," he knew that the victories wouldn't count unless they were confirmed. Landing at base at 9:30, he called to Lieutenant Chambers to accompany him by car in search of witnesses among the Americans at the front. After passing through Verdun, they took a road to Fort de Tavannes that cut through ground where French and German troops had struggled in the 1916 battle of Verdun. When Eddie found a French officer, he asked if he had seen a combat overhead that morning. He had, said the officer, and a group of other officers had watched the show through field glasses. Leaving their car, Eddie and Chambers went on foot to find them.

With a written confirmation of his twin victories and the hearty congratulations from the French commandant, and "having no further business at this place," Eddie and Chambers went back to their car. But as they neared it, they heard a shrill whining sound. An instant later an artillery shell exploded. Showered with gravel and dirt, they dived into an old shell hole with the chilling realization that the Germans had seen their car and had it within range of their guns. Hunkered in the shell hole, Eddie saw that the car was pointed the wrong way for a quick escape and cursed himself for not having turned the car around when he'd parked it. When the shelling stopped, he assumed the Germans had decided one automobile wasn't worth the shells they were expending. With seconds seeming like hours, he and Chambers dashed for the car. Expecting another barrage, Eddie got it turned around, then drove away as though he were on a dirt racetrack somewhere in Nebraska.

Back at their base before noon, Eddie felt that it had been "a good morning's work." He had improved the squadron's record by two victories and shown his men that he was not going to be a deskbound squadron commander. (If he had been clairvoyant and able to look into the future to 1930, he would have seen that for his "double-header" that morning he had earned, although delayed, the nation's highest military honor, the Congressional Medal of Honor.) But celebration of the day's triumph was necessarily brief. Of far greater significance for him and the men of the Hat-in-the-Ring Squadron was what lay ahead of them the following morning. September 26, 1918, on General Pershing's calendar and that of the AEF and America's war-weary allies, was designated D.

At 4:00 A.M., "zero hour," thirty-seven American and French divisions would launch an offensive against the Argonne Forest and along the river Meuse. In the nighttime hours before the attack, AEF artillery would fire eight hundred mustard gas and phosgene shells as part of a barrage by four thousand guns. Commanding one of the batteries was Capt. Harry Truman of Independence, Missouri. His guns and the others were to carry out a six-hour bombardment. After this, more than seven hundred tanks would advance, led by a cocky expert on tanks named George S. Patton. Closely following the tanks would be infantry.

Precisely at four in the morning of the 26th, Eddie Rickenbacker was awakened by an orderly. He told Eddie the weather looked good. Outside, gazing into the black sky, Eddie wondered how many Americans would be dead or wounded by day's end. Orders for Hat-in-the-Ring pilots called for them to attack all enemy observation balloons along the entire front and to continue the attacks until the infantry's operations were completed. Each of the flights had been assigned specific targets. Sunup was six o'clock. This meant that the planes had to be in the air at 5:30, giving them half an hour to locate the balloons just as the giant gasbags were going up.

At breakfast with his five best pilots—Chambers, Taylor, Coolidge, Palmer, and Cook—Eddie reviewed the plan for the 94th's first planned venture against balloons. Each flight of three planes was assigned two. The balloons would be found along the Meuse between Brabant and Dun. The greatest danger in such an attack came from antiaircraft guns. Planes attacking a balloon that was tethered at fifteen hundred feet could be easy pickings for Archie. The impulse of an inexperienced pilot going after a balloon was to plunge right in, fire his bullets, and get away. Veterans such as Frank Luke and Ham Coolidge who went into a balloon attack, Eddie noted, did so without thinking about the risks or terrors about them. They flew as "calmly as though they were sailing through a stormless sky." Regardless of flaming missiles from the ground, they plunged through flaming onions from below as often as necessary to set a balloon on fire with incendiary bullets. The advantage of attacking at dawn was that the planes were hard to see by men on the ground and those in the ascending balloon. And enemy planes were unlikely to be up and about–unless the Germans had an inkling that something was afoot.

First to take off at 5:30, Eddie rose into the predawn blackness. Of "the most marvelous sight" he'd ever experienced, he wrote:

> *A terrific barrage of artillery fire was going on ahead of me. Through the darkness the whole western horizon was illuminated with one mass of jagged flashes. The big guns were belching out their shells with such rapidity that there appeared to be millions of them shooting at the same time. Looking back I saw the same scene in my rear. From Luneville on the east to Rheims on the west there was not one spot of darkness along the whole front. The French were attacking along both our [American] flanks at the same time in order to help demoralize the weakening Boche. The picture made me think of a giant switchboard which emitted thousands of electric flashes as invisible hands manipulated the plugs. So fascinated did I become over this extraordinary fireworks display that I was startled upon peering over the side of my machine to discover the city of Verdun below my wings. Setting my course above the dim outline of the river Meuse I followed its windings downstream, occasionally cutting across little peninsulas which I recognized along the way. Every inch of this route was as familiar to me as the path around the corner of my old home.*

In the first faint glimmer of daybreak Eddie watched long snaky flashes of German tracer bullets as either Chambers or

Cook attacked and set ablaze the balloon that had been designated to them. Before the glare faded, a second balloon exploded. Having seen his pilots succeed beyond expectations on their first planned venture against *Drachen*, he turned north to look for a balloon nest that had been reported to be near Damvillers. He arrived with a burst of flame signaling that someone had already gotten to it.

Pleased that another *Drachen* had been destroyed, he looked to his right and discovered a Fokker flying beside him less than a hundred yards away. In an instant of deft maneuvering the German was suddenly ahead, turning about, and coming straight for him. With the guns of both planes blazing and tracer bullets looking like four burning ropes linking the Fokker and Spad, a head-on collision seemed inevitable until the German tipped down his nose to dive. It proved to be a fatal maneuver. In a sharp turn, Eddie closed on the Fokker and sprayed its fuselage with both guns. But as the plane fell toward earth, Eddie's engine started vibrating violently.

Picturing the motor quitting, the plane being forced to land in German territory, and himself a prisoner of war, Eddie breathed a sigh of relief as the plane cleared the American line and made it to the U.S. airfield at Verdun. When he landed, he realized that in the head-on duel with the Fokker, half of his propeller had been shot off. His victory over the Fokker, if confirmed by a ground observer, and ten balloons knocked out by his squadron, had been accomplished in an hour with the flight suffering no losses. Strategically, their morning's work had destroyed so many *Drachen* that the Germans would be unable to quickly replace them, leaving them at a disadvantage in aerial observation of the status of the battle on the ground.

Eddie's elation over the day's victories was soon punctured as devastatingly as a strafed *Drachen*. He learned that two of his lieutenants, Sherry and Nutt, had not returned from a patrol. Long after dark their mechanics remained on the field to fire flares in the hope that the pilots had simply lost their way. Eddie could only wait and pray that morning would bring a telephone report that Sherry and Nutt had landed safely at another base.

The call that came was from Sherry. He reported that he and Nutt had run into a flight of eight Fokkers. The Hun pilots had been so skilled and experienced and worked together with such "nicety," he said, that he and Nutt were unable either to hold their own or escape. Nutt had gone down in flames, leaving Sherry to make a break with all the Fokkers on his tail and eager for a kill. Forced lower and lower over no-man's-land, he'd crashed into a shell hole. As his Spad was turning over and shattering into fragments, he'd been thrown from the plane. When he made a dash for cover, the Germans swooped down, strafing as they came. At that moment a formation of Spads appeared, forcing the Germans to flee while Sherry scampered toward U.S. trenches.

In the morning, Sherry told Eddie, he and a group of American soldiers had found Nutt's body near his smashed plane. With several bullet holes in his back and chest, he was dead before the plane hit the ground. As the search party began digging a grave, Sherry continued, they had come under fire from a sniper and one of the men was hit in the foot. Infuriated that a German would shoot at a burial party, the men rushed the trench from which the sniper fired and clubbed him to death with their rifle butts.

That evening (September 29, 1918), Eddie recorded more distressing news in his diary. "Frank Luke, the marvelous balloon strafer of the 27th," he wrote, "did not return last night."

When no further word was received, the men of Eddie's group resigned themselves to having lost "the greatest airman in the army." What they did not know, and would not learn until long after the war was over, was that on Luke's last patrol he'd shot down three more German balloons but had been forced down in enemy territory by engine trouble. What happened next was recorded for posterity in the citation that explained why Lt. Frank Luke, Jr. of the 27th Aero Squadron was awarded the Medal of Honor:

> *After having previously destroyed a number of enemy aircraft within 17 days, he voluntarily started on a patrol after German observation balloons. Though pur-*

sued by eight German planes which were protecting the
enemy balloon line, he unhesitatingly attacked and shot
down in flames three German balloons, being himself
under heavy fire from ground batteries, and the hostile
planes. Severely wounded, he descended to within 50
meters of the ground and flying at this low altitude
near the town of Murvaux, opened fire upon enemy
troops, killing six and wounding as many more. Forced
to make a landing and surrounded on all sides by the
enemy, who called upon him to surrender, he drew his
automatic pistol and defended himself gallantly until
he fell dead from a wound in the chest.

Two days after learning that Frank Luke was missing, Eddie
was at dinner with Reed Chambers and another lieutenant. They
were interrupted by an orderly who had a message from the
group commander, Major Hanley. Eddie and two volunteers were
to report to the CO's office "forthwith" for a "most important mission." With Ham Coolidge and Wier Cook, Eddie hastened there
and was surprised to find Gen. Billy Mitchell "pacing the floor."

Mitchell explained that American troops were at that moment
engaged in an attack on Montfaucon and were advancing up a
ten-mile valley between the Argonne Forest and the river Meuse.
Their objective was a hilltop from which in 1916 the Crown
Prince of Germany had viewed the battles for Verdun. The hill
provided an extensive view for miles around.

For four days, Mitchell continued, the Americans had been
flinging themselves against the present German defenses in the
region the doughboys had named Death Valley. In the fight, several thousand Americans became marooned and ran out of food
and ammunition. What he and Major Hanley had been discussing, Mitchell said, was the advisability of sending an airlift of
supplies at daybreak. In addition to this revelation, Mitchell dis-
closed that the Army Intelligence Bureau had reported that
eleven German troop trains had left Metz at noon. Aboard these
trains, the report stated, were troops of the famous Prussian
Guard for an attack on the marooned Americans. What Mitchell

required was confirmation of the report. The mission at night was so hazardous, he said, that he would entrust it only to volunteer pilots.

Eddie told him that he, Coolidge, and Cook were just the ones to do it.

"Very well," said Mitchell. "Strike the mail railroad line on the Meuse, follow it up as far as Stenay and from there go to Montmedy and on to Metz. Note carefully every moving thing on that route if you have to fly as low as the treetops. Locate the time and place of every train, how many cars it has, which way it is headed and the nature of the load, if you can. I will wait here until you return."

To guide the planes back to base, said Major Hanley, searchlights would be kept on all through the night.

As Eddie followed Coolidge and Cook into the black sky, he saw the searchlights cutting yellow slices in the clear sky. To the north were fitful flashes of artillery fire. When he was over the area of the marooned troops, he turned toward Montfaucon. On roads below were thousands of infantry advancing to be in a favorable position by daylight to attempt to rescue the marooned troops. Turning east, he found the Meuse and followed its course at three hundred feet. Going deeper and deeper into enemy territory, he saw no German searchlights, heard no ground fire, and felt sure that he had nothing to fear. Unless his engine failed. Amazed that the distinctive sound of the Spad's motor was attracting no attention below, he passed the wide lagoons of Mouzay, forty miles into enemy territory. Ahead lay Stenay.

Observing the red glow of a locomotive's firebox, he swooped lower and prepared to count the train's cars. He was disappointed that it was not a troop train, but a line of freight wagons. Crossing and recrossing the rail yard, he found no sign of the reported trains carrying the Prussian Guard. Moving on to Montmedy, he found a train going toward Stenay and another on the way to Metz. Neither was a troop train.

Frustrated at having loaded his plane with extra ammunition for the strafing he'd hoped to do and feeling "doomed to disappointment," he calculated that if there were troop trains as reported, and if they had left Metz at noon, they would have arrived at their destinations long ago. Deciding that the intelligence about the Prussian Guard on the move had been a false alarm, he headed for home. Because he was flying at night, he would have to rely on his compass.

Expecting to reach Verdun in five minutes, he was puzzled when the city didn't come into view. Suspecting an errant compass, he gave it a tap. The pointer whirled a few times and settled in a different direction. Because the compass was useless, he searched the horizon for help from searchlights. He found no beams to guide him.

With three-quarters of an hour of gas remaining, he searched the sky for the North Star. It told him that he had been going west instead of south. If he continued on that course he would have to fly fast for two hundred miles before reaching the British line at Ypres. Keeping the star behind the rudder, he flew south for fifteen minutes, then dropped toward a bend in a stream that looked like a familiar curve of the Meuse. Following the river, he reached Verdun. Ten minutes later he saw a welcome slash of guiding searchlight in the dark and knew he was close to home. When he landed, he learned that Coolidge and Cook had returned without finding any troop trains.

General Mitchell's reply to their report was a smile and "Thank God."

At daylight the infantry that Eddie had observed advancing during the night reached the marooned troops and relieved them. On the Ypres front the British were within two miles of the town of Menin. It was a place they had been trying to take for four years. At the Argonne Forest, Americans were planning to renew a bogged-down assault as part of an Allied advance on all sectors of the Western Front.

On October 1 a large formation of 94th planes plied the skies over German lines for two hours without a fight. One covey of Fokkers appeared, but they were too far away to get in range. Frustrated and impatient, Eddie flew back to base, switched planes, and went back alone late in the afternoon. He "hung around" until dusk with no quarry. As he was about to give up the hunt, he glimpsed a *Drachen* on the ground near Three-Fingered Lake.

Counting on it being inadequately guarded as darkness approached, he sped toward it, confident that there would be no Archie to molest him. A hundred rounds, fired as he dived, set the balloon ablaze. Deciding the kill was too easy to claim as a victory, he winged toward home.

Getting there was not without excitement. Crossing the American line at Vigneulles, he found himself being shot at by antiaircraft gunners. He had unwittingly ventured into airspace that had been declared off-limits to aircraft, with orders to the gunners to fire at any plane, no matter what markings it had. Fortunately, Eddie noted, "Their aim was so bad that I did not even feel indignant at their overzealousness."

A few hours after landing and telling his men about getting the unguarded balloon, he was informed that American ground observers had confirmed the kill.

October began with a change of mission. Instead of going out to look for the enemy, the 94th's new task was to patrol American lines at no more than two thousand feet. "This meant serious business to us," Eddie noted, "for not only would we be under more severe Archie fire, but we would be an easy target for the higher Hun formations, who could dive down upon us at their own pleasure. These new orders were intended to provide means of defense against the low-flying enemy machines which came over our lines. Usually they were protected by fighting machines. Rarely did they attempt to penetrate to any considerable distance back of No Man's Land. They came over to follow the lines and see what we were doing on our front, leaving to their high-flying photographic machines the inspection of our rear."

Taking off on October 2 after the departure of six Spads in a flight led by Chambers in order to "see how the new scheme was working," Eddie trailed them two thousand feet higher "to act somewhat in a protective capacity." When the flight made a turn after several patrols of the front between Sivry-sur-Meuse and Romagne, his vigilance was rewarded with the sighting of a German two-seat Hanover plane flying low and attempting to sneak across the lines. Calculating the German's position and deciding to cut him off just behind the front, he was surprised that the quarry made no move to escape. As he zoomed toward the Hanover, he wondered if the pilot's brazenness stemmed from shrewd tactics, self-confidence, stupidity, or ignorance of the fact that an enemy was on his tail.

Wary of what appeared to be an easy victory, but could be a ruse to lure him even closer, Eddie looked for lurking enemy planes. Finding none, he fixed his sights on the Hanover's rear seat. Fifty yards away and still undetected, he squeezed the triggers of both guns, saw the man in the rear seat slump to the side, and sped past the Hanover. Turning back and prepared for the pilot to open fire on him, he sighted, squeezed the triggers, and found both guns had jammed. At that moment Reed Chambers streaked into view. Firing as he descended, he riddled the pilot and sent the Hanover down among the shell holes two miles behind the American line. Although it was a shared victory, the score was Eddie's first kill behind Allied lines.

With the jammed guns cleared, Eddie discovered eight Fokkers making for clouds that would be an ideal place from which to launch an attack on the other Spads in Chambers's flight. Hoping that the Germans hadn't seen him, he looked for an opening that would permit him to slip up on them. The plan was thwarted by bursts of German tracer bullets. Executing a double spin to dodge the attack, he dived at full throttle with the Fokkers in hot pursuit. As he braced for death either from their bullets or a headlong crash, the firing stopped. Looking around, he saw Spads arriving "in the nick of time." Leading them, Reed Chambers was in pursuit of "the whole circus" as the Fokkers climbed for the shelter of a bank of clouds.

Pulling out of his dive, Eddie joined the chase and met Chambers below the clouds. At that moment the leader of the Fokkers burst into view followed by the rest of his planes. In the ensuing dogfight, Eddie and Chambers each shot down one plane and watched the remainder of the Germans break off and speed away.

Confirmation of their shared victory and the independent scores, telephoned to the base from ground observers, awaited them when they landed.

Recording the day's actions in his diary, Eddie wrote, "Thought my days were ended."

In the afternoon of the next day (October 2, 1918), Eddie shared a victory with Ham Coolidge and got one of his own, his fourteenth confirmed solo score. Added to these were kills by Thorn Taylor, Will Palmer, and Crafty Sparks. The day's work placed the 94th's record well ahead of that of the 27th Squadron. But the achievement was marred by the apparent loss of two pilots. Hoping that they weren't killed but had crashed and been taken prisoner, Eddie put off writing condolence letters to their parents for weeks. His instincts proved correct. Both men had survived being shot down. Although wounded, they were repatriated at the end of the war.

Catching a lone Fokker north of Montfaucon on October 5, Eddie tallied victory number fifteen. But just as pleasing to him that day was word that the Hanover he and Chambers shot down within U.S. lines on October 2 had been located. The plane had landed in relatively good condition and was being guarded against souvenir scavengers, should he and Chambers care to travel to the spot about a mile north of the town to inspect it.

"Up to this time the American air force had never captured one of these two-seater Hanover machines," Eddie noted. "We were all of us anxious to fly different types of German airplanes, to compare them with our own, to examine what new devices they employed, to test their engines and to see toward what improvements their designers were tending."

With rain precluding flying that morning, Eddie noted, he and Chambers "lost no time in getting an automobile and making our way to the front line." The route took them along the eastern edge of the Argonne Forest at Varennes. "Along both sides of the road as far as the eye could reach," Eddie wrote, "the shell holes covered the landscape as thickly as in almost any part of No Man's Land. Trees were sheared of their branches and even the trunks of large trees themselves were cut jaggedly in two by the enemy's shells. Occasionally the ugly base of a dud shell could be seen protruding six or eight inches from the tree's trunk. And along the whole way strings of motor trucks were passing and repassing, some laden with ammunition, food, medical, and other supplies hurrying to the front lines, dodging as they splashed through the slimy mud. Long lines of 'empties' were coming against this stream [and others were] filled with the wounded who were being carried back to a field hospital for amputations or other surgical operations. Occasionally we would find ourselves blocked as whole processions came to a halt."

Stopping at the town of Montfaucon, they ate lunch at a YMCA hut and watched a long line of soldiers waiting to buy chocolate and cigarettes. Given directions to the location of the place where the Hanover was under guard, they hurried to their prize. Finding it in "remarkably good condition," they marveled that its pilot had been able to keep it under control and bring it in for a fairly good landing on rough ground. The nose had gone over, breaking the propeller and leaving the tail sticking up and resting against a shattered telephone pole. A few wing ribs had been snapped. American mechanics who retrieved the plane had loaded it on a truck and carted it away. The man in the observer seat had died of his bullet wounds and was buried nearby. The pilot had been rushed to a hospital with a shattered jaw.

With the Hanover loaded onto a trailer attached to their car, Eddie and Chambers left for the return trip to their base at five in the afternoon. Along the way they watched a battle in the sky between nine Fokkers and a pair of Spads, though they could not tell whether the Spads were American or French. The skirmish ended with the Spads downing two Fokkers. When Eddie and Chambers got back to base, they learned that the Spads were from the 94th. The victorious pilots were Lieutenants Kaye and Jeffers. (No relation to the author of this book, as far as I know.)

October 6 brought the destruction of a German balloon by Ham Coolidge and a chance sixteenth victory for Eddie when he happened to spot a balloon being pulled down for the night.

After being grounded by bad weather for a few days, the Hat-in-the-Ring Squadron got orders to knock out two *Drachen* that had become "very bothersome" to American forces at Dun-sur-Meuse and Aincreville. The attack would include planes of the 27th and 147th Squadrons with Eddie in command. Selecting Coolidge and Chambers to act as "balloon executioners," he ordered all pilots to rendezvous at three thousand feet over Montfaucon at 3:40 P.M. The first target would be the balloon at Dun. After destroying it, they would proceed to Aincreville.

The afternoon weather was fair. Allied intelligence reports guaranteed that the planes would encounter opposition from the greatest concentration of the enemy since the start of the war in 1914. They should expect the red-nosed Richthofen Circus and planes of the Loerzer Circus with the bellies of their fuselages painted yellow. They also might find the checkerboard design of No. 3 Jagdstaffel adorning fast new Siemens-Schuckert fighters with four-bladed propellers. And there were reports of Fokkers that had been fitted with four instead of two forward-mounted guns fixed above the engine and top wing. When fired at once they looked like Fourth of July fireworks and were known as "roman candles."

A heavy concentration of enemy aircraft along the front was necessary because Americans were on the attack at the Argonne, requiring the Germans to hold fast at the Meuse. The British bombing of German cities had become intolerable, demanding a massing of planes close to the front in an effort to stop the raiders before they could reach the Fatherland. All of this was needed to buy time so that if an armistice could be attained, the terms would not result in the loss of precious German territories that certainly would be demanded if the war ended with the Allies holding the upper hand.

Commanding fourteen Spads of the 94th, seven planes of the 27th, and eight from the 147th, Eddie took his No. 1 to several thousand feet to observe the progress of a flotilla that resembled "a huge crawling beetle." With Coolidge and Chambers in the van, the formation arrived at Dun-sur-Meuse to a welcome from "an outlandish exhibition of Archie's fury." In bright sunshine floated the targeted balloon. But approaching fast from the distant horizon were eleven Fokkers "in beautiful formation." From the opposite direction came eight more.

While pondering which flight presented more danger, Eddie looked down and saw the balloon's ground crew hurrying to draw down their *Drachen*. Peering again at Fokkers coming in from the west, he saw red noses. They were heading to the 147 formation, led by Wilbert White, Jr., nicknamed Wilbur. As the first of the Fokkers passed beneath him, Eddie fired into the plane's fuel tank. He then watched the German pilot leap from the cockpit. Attached to his back was a rope that yanked open a parachute. Wishing the pilot "all the luck in the world," Eddie again resented that the United States didn't provide such a means of escape for its pilots. But the mixture of anger at American stupidity and good wishes for an enemy immediately vanished from his mind as he could only watch in horror while Wilbur White's plane collided head-on with a Fokker. They hit each other at 250 miles an hour, causing the planes to jam together like parts of a telescope.

One of the finest and best fighters in Eddie's group, White was born on May 1, 1889, in New York City. The son of a protestant minister, he'd graduated from the University of Wooster in 1912. Married with two children, he enlisted in the U.S. Air Service on July 3, 1917, and did his training in Texas and Canada. With seven victories on his record, he was the 147th's highest scoring ace. Ironically and tragically, his seventh score had earned him a leave to return to the United States. He'd planned to do so after completing the mission on which he was killed. For his action in deliberately ramming the German on October 10 because his guns had jammed, he was recommended for the Congressional Medal of Honor. Instead, an Oak Leaf Cluster was added to a Distinguished Service Cross that was awarded for shooting down a balloon and a Fokker on September 14, 1918. The French had given him a Croix de Guerre for downing two Albatroses at Château-Thierry on July 24. The German with whom he'd collided on October 10, Wilhelm Kohlbach of Jasta 10, survived and was credited with a fifth victory.

Perhaps shaken by the horror of the midair collision, the Germans of Kohlbach's flight broke off the combat and departed. With them gone, Eddie turned his attention to the intent of the mission and was amazed to see one of his Spads diving toward the nested balloon through "a hurricane of projectiles." One of the flaming onions hit the Spad's wings and set them on fire, forcing it to land nearby. As Eddie dived to strafe the balloon ground crew, he saw another Spad whip past. It was Jimmy Meissner. Two Fokkers were on his tail.

Determined to get the "two ugly brutes who were trying their best to execute him," Eddie joined the procession and fired a long burst at the rear Fokker. As the hit German spun down, the second pulled away and fled. While all this was transpiring, Coolidge and Chambers each got a Fokker. Although the mission to shoot down two balloons had failed, Eddie flew back to base satisfied with four more victories for the 94th, but regretting that he'd been unable to help the pilot who'd been brought down by the flaming onions (Lieutenant Brotherton of the 147).

While the Hat-in-the-Ring pilots were away hunting *Drachens* and grappling with German fighter squadrons, the squadron's mechanics had accepted a challenge from Captain Rickenbacker to make the battered captive Hanover two-seater airworthy again so it could be studied and tested by 94th aviators, then used to train them in how to attack such a plane in mock combat. When the plane was ready, with its Maltese cross and other insignia left intact, Eddie notified the pilots of squadrons at other Allied aerodromes that if they happened to see the plane in the air around 94's base, they were not to attack it. The first to take it up "for a short flip," he found that the heavy plane handled well at both fast and slow speeds required to maneuver in combat, but that a skilled pilot in a lighter Spad could expect to enjoy the advantage. His surmise proved correct. In bouts of feigned battles with one of the 94th's best men at the controls of the Hanover, the encircling Spads always bettered the Hanover while learning about its maneuverability without having to worry about being shot down.

A few days after these instructive engagements began, an observer on the ground was a captain in the motion picture unit of the air service. A man who never went anywhere without a movie camera in a bag slung over a shoulder, twenty-five-year-old Merian C. Cooper had a lot in common with Eddie Ricken-backer. As a boy he'd been adventuresome and often reckless. But while Eddie dreamed of racing cars, Cooper had yearned to be a daring explorer. After a try at becoming a naval officer during a year at the Naval Academy, he'd dropped out and joined the mer-chant marine. This was followed by an interlude as a newspa-perman in the Midwest and an enlistment in the Georgia National Guard that took him to Mexico during Black Jack Per-shing's hunt for Pancho Villa. Transferring from the infantry to the Aviation Corps when the United States entered the Great War, he took pilot training and served as a photographer in observa-tion planes over German lines.

Eddie invited Cooper to spend the night with the 94th and to film the exercise with the Hanover the next day from the rear seat of a Liberty DH-9A to be piloted by Jimmy Meissner. It proved to be a day Cooper would never forget. During takeoff the Liberty's engine stopped at an altitude of fifteen feet. Barely missing tele-graph wires strung beside a road next to the field, the plane hit the roadway hard, bounded up, did a half somersault, and stopped nose-down on the other side of the road. Hurrying to the wrecked plane and expecting to find two dead occupants, Eddie almost laughed as Meissner and Cooper crawled from the smash-up unhurt.

Dusting himself off, Cooper asked Eddie if he had another plane. None was available at the base, Eddie replied, but he was sure he could requisition one from the supply station. First, how-ever, Eddie explained, there was to be a ceremony the next day at Souilly. Gen. Mason M. Patrick was to award him and twenty pi-lots of the U.S. Air Service the Distinguished Service Cross. His was for the victory he had shared with James Norman Hall in downing an Albatros on April 29.

While a band played the National Anthem, Eddie thought about the pilots whose names had been read aloud but who could not answer for deeds of heroism that had ended with their deaths, among them Frank Luke and Wilbert White. Glancing down the line of honored men, he wondered who would be the next to go. Yet one thing was certain, he mused. The heroic deeds of these great American airmen would live as long as their comrades did. With every fresh honor that was conferred, he would write, he accepted "a corresponding degree of responsibility and obligation to continue to serve comrade and country so long as life endured."

The day after the ceremony, the new Liberty was on hand and ready. With Cooper again in the rear seat, Jimmy Meissner had instructions to keep the Liberty as close as possible to the Hanover and fly to the left side of "the show" so that Cooper's camera would attain the best possible view. At the controls of the Hanover, Thorn Taylor wore a "villanious-looking" German uniform. Reed Chambers was in the rear seat. Tucked out of sight was a straw-stuffed dummy outfitted like a Boche pilot. At the climactic moment of the scenario, Chambers was to pitch it over the side in a blatant piece of propaganda to demonstrate that the "Boche aviators preferred to hurl themselves out to certain death rather than longer face the furious assaults of dashing young American air fighters."

The star of the scenario was Eddie in his Spad No. 1 with the Hat-in-the-Ring emblem on the fuselage and red, white, and blue markings along wings and tail "sufficiently glaring to prove to the most skeptical movie fan that this was indeed a genuine United States warplane." (The hues of the insignia didn't matter. The film in Cooper's camera was monochromatic; color was decades in the future.) To create an illusion that Eddie was engaged in a fight with numerous planes, Cooper had filmed a flight of Spads soaring high enough that their wing markings were impossible to discern. When all these shots were edited in sequence, the effect would be that Eddie had gone up to demolish the German formation by himself.

Real ammunition would be fired, but aimed well above the Hanover. To simulate a hit, Chambers would toss handfuls of lampblack over the side and then drop a landing flare to create an illusion of erupting flames. Moments later he would fling out the dummy.

"It was a clever plot," Eddie boasted. "The whole aerodrome was in raptures over the idea and everybody quit work to gather on the field to witness the contest." For Cooper to get shots of the Spads leaving the ground, Meissner took the Liberty up first and awaited the Spads at two thousand feet.

As the performance commenced, Eddie recalled, "It was necessary to keep an eye on the camera, so as not to get out of its beam while pulling off our most priceless stunts, and at the same time we had to be a little careful as to the direction our bullets were going. Captain Cooper was thrusting his head out into the slipstream manfully trying to keep my swifter-moving plane always within range of his camera."

The fake dogfight was repeated several times, but with ammunition running low the time had come to stage the fatal hit. Making a final turn above the Hanover while Cooper was filming close to the German plane, Eddie flew directly toward the camera with his guns aimed above the Hanover. A cloud of lampblack appeared. A flash of flame. As the dummy went over the side, Cooper leaned far out of the Liberty to film its plummet to earth, then directed his lens up to record the downward spiral of the Hanover as Thorn Taylor skillfully faked the demise of the scenario's "last of the wicked formation of hostile machines."

At this point the actors in Eddie's aerial fiction became players in what might have been a Mack Sennett slapstick comedy of errors and mistaken identity, or a French farce of unintended consequences. Eddie recalled:

> *Paying little attention as to just where we were flying, so long as open country was below us, we had not noticed that we were some miles south and west of a French aerodrome. Suddenly a puff of real Archie smoke in the vicinity of the Hanover told me that some enthusiastic outsider was volunteering his services on behalf of our little entertainment. Another and another shell burst before I could reverse my direction and get started to place my Spad close to the black machine wearing the Iron Cross of the Kaiser. Reed Chambers*

*took in the situation at a glance. He pointed down the
Hanover's nose and began to dive for a landing on the
French aerodrome below us. At the same time several
French Breguets left the field and began climbing to as-
sist me in my dangerous task of demolishing the
Hanover.*

*Diving down to intervene before any more shooting
was done I succeeded in satisfying the Frenchmen that I
had the affair well in hand and that the Hanover was
coming down to surrender.*

On the ground, Eddie explained the situation to the French. As
they all laughed, Eddie looked at Chambers and Taylor and found
the glum expressions of men who "seemed to feel that the joke
was on them."

The next day Captain Cooper departed for Paris with his films.
The completed movie was eventually exhibited in France and the
United States, but by then the Great War was over. Thirteen years
later in a movie written and directed by Cooper, airplanes provided the dramatic climax to a story about a giant homesick and
lovelorn ape named Kong who met his death after bursts of machine gun fire sent him plunging from the pinnacle of the Empire
State Building.

Eddie's captured Hanover was eventually taken to the American station at an air base in Orly outside Paris and later shipped
to the United States to be placed on exhibition.

CHAPTER 15

Finis de la Guerre

O N THE AFTERNOON AFTER STARRING IN MERIAM COOPER'S "AIR-plane movie show," Eddie felt "fed up" with a period of "eventless flying" and went off alone with "an idea of shooting down a balloon." He thought that one might be hanging north of Montfaucon. Nearing the Meuse valley around five o'clock, he found a haze so thick that the Germans had hauled down all *Drachen*. But farther south the sky was clear, and American observation balloons were up. Assuming that it was too late in the day for German planes to be out hunting, Eddie was startled to see a bright blaze in the direction of the U.S. line at Exermont. If a "late roving Hun" had made a successful balloon attack, he reasoned, the plane would make a dash for Germany on a course that would take it directly toward his position. Although he was unable to observe an enemy plane, he knew one was there because of antiaircraft bursts marking its course.

Anticipating launching a surprise attack, Eddie abruptly realized that it was he who had become a target. Streams of bullets flashed past his face and ripped into the Spad's wings and fuselage from above. Absorbed in plotting how to go after the balloon killer, he had been oblivious to his surroundings. It was now obvious that escorts for the German balloon hunter had been stalking him for quite a while. Experience had taught him that if planes were above him, others had to be below, waiting for him to go into an evasive dive. Instead, he corkscrewed up and found a pair of Fokkers of the Richthofen Flying Circus swooping down and two more holding back. This left him in the position of a slice of meat in a sandwich.

Suddenly in the fight of his life, he chose not to wait for an attack from above, but to go after one of the planes below. Nosing over, he hurtled down with both guns blasting ahead of his target. As the enemy flew into the line of fire, the plane burst into flames. As it went down, he executed a loop to go after the Fokkers above. Rather than engage, all the Germans turned in the direction of Germany. Seething at having been "badly treated by the red-nosed Boches" and embarrassed by falling into their trap, but certain that his Spad was speedier than the Fokkers, he gave chase. Three miles into German territory at a thousand feet, he calculated that the last of the Fokkers was in range and fired. The Fokker went down out of control. But the remaining pair were now safely away and leaving the fight to the skills of Archie batteries and the marksmanship of hundreds of infantrymen. With Archie bursts on all sides and rifle bullets whizzing past, Eddie turned for home to put in a claim for the two Fokkers. (One would be confirmed.)

"War flying is much like other business—one gets accustomed to all the incidents that attend its daily routine, its risks, its thrills, its dangers, its good and bad fortune," Eddie wrote in *Fighting the Flying Circus.* "A strange sort of fatalism fastens to the mind of an aviator who continues to run the gauntlet of Archie. He flies through bursting shells without trying to dodge them, with indeed little thought to their menace. If a bullet or shell has his name written on it there is no use trying to avoid it. If it has not—why worry?"

On Sunday, October 27, 1918, the name on an Archie shell was that of Ham Coolidge. It slammed into his Spad at midfuselage and blasted the plane to pieces. A classmate of Quentin Roosevelt at the Groton School and Harvard, he had been one of the top-scoring aces of the 94th Squadron. His eight victories included five planes and three balloons. Noting that Coolidge had been one of the most popular men in the service and a man who'd never shirked or complained, Eddie believed Coolidge "possessed all the qualifications of leadership and a brilliant career in any profession he might have chosen."

When Coolidge was killed he'd been hurrying to the assistance of a formation of U.S. bombers returning from a raid at the town of Grand Pre. The night before, thousands of German troops had unloaded from trains and taken positions in the town and around it. In a ferocious air battle, many of the new American-built Liberty planes deserved the nickname "flying coffins" as their poorly protected fuel systems proved shockingly vulnerable.

Two days after Coolidge was killed, Eddie took off at three in the afternoon to observe a new leader of Flight One, Lieutenant Kaye, who had been called upon to take over when Reed Chambers was rushed to a hospital with appendicitis. On that date, October 29, 1918, Eddie had no rivals in number of victories—twenty-four, by his count. Men of the original 94th who might have challenged him were gone. Lufbery, Luke, and Coolidge had been killed. Jerry Meissner had been transferred to command of the 147th. Chambers was out of action in a hospital. Bad weather in much of October that confined planes to the ground had limited chances for adding to scores. How much longer the fighting would continue was a matter being debated in the high councils of governments on both sides of the war. On October 28, Austria had asked for an armistice. The Turks were quitting in Mesopotamia. The Allies were winning in Italy. (Among the American airmen in that theater was Maj. Fiorello H. La Guardia. On leave from serving in the U.S. Congress, the future mayor of New York City was a bomber pilot.) Assessing the situation on the Western Front, the French commander, General Foch, told President Wilson's emissary, Col. Edward House, "If I obtain through [an] armistice the conditions I wish to impose upon Germany, I am satisfied. Once this object is attained, nobody has the right to shed one more drop of blood."

General John J. Pershing worried that an armistice "would re-vivify the low spirits of the German army and enable it to reorganize and resist later on." He desired unconditional German surrender and planned a new offensive along the Meuse on the first of November. To support the attack he had three batteries of 14-inch naval guns mounted on railway flatcars able to fire 1,400-pound shells twenty-five miles. In the AEF arsenal were scores of thousands of gas shells. Out of the 1.2 million Americans in France, 850,000 were combat troops in twenty-two divisions. Also at his disposal were 324 tanks and 840 planes.

As four of those aircraft took off for the lines between Grand Pre and Brieulles on the afternoon of October 30, Lieutenant Kaye was flight leader for another experienced pilot and two new men. In order to observe Kaye's baptism as a flight leader and to be on hand to help if needed, the 94th's squadron commander, Eddie Rickenbacker, stayed well behind them about a thousand feet higher. After flying two patrols between the towns without sighting enemy airplanes, he noticed a pair of Fokkers coming out of Germany at low altitude. Despite being outnumbered, they were obviously determined to attack.

With no hope of overtaking the Germans, Eddie watched a daring but failed attempt to break up Kaye's formation by attacking the rear Spad. After a few gun bursts that failed to bring it down, they turned away. As they headed toward Grand Pre, Eddie decided that Kaye's flight would get home safely and that Eddie Rickenbacker's strategy should be to make a detour over German lines and lie in wait for the Fokkers to return. When they appeared over Emecourt, they were not more than a thousand feet aboveground. Lurking at twice that altitude, he let the two Germans go by, presenting him with the opportunity to swoop down on them at full speed. After a short burst of fire into the fuselage of the nearer Fokker sent it spiraling down, he saw the red nose of the Richthofen Circus.

As the second plane dived for the ground, Eddie began a steep climb toward the west and home. Expecting a storm of Archie and machine gun fire, he was surprised and relieved that very little came his way. Unscathed, he was soon over the village of St. George, still inside German lines. There at the edge of the small community was a *Drachen*, "sleeping" in its nest with its ground crew and defending gunners nowhere in sight. Diving to within a hundred feet and with both guns firing, he peppered the huge rubber sausage with bullets and pulled up to prepare for another attack. But as he leveled off, he saw the balloon burning.

Eddie's satisfaction with the kill didn't last long. Looking at his watch, he realized that he'd been flying for two hours and ten minutes—the maximum time permitted by the Spad's fuel load when he'd taken off. Throttling down to the slowest possible speed in order to conserve gas, he managed to creep to Verdun in darkness and began searching for a spot to land. Five minutes beyond the time when he should have run out of gas and still ten miles from his base, he fired a red flare to signal that he was in trouble. At the moment the engine sputtered and stopped, he saw the aerodrome's landing lights go on. Barely clearing an adjacent road with the wind at his back, he felt the wheels hit the ground with a thud. The Spad rolled to a stop less than a hundred feet from its hangar.

The next day, October 31, 1918, was too rainy for flying, but Eddie's mood brightened late in the afternoon when an order came for the Hat-in-the-Ring pilots and all other squadrons to be in the air at daybreak to protect an infantry advance from Grand Pre to Buzancy. To Eddie this meant that he and his men would be both participants and witnesses in an action that might be the last great attack of the war.

This feeling was reinforced at 3:30 on the morning of November 1 with the unleashing of an Allied artillery barrage that one observer described as the striking of "a million hammers." In the darkness before dawn, as the aviators were donning flying suits, stacks of newspapers were being delivered to the 94th containing stories of Turkey's surrender and accounts of Austria's appeal to the Allies for a cessation of hostilities. Grabbing all the copies that would fit into the office of Spad No. 1, Eddie walked to the plane to await clearance to take off at 5:30. The word that came was disappointing. The valley of the Meuse was socked in by fog. The squadron would have to wait until it thinned. Takeoff clearance came four hours later.

Eddie vividly recalled that morning in *Fighting the Flying Circus*:

> *Arrived over the front lines near the town of Lapelle, I flew at an altitude of only a hundred feet above the ground. And there I saw our Doughboys after their victorious advance of the morning crouching in every available shell hole and lying several deep in every depression while looking forward for a snipe shot at any enemy's head that came into view. Others were posted behind woods and buildings with bayonets fixed, waiting for word to go forward. As I passed overhead I threw overboard handfuls of morning papers to them and was amused to see how eagerly the Doughboys ran out of their holes to pick them up. With utter disdain for the nearby Hun snipers, they exposed themselves gladly for the opportunity of getting the latest news from an airplane. I knew the news they would get would repay them for the momentary risk they ran.*

> *Dropping half my load there I flew over the Moselle Valley where I distributed the remainder of the papers among the men in the front lines of that sector. Returning then to the region of Buzancy I caught sight of a huge supply depot burning. A closer view disclosed the fact it was German and German soldiers were still on the premises. They were destroying materials that they knew they would be unable to save. In other words they were contemplating a fast retreat.*

> *A few dashes up and down the highways leading to the north quickly confirmed this impression. Every road was filled with lorries and retreating artillery. All were hurrying toward Longuyon and the German border.*

> *All the way up the Meuse as far as Stenay I found the*

same mad rush for the rear. Every road was filled with
retreating Heinies. They were going while the "going
was good" and their very gestures seemed to indicate
that for them it was indeed "finis de la guerre."

The following day Eddie was granted three days' leave in Paris. He found the streets, boulevards, and cafés in "gaiety unrestrained." The Place de la Concorde and the Champs-Élysées were crammed with captured German guns and even airplanes. Everywhere he looked were flags and bunting. On his third day in Paris he was joined by Lois Meredith for a shopping spree. For her it was a hat. He paid 1,450 francs for a "wonderful" officer's overcoat. They had lunch and went for "quite some ride" around the jubilant city. With the ending of the war so near, Eddie joked, "This would be a bad time to get killed."

Returning to base on November 5, Eddie learned that he hadn't missed anything. Rainy skies had kept the squadrons from flying. They were still grounded on the seventh when a United Press correspondent told Eddie that a German peace delegation bearing a white flag had crossed no man's-land between Haudry and Cheme on the La Chapelle road to sign the armistice. As Eddie pondered this welcome report, he hoped that with peace actually in sight, everyone on all sides would exhibit "a desire to live and let live" and that his pilots would "prefer to survive rather than run the risks of combat flying now that the war was fairly over."

Instead, Eddie found the men of the Hat-in-the-Ring Squadron "infatuated with fighting." They begged him for permission to go out at times when a glance at the fog and rain showed the foolishness of such a request. "Not content with the collapse of the enemy forces," he wrote, "the pilots wanted to humiliate them further with flights deep within [Germany] where they might strafe airplane hangars and retreating troops for the last time. It must be done at once, they feared, or it would be too late."

No one was hungrier to take a last nibble at the Germans than Cedric Fauntleroy. Disregarding terrible weather conditions on Saturday, November 9, he, Lieutenant Dewitt and Lieutenant Cook pleaded with Eddie to allow them to go after a *Drachen* that had been reported "swinging back of the Meuse." Eager to accompany them was a Major Kirby. Scheduled to take command of a new squadron but with no experience flying over enemy lines, he had come to the 94th in the hope of doing so before the shooting stopped.

"Full of misgivings," Eddie gave permission. When the four planes hadn't returned two hours later, and with darkness falling, he had the landing lights turned on. During the night a report was received that a Spad had collided with a French two-seater near Beaumont late that afternoon. Confirming that no Spads had been flying but his own, Eddie was filled with "woeful conjectures" as to which of the four pilots had been killed.

With no further information and none of the 94th's planes having returned to base the next morning, Eddie had to concern himself with preparations for a medals award ceremony to take place at eleven o'clock. Pilots of the 94th and other squadrons would get the Distinguished Service Cross from Gen. Hunter Liggett. As Eddie received two more palms for his DSC, he feared that the pilots of the overdue planes had met some form of disaster—killed in the air or in a crash, fallen and wounded somewhere in no-man's-land, or captured. Plagued by thoughts of the culpability that must rightfully be his if any of these calamities had occurred, he found no joy in congratulations on his citations.

Bundled against the cold wind and rain in his new officer's overcoat, he wandered onto the field and peered through swirls of fog. He felt a flash of anger at the sight of a plane on the field. Determined to find out what "idiot" was thinking about flying in such weather, he strode angrily toward the plane, then stopped and gazed in amazement at Fauntleroy's No. 3 on its fuselage. Finding the Spad's office unoccupied, he ran to the hangar. Startled mechanics told him that Fauntleroy had just landed and was in the squadron office filing a report, that Captain Dewitt had made a crash landing behind American lines and was safe, and that Major Kirby had phoned from an aerodrome near the Meuse to report that he had shot down an enemy plane and would return to home base when the fog lifted.

Kirby's "first remarkable victory," Eddie noted, gave the 94th the distinction of claiming the first and the final victories of an American squadron in the war. Between his shared score with James Norman Hall on April 29 and Kirby's victory on November 10, the Hat-in-the-Ring Squadron had completed more flying hours at the front and had shot down sixty-nine planes and balloons—more victories than any other American squadron.

Twenty-six were credited to Eddie Rickenbacker, fourteen of them in October. When word came to the 94th on the night of November 10, 1918, that an armistice had been agreed to, effective at 11:00 A.M. the next day, he was America's undisputed ace of aces.

"We all went a little mad," Eddie wrote of the events following a phone call that the war was over. "Shouting and screaming like crazy men, we ran to get whatever firearms we had, including flare pistols, and began blasting up into the sky. It was already bright up there. As far as we could see the sky was filled with exploding shells and rockets, star shells, parachute flares, and searchlights. Machine guns hammered; big guns boomed. What a night!"

The celebration finally ended with everyone piled into a human pyramid in the muddy airfield. The heap of giddy young men was, Eddie said, "a monument to the incredible fact that we had lived until now and were going to live again tomorrow."

The order from the American air service high command was that all pilots should stay on the ground on the eleventh. The historic morning turned out to be muggy and foggy, but an hour before the armistice was to go into effect, Eddie sauntered to Spad No. 1's hangar. He told the mechanics to roll the plane out so that he could "test the engine."

Forty-five minutes later, he recalled in his autobiography, he was piloting Spad No. 1 less than five hundred feet over no-man's-land near Conflans. He saw the Americans and Germans crouched in trenches. Precisely at eleven o'clock, brown-clad doughboys and Germans in gray-green rushed from the trenches toward each other, casting aside weapons, chucking helmets into the air, and throwing their arms wide to invite and give hugs.

"It was the *finis de la guerre*," he wrote in *Fighting the Flying Circus.* "It was the *finis d'aviation.* It was to us, perhaps unconsciously, the end of that intimate relationship that since the beginning of the war had cemented together brothers-in-arms into a closer fraternity than is known to any other friendship in the world."

CHAPTER 16

Earthbound Again

B Y EDDIE RICKENBACKER'S ACCOUNT HE HAD ENDURED 134 "AER-
ial encounters" in which he and each of his opponents
shared the objective of shooting the other down. Except for holes
he'd found in wings, rudder, and fuselage after landing, there was
no reckoning how many bullets had missed but come close to
getting him. None had wounded him. His Hat-in-the-Ring gang
had been in the thick of it from the start—first American combat
aviators to breach enemy lines, the first kill, and the last, for a
squadron total of sixty-nine. The 94th had produced the first
American ace (Douglas Campbell). By war's end Eddie's victories
had earned him the title American ace of aces. He'd been
awarded the French Legion of Honor, the Croix de Guerre with
four Palms, and the U.S. Distinguished Service Cross with nine
Oak Leaves. He lacked only the Congressional Medal of Honor.
This oversight would continue for eleven years and 360 days.
President Herbert Hoover presented it at Bolling Field, Washington, D.C., on November 6, 1930. It cited Eddie's "conspicuous gallantry and intrepidity above and beyond the call of duty" for his
double victory on September 25, 1918.

During the next world war many combat pilots would be

credited with more victories, but their achievements occurred over four years of combat in planes flying at 350 mph, firing multiple .50-caliber automatic machine guns and even cannons. Eddie's official twenty-six were won in wood-and-canvas planes at 100 miles per hour with two rifle-caliber guns during a period of seven months, more than two of which he'd spent in a hospital because of his ear trouble.

On the day the guns went silent on the Western Front, the American people hailed two certified heroes, the dashing, romantic aviator Eddie Rickenbacker and a homely farm boy from Tennessee. When tall, gangly, redheaded, twangy voiced, slow talking, thirty-year-old draftee Alvin Cullum York of Fentress County showed up for basic training at the U.S. Army's Camp Gordon in the pine flats of Georgia on November 15, 1917, he appeared to be a prime example of the hillbilly. Eleven months later he was Sergeant York. With a Medal of Honor and every other available decoration for valor in war, he was the most honored American foot soldier since Teddy Roosevelt led his Rough Rider cavalrymen in a gallant charge up the San Juan Heights in the Spanish-American War. Roosevelt had lusted for battle. Alvin York had tried to avoid it as a conscientious objector who believed that to kill a man, even in wartime, went against the Ten Commandments and everything preached by the Church of Christ in Christian Union.

Two months after the United States declared war on Germany, Alvin's pacifist faith had a collision with history in the form of a card sent by the U.S. government requiring him to make himself available for service in the U.S. Army. Advised to claim conscientious-objector status by the postmaster, Rosier Pile, Alvin scribbled his answer—"Don't want to fight"—and sent it back. The government's reply was that because the Church of Christ in Christian Union was not on any list of recognized churches that could claim C.O. status for its members, Alvin would have to join in the war to "keep the world safe for democracy" as a foot soldier in Company G, 328th Infantry Regiment of the 82d "All American" Division.

Five months later in the Argonne Forest, German soldiers discovered how well Cpl. Alvin York handled a rifle. Part of a squad sent on a surprise attack against a German machine gun nest, Alvin and his men captured a group of fifteen to twenty Germans, including a major, without firing a shot. But as they were being led away, the major shouted to other Germans to open fire. "There were over thirty of them in continuous action," Alvin recalled, "and all I could do was touch the Germans off as fast as I could. I was sharpshooting. I don't think I missed a shot. It was no time to miss." When a German lieutenant and five of his men lunged from a trench with fixed bayonets, Alvin first aimed at the last of them, then the next farthest, and so on. With all six killed, the major said to Alvin that if he would "just stop shooting," he would order his men to surrender. As they laid down their weapons and raised their arms, Alvin counted 132 prisoners. Dead on the field were twenty-eight more, along with thirty-five machine guns and a cache of arms and ammunition.

Promoted to sergeant, Alvin was awarded the Medal of Honor, the French Croix de Guerre, and the Italian Croce de Guera. Sent home as a certified hero, he received offers of vast amounts of money to endorse products, to star in the Ziegfeld Follies, and for the right to turn his life story into a movie. Alvin rejected them all. "This uniform," he said, "is not for sale."

Because of his fame as ace of aces, Capt. Eddie Rickenbacker also found himself an object of interest to people he called "well-wishers, hero-worshipers and fast-buck operators." He wrote of this phenomenon, "I knew that with the title 'American Ace of Aces' would come an awesome responsibility. Because of it I now represented the spirit of American aviation, especially to the youth of the nation, and I must never permit that image to be cheapened. I knew that it would be easy to go from hero to zero."

He did make one concession to a supplicant who had a monetary interest in Capt. Eddie Rickenbacker. He'd signed a contract on November 17, 1918, with Laurence La Tourelle Driggs of the Frederick A. Stokes Company of New York to write a book about his experiences in the war. He turned down an appeal by Edgar Wolfe of the Wolfe publishing dynasty in Columbus, Ohio, to endorse a public subscription drive to buy a house for the Rickenbacker family in their hometown. "Although I was proud of my birthplace," Eddie noted, "I did not plan to live there the balance of my life." Neither was America's ace of aces receptive to offers to lend his name to advertisements for chewing gum, cigars, cigarettes, or clothing.

What Eddie wanted was to remain with the Hat-in-the-Ring Squadron. When it was ordered to make ready to move into Germany no later than November 20 as part of the Allied occupation, he immediately flew in No. 1 at the head of an advance planning group to Coblenz, Germany, with the intention of remaining with the 94th until it was sent home. But a week after the squadron was established at a former German air base, he was informed that he was being ordered back to the States to lead a nationwide Liberty Bond drive. Unhappy with this news, he rushed to 1st Pursuit Group headquarters to see about having the order revoked.

Told that the decision had come from army headquarters in Washington, D.C., Eddie saw that his only hope lay with Billy Mitchell. The matter was discussed at a Thanksgiving Day dinner with Billy as guest of honor in the 94th mess hall. Very well fed, Mitchell departed with a pledge to "go all the way up to Pershing if anyone interfered with the squadron's plans."

As the issue hung in the balance through mid-December, Eddie worked on his book, dictating accounts of aerial combat to Driggs. But on December 17 he was informed that the order to return to the United States stood. On Christmas the squadron gave him a farewell dinner and a silver cup. Up early the next morning, he was driven to Bar-le-Duc to catch a train to Paris. That night he dined at Ciro's and took in the show at the Folies Bergere. On December 27, after doing some shopping, he returned to his hotel and found two messages. One was from Billy Mitchell, listing people Eddie should see and what he should say in America. A cable from the *New York World* expressed interest in the newspaper obtaining rights to run prepublication excerpts of his forthcoming, excitedly anticipated war memoir.

Crossing the Atlantic on the *Adriatic*, Capt. Edward V. Rickenbacker was America's most famous aviator since Wilbur and Orville Wright's airplane in sustained, controlled flight had definitively signaled the severing of humanity's earthly bonds. Fifteen years later Eddie and the men of the Army Air Service—along with pilots of the RAF, France, the Red Baron's Flying Circus, and other aviators on all the fighting fronts who'd climbed into airplanes of different sizes, shapes, and colors—had recast the nature of warfare. The largest of these aerial armadas was that of the RAF with 27,333 officers, 263,410 other ranks, 22,647 planes, and nearly 700 aerodromes. At the signing of the armistice the United States Army Air Service had 195,024 personnel, of which 20,568 were officers. The AEF had a fleet of 3,538 planes, but only 25 percent of these were American built. Stationed at bases in France on November 11, 1918, were 45 squadrons with 740 planes, 765 pilots, 1,481 observers, and 25 gunners. Five U.S. daytime bomber squadrons were equipped with American-made de Havillands powered by Liberty engines.

The overall commander of these U.S. units was Brig. Gen. William "Billy" Mitchell. In the spring of 1918 he had lost the chauffeur services of the man who was now the American ace of aces, on his way home to a hero's welcome. Reluctantly.

Describing "Captain Eddie" as the *Adriatic* plied the wintry waves of the Atlantic Ocean, biographer Finis Farr saw Eddie taking inventory of his assets and evaluating his future: "In assets, he had only his skill as a driver, pilot, and mechanic. Financially he had scraped the bottom of the till. The savings of his racing days had been used up in caring for his mother and eking out his meager Army pay. To put it briefly, he was broke. He could always make money as a racing driver; but he had decided that racing, for him, was a closed chapter."

On a stopover in England, Eddie had turned down a lucrative offer from his old friend Louis Coatalen of the Sunbeam company to resume racing to promote its cars. In looking ahead, Eddie saw few immediate prospects in aviation, but green pastures in the future of automobiles. Surely, he supposed, there would be room for him and an automobile of his design, but not just any auto. His would be the "great American car." All he needed was money.

When the *Adriatic* docked at Hoboken, New Jersey, on February 1, 1919, newspaper reporters and photographers scrambled aboard.

"What about flying the Atlantic?" Eddie was asked. "Do you think anyone can do it? Or is it a pipe dream?"

"If the United States Army wants a man to fly across the Atlantic, and will provide the necessary support," Eddie replied, "I am willing to do the job."

What were his views on the war? And the future?

"It makes a fellow think to see so many men die. It makes him think about the meaning of life. Like many others who have gone through battle, I feel that from now on I shall take a greater interest in this country–especially in the young people. It's the young who count. I am going to take the duties of citizenship much more seriously than I used to, and I will take more interest than ever before in helping elect the right kind of men to run America."

Whisked from the clutches of the eager reporters by a plainly anxious sergeant of the military police, Eddie was told that he'd been ordered to report to the army provost immediately. Escorted to the anteroom of an office on the pier, he was told to take a seat. After a moment the door to the inner office opened. A lieutenant general emerged. "Rickenbacker," he commanded, "come in here."

Convinced that he was in deep trouble, Eddie stepped into the office. Standing beside a woodburning stove was the woman whose letter had cautioned him to fly low and slow. That night at a banquet in his honor at the Waldorf-Astoria Hotel, a congressman presented Eddie a pair of platinum air service wings studded with diamonds and sapphires. When the applause stopped and the audience waited eagerly for Eddie to make a speech, he searched the room for his mother. Holding up the wings, he said only, "I give them to you, Mother."

Ensconced with his mother and sister Emma at the army's expense at the Waldorf prior to the start of the Liberty Bond tour, Eddie found himself besieged by visitors, bellboys with telegrams, phone calls, letters, and invitations to luncheons and dinners from the cream of New York's high society. From towns where he had raced cars, delegations expressed eagerness to have him visit. Almost every day he fended off theatrical agents offering bookings on the vaudeville circuit. The most persistent show business suitor was Carl Laemmle. Head of Universal Studios, he implored Eddie to appear as himself in a motion picture. Unwilling to take no for an answer, Laemmle assigned his young assistant Irving Thalberg to the task. Trailing Eddie on the bond tour with a certified check for one hundred thousand dollars, Thalberg booked adjacent compartments on trains and next-door rooms in hotels. "I could just see myself up there on the screen," Eddie recalled disdainfully, "making movie love to some heroine." Fully aware of his potential influence upon America's youth, he felt that by depicting himself in the movies he would "degrade both my own stature and the uniform I so proudly wore." Threat of a lawsuit sent Thalberg back to Mr. Laemmle in Hollywood empty-handed.

Welcome callers to Eddie's hotel were congressional and military leaders. On the subject of the deplorable condition of military equipment provided to the army and its inferiority to that of Britain, France, and Germany, he "pulled no punches." The idea of a U.S. Army–sponsored transatlantic flight received "no encouragement."

As the date for the start of the Liberty Bond tour approached, Eddie acknowledged that his inexperience as a public speaker demanded urgent attention. To help him put his thoughts in the form of a script, he turned to a newspaperman he'd befriended in France.

Born in Manhattan, Kansas, in 1880, Alfred Damon Runyan had seen his name altered by men in the newspaper trade. A printer's error turned the "a" in his last name to "u." An editor had crossed out "Alfred" from a too-lengthy byline, leaving Damon Runyon. Claiming to have been kicked out of school in either the fourth or sixth grade, he was a newspaperman at age fifteen and a chain-smoker of Red Eye and oval Turkish cigarettes. His first byline had appeared in the *Pueblo (Ariz.) Evening Post* when he was seventeen. The following year (1898) he was a war correspondent with the 13th Minnesota Volunteers in the Philippines. After kicking around San Francisco and Rocky Mountain papers, he was hired by William Randolph Hearst's *American Weekly*.

Before long his prowess as a sportswriter garnered him billing in
Hearst advertising as "the greatest baseball writer in the country."
In 1916 he'd covered Black Jack Pershing's pursuit of Pancho
Villa. In France in 1918 to cover the battle of the Argonne, he had
considered it his professional obligation to meet the American
ace of aces, "Captain Eddie" Rickenbacker.

Recruited by Eddie for instruction on how to prepare a speech,
Runyon introduced his pupil to the device of arranging each
point of the talk on a separate small card. Using them as an outline, the actual speech would be given extemporaneously. Eddie
found that the cards worked well. His next problem was the manner in which he spoke. Delivery was "flat and dull." This could
be remedied only by an elocutionist. Runyon recommended
Madame Amanda. A vocal coach for foreign stars of the Metropolitan Opera, she was, in Eddie's words, "a stout woman." Her
method was to require him to speak from the Met stage with her
in the "chicken roost" in the topmost balcony. She also insisted
that he get a book entitled *Modern Eloquence* and practice speaking in front of a mirror. Conceding that there was also much to
learn about appearing in public besides speaking, he bought a
book on etiquette.

These new skills were tested on March 23, 1919, at Boston's
prestigious Symphony Hall. As the governor of Massachusetts,
Calvin Coolidge, rose to introduce him, Eddie was "scared to
death." But the longer Coolidge talked in a "high, whiny voice,"
Eddie wondered how Coolidge had ever gotten elected. Self-
confidence swelled. Guided by headings and phrases on his
prompt cards, he led the increasingly rapt audience of six thousand through his war, from driving for Pershing and Billy
Mitchell to learning how to fly, his first combat, first victory, the
one that had elevated him to ace of aces, and the last.

As the tour made its way across the country, adherence to the
basic script was not always possible. During his appearance at
the Metropolitan Opera House in New York he had to discard a
large portion of the rehearsed talk and extemporize when the
bulb in the projector burned out. When some appearances drew
disappointingly small turnouts for the laudable cause of buying

Liberty Bonds, he found it "heartbreaking to stand up on a stage and talk to empty seats." Yet in towns and cities where the people came, he was energized anew. At the conclusion of the tour on May 30, he found that the experience had reintroduced him to the country and its people.

He'd also learned the difference between the popular view of a famous race driver before the war and what the public expected of a hero of that war. He found "the frenzy, the adulation, the pressure were all taking their toll." Reliving the war in the talks resulted in dreams about it, including having a nightmare on a train about a dogfight that was so vivid it ended with him tumbling from his upper berth. On another train he was amazed that a Pullman porter shoved a twenty-dollar bill at him and asked him to autograph it. The porter proudly showed it off, resulting in many of the train's passengers producing currency to be signed. Even more astonishing was a simulated airplane in a parade held in his honor in Los Angeles that was made of flowers. "It was stunningly beautiful," he wrote, "but I felt like an idiot riding in it for three hours."

At the conclusion of the bond tour he was promoted to major and discharged from the army. Considering his captain's bars "earned and deserved," he chose not to adopt the new title. In becoming a civilian again he faced the question of what to do with his life. He did not want to return to racing. The bond tour had left him determined not to take any job offered on the basis of his publicity value. He was interested in both military and civilian aviation, but he'd seen that the federal government had no interest in his ideas on the development of either. Individuals in the budding aviation field and those in the booming automobile business who expressed an interest in Eddie Rickenbacker proved to be more concerned with adding a hero's name to the company letterhead than in what he might contribute as a mechanical engineer. Deals were offered that were either illusory from the start or eventually disappointing in reality.

"The boys" who had gone to war singing George M. Cohan's "Over There" were coming home to a country that posed the musical question "How are you gonna keep 'em down on the farm after they've seen Par-ee?" Going off to war, doughboys who'd imbibed corn whiskey at home had drowned their cares with fine French wines, champagne, Scotch whiskey, and even German beer. Coming home in 1919, they found a country that had turned off spiritous spigots with a constitutional amendment that banned manufacture, sale, and consumption of alcoholic drinks. Another amendment that would take effect in 1920 granted women the vote. Fears of economists that returning troops would not easily find jobs proved unfounded. Except for the booze business, American industry was enjoying a boom that lifted the stock market to heady and unexplored heights. And the United States was a nation in the first throes of an endless love affair with the automobile.

It was also a country infatuated with "the boys" who'd won the Great War and made the world "safe for democracy." Huge crowds greeted ships that brought them home by way of the port of New York. Parades honored them everywhere. Thousands of soldiers passed in review, then went home, put away their uniforms to resume prewar lives or begin new ones, and faded into anonymity. A few could not. Fate and traits of character had made them heroes. Everyone knew their names: Black Jack Pershing, Wild Bill Donovan, Douglas MacArthur of the Rainbow Division, Billy Mitchell, Father Duffy of the Fighting 69th, Sgt. Alvin York, the flying ace Douglas Campbell, and others–but especially the American ace of aces, "Captain Eddie" Rickenbacker. He was not only valiant, victorious, and handsome, but master of the new age of the automobile and the airplane.

If what Henry Ford had said was true, that machinery was "the new Messiah," Eddie Rickenbacker had become an apostle of the power of the internal combustion engine on land and in the sky. Introducing Eddie on the occasion of another dinner given in his honor at the Waldorf-Astoria Hotel by the American Automobile Association, Secretary of War Newton D. Baker had called him "one of the real crusaders of America–one of the truest knights our country has ever known." At a banquet of the Automobile

Club in Columbus, Ohio, Eddie was given a pair of aviator's wings made of platinum, 156 diamonds, and 66 sapphires. The local newspaper, the *Citizen*, ran an eight-column headline: WINGED KNIGHT RETURNS HOME IN TRIUMPH.

When Eddie escorted Elsie Janis to supper at the Hotel Astor roof garden, he and the star of Broadway musical comedies were called to the bandstand to acknowledge a standing ovation. A newspaper would later report that the dashing, bachelor ace of aces and the stage star were engaged, requiring Eddie to issue a denial. If he went to the theater to see Fay Bainter in *East Is West*, John and Lionel Barrymore in *The Jest*, or George White's *Scandals of 1919*, he could expect a burst of applause as he made his way to his seat. Invited to New York's Bayside Yacht Club, he met a comedian who did a golf act in the Ziegfeld Follies. W. C. Fields liked Eddie so much that he telephoned two of the show's chorus girls to join them at Travers Island for a picnic on the beach. Eddie noted that while driving back to Manhattan the foursome made a stop at a "wayside inn" for "many drinks." On a visit to Los Angeles, movie stars flocked to be seen with him, including the screen's most famous swashbuckler, Douglas Fairbanks. A throng of photographers eagerly snapped pictures of the hero of screen sword fights and a hero of real battles in dogfights in the skies over the Western Front.

After eight months of the "adulation and anxiety, encouragement and disappointment, and incessant travel" selling Liberty Bonds, it was natural that Eddie should celebrate, wrote biographer Finis Farr. But the tour had tended to erode his mental and physical equipment, which he kept going with nerve and stamina rather than reserves of strength. Instead of what he had gone through since the armistice, continued Farr's analysis of Eddie in the summer of 1919, "a wise physician would have prescribed six months of relaxation in some Adirondack lodge, where nothing at all would be seen except the activities of squirrels, chipmunks, and deer." His diet would be controlled, and there would be no eating on the run, no more cabaret life, and no arguments and anxieties. This activity may not have been good for his health,

Farr wrote, "but it gave him a feeling of excited anticipation." As the summer approached its end, he "had reason to expect a dramatic adjustment of his affairs."

Invited to spend some time at a friend's home in New Mexico, Eddie saw an opportunity to both relax and think about what to make of his life. A few days after arriving he bought a secondhand Model T Ford, a sleeping bag, and everything else he thought he would need for camping alone in the desert. As the rugged respite stretched into weeks, he recognized that one of his steadfast aspirations had been to build an automobile of his own design. This had been the underlying motivation throughout his racing career. He had frequently changed jobs so he could study different car designs. In evaluating their performance he'd seen ways to improve on them, but the results accrued to others—Frayer-Miller, Columbus Buggy, Fred Duesenberg's Mason Automobile Company, Maxwell, and Louis Coatalen's Sunbeam Motor Works. Ruminating on the kind of car he would design and build, he envisioned engineering a high-speed motor that would overcome industry objections to excessive vibration and gasoline consumption. His car would have a lower center of gravity for both safety and comfort. It would have a four-wheel brake system. It would be called Rickenbacker, and he would personally ensure that it would be "worthy of the name." All he needed was the money to build it.

For a man closely identified with cars and airplanes, Eddie did almost all of his traveling by train. It was the beginning of the golden era of railroads. They spanned the continent, linking the financial powers of Wall Street and the great industrial cities of Pittsburgh and Chicago and the automobile capital, Detroit. On one of Eddie's trips to the Motor City, he encountered the head of General Motors, William C. Durant. Eddie knew his son Clifford. An amateur race car driver, he'd met Eddie in California before the war. Since then Clifford had married Adelaide Frost. Stories about Clifford in newspapers invariably described him as a "millionaire sportsman."

During the trip to Detroit, Eddie and Durant chatted generally about business conditions and the auto industry in particular.

Durant suggested that Eddie call on him at GM headquarters at Columbus Circle in New York. Eddie said he would. When he did, Durant was blunt. "Well, Eddie," he asked, "what do you think you can do for us?" Durant made promises that weren't kept. Possibilities of employment came from other firms, including a position promoting the Curtiss aircraft company, a proposition from a tiremaker in Pittsburgh, and a vague interest in him expressed by the Refiners Oil Company. None materialized.

Early in October, Eddie went to dinner in Detroit with an old friend. Former race driver, creative engineer, entrepreneur, and "great salesman," Harry Cunningham had run a successful agency for the EMF automobile. The firm had been formed by and named with the initials of the last names of its founders, Barney Everitt, William Metzger, and Walter E. Flanders. Everitt's primary interest was auto bodies. Flanders was a production expert who had been responsible for the Ford assembly line. Soon after the company was formed, Metzger virtually retired. EMF had recently been bought by the Studebaker wagon company. This resulted in changing the car's name to Studebaker.

Excited by Eddie's description of a future Rickenbacker auto, Cunningham met with Everitt and Flanders to discuss providing finances. They agreed to invest $200,000 for the design and building of the prototype of a six-cylinder car that would tap the middle price bracket of $1,500 to $2,000, leaving the low-priced market to Henry Ford's Model T and the limited high-cost field to Cadillac and Packard. Eddie wanted the Rickenbacker to become the automobile of "the white-collar worker, the junior executive, the fairly prosperous farmer and the woman of taste," as well as people who "recognized fine engineering and workmanship."

Although the Detroit-based enterprise was called the Rickenbacker Motor Company, the firm's president was Everitt. Eddie bacame vice president and took charge of the aspect of the auto business that he knew best, with the title of director of sales. Work on designing the prototype began in early 1920 with the goal of introducing the Rickenbacker to the market in 1922.

As planning for the car went on with little for its namesake to contribute to that process, Eddie found himself tempted by a lucrative offer from W. C. Durant of General Motors to be the chief of sales in California for the company's slightly-lower-than-middle-market car, the four-cylinder Sheridan. The job entailed establishing Sheridan dealerships throughout the state. He accepted the position at the end of 1920 and chose not to locate his base of operations in Los Angeles, but in San Francisco. Recognizing that his fame as America's ace of aces would garner attention from the general public and the press as he traveled the state in search of potential dealers for the Sheridan, he chose to do so in a one-seat Italian-made Bellanca biplane that he leased from a small San Francisco company. To make the plane more powerful, he installed an American six-cylinder engine. Landing in the cow pasture nearest a town, he would be greeted by the prospective dealer, a wide-eyed crowd of townsfolk, and a photographer from the local newspaper. When a dealership agreement resulted, an advertising campaign began to stimulate interest in the car's arrival. A full-page newspaper ad a few days in advance blared "Sheridan is coming." Upon the installation of the car on the dealer's property, an ad announced "Sheridan is here," next to a photo of the car. By year's end twenty-seven dealers in California had sold seven hundred Sheridans.

Between sales excursions, Eddie made round-trips to Detroit. When the prototype was ready, he became the test driver. To be certain that it could be driven by nonprofessionals, he found people who had never been behind a steering wheel and let them take it for test drives. In the fall of 1921, Rickenbacker Motor Company announced a public stock offering that resulted in sales of $5 million worth to about 13,000 investors, with Eddie and his three partners retaining about 25 percent of the shares. The capital allowed them to buy a building and begin production of the Rickenbacker.

For the opening of the New York Automobile Show in the first week of September 1922 at the Grand Central Palace on Lexington Avenue, the entire output of the factory (three cars) was on display on the fourth floor. The touring car was priced at $1,428. A coupe roadster was $1,485. The top-of-the-line sedan sold for $1,995. Each had a high-speed engine and low-slung body. The sales slogan was "A Car Worthy of Its Name." The radiator orna- ment was a facsimile of the insignia of the Hat-in-the-Ring Squadron. Orders for the car flooded in.

Songwriter Leo Wood became so enthralled with Eddie's auto- mobile that he wrote a tune about it entitled "In My Rickenbacker Car." Published in 1923, the sheet music offered a cover that pictured a man and woman out for a drive, passing under the overarching branches of a tree, and an inset photo of Eddie as America's ace of aces. Wood penned these lyrics:

> *I used to worry 'cause I had no girl, no precious pearl,*
> > *with whom to whirl;*
> *But dancing don't mean a thing now to me,*
> *For I've found someone to keep me company;*
> *And ev'ry moment that I find to spare,*
> *With this new pal of mine I gladly share.*

> *CHORUS:*

> *Over hill and dale together merrily we go;*
> *We should worry 'bout the weather,*
> *Summer's sun or winter's snow;*
> *And she's not a bit expensive like most sweethearts are;*
> *Always there when I need her, all I do is feed her.*
> *It's my Rickenbacker car. Oh car!*
> *Merrily I toll along, roll along and there's nothing*
> > *wrong.*
> *Merrily I roll along in my cracker-jacker*
> > *Rickenbacker,*
> *She won't jar your vacation for there's no vibration.*
> *In my Rickenbacker car.*

On the optimistic day of the debut of a car that Eddie believed would be worthy of its name and the Hat-in-the-Ring insignia on its radiator, the floral decorations that adorned the area where the three cars were displayed had been arranged by Adelaide Durant.

Having divorced her playboy husband, Clifford, she had spent some time in Paris before settling in New York City. Because she and Eddie had become acquainted when he and Clifford had been racing cars in California before the war, they found they had mutual friends in New York who were pleased to invite two unattached, sophisticated, stylish, and good-looking people to dinner parties and other glittery events of a decade that was already being celebrated as the Roaring Twenties.

In 1920 a composer of popular songs wrote a tune that captured the mood of the country. Jerome Kern's song urged Americans to always look for the silver lining and try to find the sunny side of life. For the majority of Kern's countrymen, the sun seemed to shine everywhere. The whole country appeared to be taking part in a frenzied determination to blot out the horrors of the war and get on with enjoying the peace and prosperity that had been secured by the blood of so many young men that they were given a name: the Lost Generation.

In 1917, twenty-one-year-old F. Scott Fitzgerald had dropped out of Princeton University to enlist in the army. He'd served as aide-de-camp to Brig. Gen. John Ryan, but had not gone overseas. A civilian again in 1920, he published a largely autobiographical novel. Titled *This Side of Paradise*, it served as a rallying cry for rebellious, alienated youth. It enshrined the author in history as the embodiment of the 1920s. An older generation reading him discovered to its shock and horror that the youth of the nation, and especially the young women, apparently intended to live by a totally different moral code. Their social creed took the form of liberal sexuality in "petting parties" and casual kissing. They danced to jazz, zoomed about in racy cars, did excessive drinking, donned open galoshes that flapped when they walked or danced, giving the language of the twenties the word "flappers," and openly smoked cigarettes.

In 1919, American women had marked a milestone in a long struggle for equality with men with ratification of the Nineteenth Amendment. When it took effect in 1920, they were given the right to vote. Many women also interpreted their new status as liberation from other strictures. The result was the appearance of a figure historians labeled "the New Woman." Those who went to the polls for the first time helped elect Warren G. Harding president and quickly claimed an equal footing with men in all other aspects of life. This "new woman" in the pages of *This Side of Paradise* wore her hair and skirts short, ate three-o-clock-after-dance suppers, and danced in a way that appalled the older generation. The main character of *This Side of Paradise*, Amory Blaine, was a "romantic egotist" who saw himself as a "slicker," defined as someone who had a clever sense of social values, dressed well, got into activities in order to "shine," and went to college to show "in a wordly way" that he was "successful." Amory felt that modern life no longer changed century by century, but year to year and ten times faster. But it wasn't enough. "My idea," he declared, "is that we've got to go much faster." Nothing was more representative of that attitude in a decade that was also called "the Jazz Age" than young people zipping around in a fast automobile. In *Only Yesterday*, a chronicle of the twenties, Frederick Lewis Allen, wrote, "The automobile offered an almost universally available means of escaping temporarily from the supervision of parents and chaperons, or from the influence of neighborhood opinion."

Although Eddie Rickenbacker and the former Mrs. Clifford Durant were older than the average "flaming youth" of the middle years of the Roaring Twenties, and well past worrying about supervising parents and chaperons, they inhabited a small universe in which fast cars had been central. And they were familiar with the vicissitudes of automobile manufacturing and selling.

They also had the Midwest in common. He was born and raised in Ohio. Adelaide was from Grand Rapids, Michigan. Her father was Stoel Meech Frost. When his wife passed away young, Adelaide and a sister, Phoebe, were raised by a grandmother. A talented singer, Adelaide met Clifford Durant in Detroit. Soon after they married they moved to Los Angeles and settled into a lifestyle befitting his wealth, including a huge house with extensive grounds and many servants to attend to the needs of numerous guests at frequent parties, including Eddie. When the marriage failed, she was so well liked by her father-in-law that Durant es-

tablished a trust fund for her in gratitude for "doing her best in a
lost cause." Money, charm, and beauty made her a very popular
figure in the social circles of a city that was the effervescent center of a country in the throes of a prosperity that everyone expected to be endless.

Being a dashing war hero and single, Eddie had returned from
France to plunge zestfully into the swirling tides of the place his
friend Damon Runyon called Baghdad on the Hudson. He could
have a good time anytime, whether he was sipping drinks in a
roadhouse with a couple of leggy showgirls summoned by W. C.
Fields, formally decked out for dinners in the townhouses of the
very rich, having supper at Justine Johnson's Little Club just off
Times Square, lounging in one of the hundreds of watering holes
called speakeasies that sprang up to slake thirsts despite Prohibition, or at parties that he threw in his suite at the Commodore.
With the success of the Rickenbacker Motor Company, his social
circle had widened to include the New York–based representa-
tives of the automotive industry and Wall Street financiers. When
he was seen out on the town in the company of an attractive
woman, whether Elsie Janis or an adornment of New York's café
society, he could count on a newspaper story or stories appearing
to state with certainty that she was soon to become Mrs. Captain
Eddie Rickenbacker.

Three years after the armistice he was thirty-two years old and
as trim as the day of his first flight in a Nieuport fighter plane. Experiences of the war had added creases to the corners of his eyes
and mouth. His hair was thinner and a little farther back from his
brow, imbuing him with a rather intellectual look. The aviator
who'd worn a Paris-tailored uniform was now a man of the world
of business in a conservative suit with a discreet necktie and gray
fedora. He'd gone from harum-scarum boyhood, devil-may-care
twenty-year-old race car driver, aviation novice, and America's
heralded ace of aces to successful automaker. And now he was
ready to give up a life of living in hotels and selling himself and
cars in what he called "the personality market." It was time, he
recalled in his autobiography, to "dare to think about taking on
the responsibilities of a wife and family."

Explaining how he chose Adelaide Frost Durant, Eddie employed an aviation analogy. He wrote, "Dan Cupid shot me down in flames." Biographer and friend Hans Christian Adamson preferred auto racing language: "Eddie, who had been so reluctant all these years to speed down the roaring road of romance to the finish line at the altar, suddenly saw Cupid wave the starter's flag, and he was off in the typical Rickenbacker headlong rush. It was not a case of love at first sight, however, because he had known Adelaide for many years. None of Eddie's or Adelaide's friends ever quite learned how they became engaged, because it all happened with lightning speed." In December 1921 as he prepared for the auto show, he was heart-whole and fancy-free. When the show closed in January he was engaged to be married in the fall.

The wedding took place on September 16, 1922, in Greenwich, Connecticut, with the Reverend Jacob Pister officiating. Pastor of the Rickenbachers' Lutheran church in Columbus, Ohio, he had christened and confirmed Eddie. The wedding, Eddie wrote in his diary, was the "opening of a New chapter in the Book of Life." Adelaide "looked beautiful and inspiring." Immediately after the ceremony the newlyweds went to New York to begin their honeymoon on the White Star ocean liner *Majestic*, bound for Europe.

Based in Paris, Mr. and Mrs. Rickenbacker traveled to the Argonne Forest battlefield. He pondered the deaths of so many men in the conflict of 1914–18 and wrote in his diary that he would like to see the day when statesmen and government officials, not a generation of young men, suffered from the mistakes that resulted in war.

On October 3, 1922, the Rickenbackers checked into the Adlon Hotel in Berlin. Informed that Eddie Rickenbacker had arrived in Germany, the aviator who had succeeded Baron von Richthofen as Germany's ace of aces, Ernst Udet, invited Eddie to dine with him, Hermann Goering, and a third former pilot, Erhard Milch. During the meal Goering spoke at great length, telling "Herr Eddie" there would be a new "German empire" that would be created by airpower. It would begin with Goering and other airmen of the war teaching gliding as a sport to young men. The new Germany would build a fleet of passenger planes that could be converted to bombers. When the time was ripe, an air force would be established. In the next war, Goering said in a chilling tone, the airplane would deliver the decisive blow at the very beginning.

The rest of the honeymoon took Eddie and Adelaide to Nice, Cannes, Rome, Naples, Pompeii, Florence, Turin, and Venice. Back in Paris in early November, Eddie ran into one of the war correspondents he'd met in France, Webb Miller of the United Press. Over drinks in the Ritz bar they discussed European politics. Miller was worried that Italian fascists and their bombastic, lantern-jawed leader, Benito Mussolini, portended trouble. Eddie recalled Goering's boasting of a future German air force spearheading a new German empire. When he told Miller that he and Adelaide would be taking in the auto show in London and that they would be flying to England in a plane of the recently organized British Airways, Miller pointed out that there had been a head-on collision on that very London–Paris route over Beauvais in which six people had been killed, and that John Galsworthy had proposed in London's *Times* that because planes were so dangerous, they should be banned. Eddie dismissed both reports with a shrug and a laugh.

Although the Rickenbacker car was not displayed at the British auto show, Eddie showed a great deal of interest in lighter weight European models. But on the evening of November 11, the fourth anniversary of the armistice, his thoughts were not on cars. As he joined a celebration at the Savoy, he recalled watching planes of the Royal Air Force and getting the idea to form a squadron of race car drivers. As to the festivities, he wrote in his diary, "At the Savoy every inch of space reserved for guests, all in their best, beautiful women and handsome men played as Kids; it was a Gala night for all but the poor and unemployed, ex-soldiers selling shoestrings, matches; how the spirit of Humanity would be benefitted, if the millions spent on pleasure could be given to a better cause and the spenders stayed a night at Home."

Other London diversions for the honeymooners included a performance of *The Cat and the Canary*, dancing at the London branch of Ciro's, shopping at Harrods, and watching cloth-capped jobless men toting the red flag of revolution in an orderly demonstration in front of the prime minister's house on Downing Street. The American Club was pronounced "a nice place with plenty of Americans." During a luncheon at the Royal Automobile Club he listened to chatter about cars while thinking about how an airplane could be used to pull "one of the greatest advertising stunts ever put over in the auto industry." He envisioned building "a three-motor plane, with body hinged at the wings and long enough to transport one of our [Rickenbacker] cars ready to drive away upon landing." The homeward crossing was on the liner *Majestic.*

Before sailing off to Europe with his bride, Eddie had asked the Rickenbacker Motor Company's office manager in Detroit to find him a secretary who was "willing to work and wasn't interested in getting married for several years." Awaiting him upon his return was Miss Marguerite Shepherd, "an attractive, well-educated and serious young woman" from Hamilton, Ontario, Canada. Over the next forty-four years, "Sheppy" would serve as his office manager, the Rickenbackers' personal accountant, and archivist of Eddie's activities, "good and bad, fortunate and un-fortunate, as reported both in print and photographs."

To sell the car worthy of its name, Eddie took to the air, but the plane was "a big German aluminum Junkers," piloted by Eddie's friend Eddie Stimson. News that ace of aces "Captain Eddie" was heading toward a city or town invariably drew huge crowds to whatever field had been designated for landing. In most places one of the local service clubs arranged a gathering in his honor. He provided audiences stories about his war along with a pitch for his automobile.

Thirty-five years after the debut of the Rickenbacker, Eddie recalled in his autobiography, "We had a phenomenal growth; at its peak the Rickenbacker Motor Company had some 1,200 distribu-tors and dealers in the United States and about 300 throughout the world. In our first two years we built and sold fifty thousand cars. Profits were low, for we had to build a better car and sell it for less in order to compete. Our original capitalization of $5 million was small potatoes compared to that of the big manufacturers."

In 1924 the Rickenbacker car caused "pandemonium" in the auto industry as the first passenger car with a four-wheel braking system. Having driven race cars with four-wheel brakes, Eddie was convinced of their superiority. To him it was "a simple, straightforward matter of arithmetic: four is greater than two." Although his partners exhibited "reluctance," they agreed to secretly design and manufacture a stock of such cars, then spring the four-wheel brake on the industry in full-page ads all over the country. The stunt was, said Eddie proudly, "the automotive sensation of the year." He quickly learned that it was an unwelcome surprise. He later wrote:

> *What I did not realize in my bullheaded determination to bring the superiority of four-wheel brakes to the nation was that the other automobile companies could not afford to be taken unaware. The industry had hundreds of millions of dollars' worth of auto-mobiles with two-wheel brakes in inventory or production. There were cars in showrooms, cars on the assembly line and cars in pieces en route to the assembly line. To sell these cars the entire automotive industry had to convince the public that four-wheel brakes were inferior, even unsafe.*
>
> *The Studebaker Corporation, a major manufacturer, took out full-page ads in newspapers all across the country attacking the four-wheel brake system as extremely dangerous. In every community, all the other dealers and salesmen ganged up on the Rickenbacker car and its four-wheel brakes. Some said that the car would turn over on a curve when the brakes were applied. Others claimed that all four wheels would skid, rather than grip. Some said that the four-wheel brakes would stop the car too quickly, throwing the occupants against the dashboard and injuring them.*

This adverse publicity immediately affected sales of the Rickenbacker. But because of the company's publicity campaign, Eddie's firm couldn't suddenly backtrack on its claim that its four-wheel brakes were superior. The only thing to do was "stick it out" and try to sell the cars that had been produced. To make the situation worse, the country's economy had slipped into a recession, resulting in a sharp dip in sales of all makes of cars. This left Eddie, his partners, and the stockholders facing the grim reality of dealers unable to move cars.

"When the dealers are solvent, the company is solvent," Eddie noted. "When the dealers go broke, the company goes broke." In an effort to "shore them up," he put all the money he had into the company. When it was gone, he borrowed from banks and suppliers. His personal debt soon totaled a quarter of a million dollars. But the company continued to founder. Dealers went out of business. The value of Rickenbacker Motor Company plummeted. In the midst of this crisis, Walter Flanders was killed in an accident.

Forced to realize that his "dream bubble had blown up" in his face, seeing no hope of regaining the position the company had enjoyed in its first years, and noting squabbling by the officers of the firm, Eddie decided that the only thing he could do was resign, in the hope that "a miracle might happen" and the company would survive. Within a year it was bankrupt, and Rickenbacker joined a long roster of failed automakers.

While Eddie's automotive dream bubble was still inflating, American aviation, civil and military, was literally taking off. Among the events and developments was proof of the value of the parachute. When U.S. airmail pilot C. C. Eversole's plane lost its propeller and went into a dive and spin near Minneapolis, Eversole made the first emergency bailout and floated to a safe landing from eight hundred feet. Three days later, Lt. W. D. Coney made the first transcontinental flight within twenty-four hours. He went from San Diego, California, to Jacksonville, Florida, in twenty-two hours and twenty-seven minutes. The next day Jack Knight and E. M. Allison made the first coast-to-coast airmail

delivery, leaving San Francisco on February 22, 1921, and landing in New York on February 23, in a flight of thirty-three hours
and twenty minutes.

Acting on a recommendation by an interdepartmental sub-
committee established to look into federal regulation of "air navigation," President Harding in a message to the Congress on April
12, 1921, asked for creation of a Bureau of Aviation within the
Commerce Department. It was the beginning of a process that resulted in passage of the Air Commerce Act of 1926 that also appropriated funds for the development of aviation branches of the
army and navy. This was preceded by establishment of the President's Aircraft Board by Harding's successor, Calvin Coolidge,
"for the purpose of making a study of the best means of developing and applying aircraft in national defense."

The leading figure in promoting military aviation was Eddie's
wartime commander, Brig. Gen. William "Billy" Mitchell. Two
years after the armistice, Eddie still nursed resentment of the
manner in which Mitchell had humiliated him in front of a
French general in the matter of Eddie having damaged Mitchell's
Mercedes automobile. At the time Eddie had made up his mind to
get even someday for Mitchell having used him to show the
French officer how tough a commander he could be.

The opportunity presented itself during the 1920 World Series
at Ebbets Field, Brooklyn. Invited to come up from Washington,
D.C., and join Eddie and a group of mutual friends for a game between the hometown Dodgers and the Cleveland Indians,
Mitchell arrived at Eddie's suite in New York's Biltmore Hotel in
full uniform. Eddie looked at "six rows of ribbons and a swagger
stick" and thought Mitchell was "hotter than a firecracker." After
the game, Mitchell proposed they all go out on the town. Eddie retorted, "Nuts to that. I'm not going out with a billboard like you.
Change into civvies and I'll go out with you."

With Mitchell in a borrowed suit, shirt, tie, socks, shoes, and
hat, the festive group spent a few hours drinking, primarily in
speakeasies and spas that Eddie described as "one gyp-the-blood
to another." Well lubricated, Eddie decided that the time had
come to settle the matter of the dressing-down he'd suffered for

the benefit of the French general and Mitchell's ego. But as he was about to get the thing off his chest, Mitchell blurted, "Eddie, there's something I've always wanted to tell you. I owe you an apology. You remember when I bawled you out in France? I've been sorry for it ever since."

"Bill, goddamn it," Eddie replied, "now we're friends! I was about to tell you that you owed me an apology. Up to now we have not been friends. You may have thought we were, but I know better so far as I was concerned. Now everything is out the window. We'll start over."

Several months later Mitchell flew a Glenn Martin bomber in a series of army-navy aerial bombardment tests. Between July 13 and 21, 1921, he demonstrated the effectiveness of bombing by sinking the captured German destroyer *G-102*, the light cruiser *Frankfort*, and the battleship *Ostfriesland*. To underscore the vulnerability of warships to aerial attack, on September 5, 1923, army bombers destroyed the navy surplus ships *New Jersey* and *Virginia* in tests off Cape Hatteras, North Carolina. The outcome embarrassed the top brass of the Navy Department.

Concerned by the lack of defense preparedness of the Army Air Service and the low quality of planes and equipment, Mitchell published *Our Air Force, the Keystone of National Defense* (1921) and *Winged Defense* (1925). He also used the colorful personality that had made him popular with the press during and after the war to publicly direct bristling criticism at the War Department's highest echelons. In retaliation, the brass revoked the temporary rank of brigadier general he'd gained during the war. Once again a colonel, he was transferred from the limelight of Washington, D.C., and given the minor post of air officer of the VIII Corps area in faraway San Antonio, Texas. Refusing to be silenced, he took public notice of the loss of the navy's new dirigible *Shenandoah* in a storm in September 1925. A statement given to an eager press blamed the disaster on "incompetency, criminal negligence, and almost treasonable administration of the national defense by the War and Navy Departments." He demanded that the air services of the army and navy be united in a separate, independent U.S. Air Force.

This provoked countercharges of insubordination and the convening of a court-martial. Mitchell's final supporting witness was America's ace of aces. Pulling no punches as he repeatedly clashed with the panel of judges that included Gen. Hugh A. Drum and Maj. Gen. Douglas MacArthur, Eddie provided some recent history.

"Because of the cowardice and stupidity of our own War Department and government authorities," he lectured, "when the Wright brothers went to the government with their new invention, they were refused encouragement and had to turn to France. France saw the possibility. When we entered the war, we had no aircraft industry. Hundreds of lives of our fliers were sacrificed needlessly by defective planes and obsolete equipment in training camps thousands of miles from the front. This nation owes General Mitchell a debt of gratitude for daring to speak the truth. He has learned his lesson from the only real teacher—experience."

He concluded with a passionate plea. "Unified air service," he said, "is the life insurance of our national integrity."

Convicted with a dissenting vote cast by MacArthur, Mitchell resigned from the army and retired to a farm near Middleburg, Virginia.

"That was his reward," Eddie noted, "for the great service he had given his country."

Carrying on his campaign to promote airpower, Mitchell saw the dangers to the United States of being outstripped militarily by other countries. Citing Japan as the gravest future threat, he envisioned Japanese planes attacking the Hawaiian Islands from aircraft carriers. Ignored by Washington, he died in New York City on February 19, 1936. Some vindication of his plea for an independent air force came in the creation of an Air Force General Headquarters in March 1935. After the Japanese sneak attack on Pearl Harbor on December 7, 1941, many of his ideas were adopted by the Army Air Corps in World War II. Further validation of his contribution to the nation occurred in 1946 when Congress authorized a special medal in his honor. Presented to his son two years later by Gen. Carl Spaatz, chief of staff of a newly established independent Department of the Air Force, the medal cited Billy

Mitchell's "outstanding pioneer service and foresight" in the field of American military aviation.

As Mitchell was battling War Department intransigence in 1925, Eddie was enmeshed in the struggle to save the Rickenbacker Motor Company. When he resigned from the firm with the hope that his going would keep the company afloat, he was a thirty-five-year-old married man with a personal debt of a quarter of a million dollars and no job. Friends recommended that he file for bankruptcy. He refused. Vowing to pay off his debts if he had "to work like a dog to do it," he said: "Here in America failure is not the end of the world. If you have the determination, you can come back from failure and succeed."

While contemplating the future, Eddie received a phone call from an old friend. Frank Blair, president of the Union Guardian Trust Company of Detroit, asked Eddie to come in for a chat. When Eddie arrived, Blair got to the point immediately. Noting that Eddie was a young man, he was certain that Eddie would find a new line of endeavor. Should he need financing from Union Guardian Trust Company, Blair said, "I'm pretty sure we'll be able to help you."

Gratified that there was still someone who believed in him, Eddie left Blair marveling that despite his having gone broke to the tune of a quarter of a million dollars, a banker had told him that his credit was good. Feeling "as spry and chipper as a young man just beginning a new business," all he needed was a "line of endeavor" to which he could bring a life's experience.

CHAPTER 17

The Brickyard

A MUSED BY THE PARADOX OF BEING UNEMPLOYED, A QUARTER MIL-
lion in debt, and having been told that if he returned to
Frank Blair's bank with a business plan his credit was good, Eddie saw potential in the Allison Engineering Company of Indianapolis, Indiana. It was "a little gem of a plant" that had started
out building racing cars but had shifted into other activities, including making a special bearing for aircraft engines, gears for
navy dirigibles, and superchargers for General Electric. The
company's semiretired founder, James A. Allison, spent most of
the year living in Florida. He joked that he came back to Indianapolis in the summertime just to remind employees of his
ownership of the company by occupying a desk that he could "put
my feet on," and to watch the races at another Allison business
enterprise–the Indianapolis Speedway.

What Eddie wanted to know in 1927 was whether Allison
would be interested in selling the engineering company. If Allison
went for the idea, the true buyer would be the Union Guardian
Trust Company of Detroit, with Eddie acting as its agent for a percentage of the deal. Allison heard Eddie out, then presented an alternative. It was, he said, "tailor-made" for Eddie. Noting that one

of his original Speedway partners, Frank Wheeler, was dead and the other, Carl Fisher, was "spending all his time developing Miami Beach," Allison asked Eddie, "Why don't you take over the Speedway?"

When the racetrack opened in 1909 it was 320 acres of country land that Allison and his partners had bought for seventy-two thousand dollars. In 1927 the Speedway property was virtually surrounded by Indianapolis. The land's value had multiplied several times. Real estate speculators were eager to acquire it for subdividing into housing developments. Rather than see the Speedway's demise, Allison offered Eddie a thirty-day option to purchase it for seven hundred thousand dollars.

As Eddie contemplated the possible demolition of the Speedway, he found himself awash in "nostalgic scenes of color and excitement" of racing in the "500" for the first time in 1911 and relieving Lee Frayer at the wheel of their Red Wing Special. He recalled the following year's race, won by Joe Dawson in a National, and how his own car had broken down on the forty-third lap. He also thought about Eddie Rickenbacker, ace of aces, driving the pace car in the first 500 after the war, and again in 1925, proudly pacing cars again in a Rickenbacker Straight 8.

If the Indianapolis Speedway passed out of existence, its loss would be felt with grief and nostalgia across America. Also gone would be a priceless proving ground for the development and improvement of features that increased the performance, economy, and safety of the American automobile. Practically every major innovation in cars had been tested on the Speedway's brick our face. Preserving "the Indy" would be not only a contribution to America and a financially sound enterprise, but a personal thrill.

Taking Allison up on his offer of a thirty-day option, Eddie reasoned that he could surely find backing in Indianapolis. The city had been the cradle of the American automotive industry. It produced the Marmon, American, Pioneer, Stutz, Empire, and the eminently successful Willys-Overland. Yet, despite this illustrious history, Eddie found no enthusiasm among Indianapolis money men. As word spread that he was trawling for financing, Eddie noted that real estate developers were moving in "with their bushel baskets" of cash, eager to pick up the option when it expired. Determined not to lose the opportunity, Eddie asked Allison for another month. Taking a bite of plug chewing tobacco, Allison said, "Eddie, why don't you go back to Detroit and put this thing through? Yes, take another thirty days."

Rushing to the city that had eclipsed Indianapolis as America's motor capital, Eddie met with Frank Blair. The way to proceed, Blair proposed, was by floating a $700,000 bond issue in the state of Michigan at a rate of 6.5 percent. The bank would hold 49 percent of the common stock as its fee for handling the bond issue. Eddie would have 51 percent. All of this depended on approval of the State Bond Department. The process took four weeks, but on November 1, 1927, Edward Vernon Rickenbacker was in control of the Speedway.

Exhilaration over the acquisition was dampened shortly after the completion of the deal when word came from Florida that James Allison had dropped dead of a heart attack. This left Eddie wondering what would become of the company that he had been interested in buying before Allison switched his attention to the Speedway. Allison's executors informed him that Allison Engineering Company would be sold at auction. Noting that "just about everybody in the aircraft industry" or who wanted to get into it was after the company, Eddie learned from friends what the contenders were bidding and managed to stay ahead of them by five thousand dollars until he won the right to buy the company. He pledged ninety thousand dollars that he did not have. Turning to the Indianapolis financiers who'd shunned the Speedway, he found them eager to back his purchase of Allison Engineering. With their eyes on the company's surrounding excess real estate, they accepted a promissory note for a loan of ninety thousand dollars.

He was now the owner of Allison Engineering and majority holder of the Speedway. With a draw of five thousand dollars a year from the Speedway corporation, he would devote eleven months of the year to other business interests and spend the month of May promoting the 500.

Keenly aware of the importance of the surface of race car

tracks, he examined the brick paving of the Speedway and ordered it covered with Kentucky rock asphalt. This made it much smoother and gave it a "greater coefficient of friction" because tires gripped the surface. Having seen the dangers of speeding cars going over walls, he had the Speedway's walls rebuilt and strengthened with steel supports. He also had the curves rebuilt to improve the angle of the bank.

Because the Speedway was idle 364 days a year, he put an eighteen-hole golf course in the middle of the infield oval formed by the track. It eventually brought in ten thousand dollars a year.

Exploitation of the Speedway as "the world's greatest outdoor testing laboratory for the automotive industry" was put in the hands of publicity consultant Steve Hannagan. While the Indy 500 attracted news coverage in newspapers and from newsreels, there was no interest in the yearly event from the country's newest and greatest means of communication. When radio burst onto the scene in 1920, it became a national craze that no subsequent new product matched in rapidity and breadth of sales in so short a time, including TVs, computers, and microwave ovens. Two years after they went on the market, annual sales totaled $60 million. By the end of the decade the sum would be $842,548,000, an increase of 1,400 percent. The idea that a radio could become a common household item in the same sense as the piano and phonograph had been that of a former shortwave operator for the Marconi Company, David Sarnoff. On April 14, 1912, he had been at his Marconi "wireless" atop the Wanamaker department store on lower Broadway in New York City when the ocean liner *Titanic* radioed that it had hit an iceberg and was sinking. In 1916 he suggested to the head of the Marconi Company in the United States, Edward J. Nally, that a receiver could be designed "in the form of a simple 'Radio Music Box' placed in the parlor or living room." Music on the radio would stimulate sales of phonographs and records to play on them. The result of this proposal was the formation of RCA (Radio Corporation of America) with sales of RCA radios in 1922 exceeding Sarnoff's sales forecast for the first year of $7.5 million. In 1922, RCA sales had tallied $11 million. In that year the number of radio stations jumped from eight in

January to seventy-six in July. By the end of 1922 there were five-hundred stations across the country, many of them linked by "networks" based in New York.

That radio could bring sports events into homes was demonstrated on July 2, 1921, from Boyle's Thirty Acres in Jersey City, New Jersey. Sarnoff ran the equipment for a blow-by-blow account of a prizefight between U.S. heavyweight champion Jack "Manassa Mauler" Dempsey and French champion Georges Carpentier. Millions of Americans were tuned in as Dempsey won with a fourth-round knockout.

The broadcast not only proved that radio could cover sports events, it established RCA's network, the National Broadcasting Company, as a leader in coast-to-coast programming of all kinds. In 1927 the president of NBC was Merlin H. "Deac" Aylesworth, an old friend of the new owner of the Indianapolis Speedway. Determined that the Speedway "take its rightful place in the parade of youth," but understanding that putting the Indy 500 on radio was "a hard sell," Eddie invited Aylesworth to be his guest at the first race run under his stewardship (1928).

The dubious radio executive's first evidence of the popularity of auto racing was two rows of cars lined bumper-to-bumper all the way from Indianapolis on the road to the Speedway. The clincher in persuading Aylesworth that auto racing belonged on NBC was the contest itself. Run in a rainstorm that slickened the track and brought out a caution flag at the 425-mile mark, it ended with a veteran driver, Lou Meyer in a Miller Special, barely beating rookie Lou Moore. Back in New York, Aylesworth ordered plans for broadcasting the Indy 500. Consequently, in 1929 millions of Americans heard announcers describe who was in the lead and by how much to the background noise of speeding cars that sounded like swarms of angry mechanical insects. That people would tune in to *hear* an auto race made as much sense to some Americans at the time as perplexed listeners were a decade later by the popularity of a radio program starring ventriloquist Edgar Bergen. As he bantered with a dummy named Charlie McCarthy, they asked their fans how they could be sure that Bergen's lips didn't move when Charlie talked. Others would later scratch puzzled heads when Major Bowes's *Amateur Hour* routinely put on tap dancers.

On January 4 in the year that Eddie resigned from the Rickenbacker Motor Company, a boy was born in New York City who had the destiny of becoming an adopted son of Mr. and Mrs. Eddie Rickenbacker. Named David, he would have a younger brother. Also adopted, William was born on March 16 in the year that Eddie took over the Speedway. Neither was named after Eddie because he didn't want a son to be saddled with being called "junior." He'd never been comfortable being called "Eddie" because he thought it "depicts a little fellow." He preferred to be called Rick, and was by those closest to him. But fame had decreed that the world know him as Eddie. He and Adelaide gave David the middle name Edward. William's was Frost, after his mother's family name.

The boys' equally forceful adoptive parents brought volcanic personalities to a marriage that friends described as a "union of equals." To have more room, the Rickenbackers moved from an apartment on Jefferson Avenue in Detroit to a house in Grosse Pointe, bought at a bargain price from a man who had gone broke in the car business. But in the summer of 1929, Eddie sold it and used the money to buy a large house in Bronxville, a Westchester County suburb of New York City. The change was the result of Eddie taking a job created for him at General Motors at a salary of twelve thousand dollars. He was to be special assistant general sales manager for a new line of GM cars called the La Salle. Made by the Cadillac division for the upper-medium price range, it had a V-8 engine. Before he could begin work in selling it, he was called upon to deal with lagging sales of the Cadillac. Among his contributions to GM was a recommendation that the sale of used Cadillacs be treated "as a business of itself" in which they profited from two sales of the same car—new and used—with part of the money from both new and resold cars going into GM coffers to help fund the manufacture of new cars.

Learning that the Fisher Brothers, makers of auto bodies for GM cars, had set up an investment trust for the purpose of breaking into

aviation, Eddie seized the opportunity to cash in on his purchase of
Allison Engineering and the firm's contract with the navy. If the
Fishers took the company off his hands and then sold it to General
Motors, he would no longer have to carry the financial burden of
owning the company. If the deal materialized, he saw no reason
why he shouldn't also collect a fee from the Fishers for putting
Allison in their hands to be passed on at a profit to GM. When the
transactions were completed, he pocketed nine thousand dollars.

Early in 1929 the executive vice president of GM, Charles E.
Wilson (later the head of GM), whispered to Eddie that General
Motors intended "to take a position in aviation" by acquiring the
Fokker Aircraft Corporation of America. Wilson wanted to know
if Eddie would "look into" Fokker and advise on the feasibility of
the scheme. For Eddie the conversation with Wilson was charged
with irony. Having shot down eleven planes of Anthony Fokker's
design, destroyed one on the ground, and dodged death in dogfights with Fokkers in the skies above the Western Front, he was
being asked to explore doing business with the American branch
of the German aircraft firm.

After examining the American Fokker corporation's trimotor,
linen-sheathed, steel-tubed-fuselage model F-10 with wings of
laminated wood, Eddie judged it favorably and then arranged a
meeting between Fokker and Wilson. His reward when Fokker
became a division of General Motors was being named vice president in charge of sales, with an office in New York City. It was
this job that resulted in the Rickenbackers' move from Grosse
Pointe to Bronxville.

The position would eventually land Eddie in a position to become a dynamic pioneer of commercial aviation in the United
States.

CHAPTER 18

Voice of Aviation

T RAVELING THE COUNTRY, FIRST TO SELL RICKENBACKER AUTOMO-
biles and then the La Salle and Cadillac, the war hero the
nation called "Captain Eddie" discovered that the people in small
towns and cities he visited were usually more interested in him
than in his cars. Everywhere he went he was asked to speak to
civic clubs, chambers of commerce, American Legion posts, and
school assemblies. Rather than talk about his war experiences,
he expounded on the two topics dearest to him—automobiles and
airplanes. He predicted that by 1950 there would be 50 million
cars in America, crisscrossing the nation on six lane highways
that bypassed towns and cities. Eventually there would be so
many cars jamming the roads, he said, that Americans in a hurry
would look for highways in the skies. He forecast that in this
ocean of air, anyplace in the United States that did not have a
community airport would suffer the fate of towns in the Old West
that did not welcome the advent of the railroad.

Speaking to the Board of Trade in the nation's capital on November 22, 1928, he said it was "a source of shame" that the District of Columbia did not have an airport. Declaring that the world
was on the "threshold of a new era," he told the businessmen:

*There has come into our lives a science which is go-
ing to be a blessing to every human being, the science of
aviation. It is for you to recognize its existence today.
Already it has come and is going beyond you. There are
35,000 miles being flown every day in this country by
airmail, passenger, and transport planes, a greater
mileage than is being flown in all the rest of the world
combined. See it, recognize it and grasp the opportunity
it offers. This new science will someday be the biggest industry in the world. It is your duty and obligation to
prepare for what is coming, what in fact has already
come. Passengers, mail, parcel post, express and light
freight are going from the steamships and the railroads
into the air.*

Less than a month later a ceremony was held at Kitty Hawk,
North Carolina, to mark the twenty-fifth anniversary of the first
airplane flight by the Wright brothers. In that quarter century the
airplane had signaled a revolution both in warfare and transportation. Eddie could support his claim that progress would be
inextricable from the airplane by citing that on April 4, 1927, regular commercial airplane service had been initiated by Colonial
Air Transport between New York and Boston. The certainty that
passengers would fly across the Atlantic was opened sixteen days
later by Charles A. Lindbergh's solo flight from New York to Paris.
On October 19, 1927, Pan American Airways began passenger
service between Key West, Florida, and Havana, Cuba. In August
1929 a Russian plane, *Land of the Soviets*, had demonstrated international long-distance aviation by flying 13,300 miles from
Moscow to Seattle and on to New York in a flight time of only 142
hours.

Always alert to opportunities to promote aviation, open to
making extra money to help support his family, and keenly aware
of his continuing fame as America's ace of aces, Eddie welcomed
an unusual opportunity to do all three. An adventure cartoon

strip drawn by artist Clayton Knight, and following story lines that Eddie suggested, *Ace Drummond* was carried by 135 newspapers between 1935 and 1940. The popular adventures of a title character based on Eddie and his exploits in the war were also published in thick, pocket-sized volumes for children called Big Little Books.

In 1936, *Ace Drummond* moved to the movie screen in an adventure serial produced by Universal Pictures (the company founded by Carl Laemmle, who had offered Eddie one hundred thousand dollars to star in a movie as himself in 1919 and had been turned down). Codirected by Ford Beebe and Clifford Smith, scenarios of the weekly episodes were written by Wyndham Gates, Ray Trampe, and Eddie's literary wartime friend, James Norman Hall. (Four years earlier, Hall and WWI flier Charles Nordhoff had published a bestselling sea adventure entitled *Mutiny on the Bounty.*)

The role of Ace Drummond was played by John "Dusty" King. He was supported by Jean Rogers, Jackie Morrow, Noah Beery, Jr., James B. Leon, C. Montague Shaw, Al Bridge, and Guy Bates Post. The plot was typical of Saturday matinee serials made for kids: Seeking to expand operations into the Himalayas, International Airways is being thwarted by a criminal known as the Dragon. Ace Drummond is brought in to stop him. His efforts are complicated when the daughter of an archaeologist goes missing during a search for a "lost city."

A lackluster serial that went unmentioned in Eddie's autobiography, it was occasionally enlivened by inclusion of exciting scenes of biplane dogfights. As to the comic strip, Eddie's book recorded that it "provided a lot of fun as well as profit."

While flying around the country in the 1920s to promote auto sales, the man who would inspire Ace Drummond had several "hair-raising flights" that would have had kids at Saturday afternoon picture shows on the edge of their seats. To help a friend, John M. Larsen, "sell the Post Office Department on an airmail and passenger operation," he flew with Larsen on a cross-country tour in a Junkers four-passenger low-wing monoplane

built of a new aluminum alloy called duralumin. Eddie believed
the lightweight metal held the solution to some of the major problems in building sturdy but lightweight aircraft.

The tour was to be made in three planes piloted by Harold
Harney, commander of the 1st Pursuit Group in the war, Bert
Acosta ("a famous name in aviation"), and Samuel C. Eaton. Passengers were Edward E. Allyne, director of an aluminum company, and his wife, daughter, and son. During a stopover in
Cleveland, Eddie arranged for Harney to take the Allyne family
for a sightseeing flight over the city. To Eddie's horror, the takeoff
ended in the plane smashing into a telephone pole. No one was
injured, but the plane was wrecked.

A few days later in Omaha the weather was so hot (hot air is
less dense than cold air, decreasing lift) that the plane carrying
Eddie and Harney couldn't get up enough speed to lift off. As it
slammed into a house, a two-by-four board was driven through
the fuselage and barely missed Eddie's head. Again the plane was
a hopeless ruin.

Flying from Los Angeles and hoping to reach El Paso, Texas,
by nightfall Eddie was with Eaton, who piloted. Flying low along
the Mexican border, Eddie saw orange flashes and puffs of smoke
beneath the plane. He deduced that Mexican border guards believed they were "the forefront of a gringo invasion."

Over the Sacramento mountain range between El Paso and
Roswell, New Mexico, the gas pump broke. While the engine
sputtered and the plane headed toward a ridge, Eaton was frantically using a manual pump to feed gas into the carburetor. The
plane "scraped" over the mountain.

After stops at Kansas City, St. Louis, and Eddie's hometown,
Columbus, Ohio, Eddie's plane made an emergency landing on a
field near Bellefonte, Pennsylvania. Leaving Bert Acosta to fly the
plane to New York, Eddie and Allyne finished the trip by train. A
few days later another duralumin-made plane crashed and
burned at Morristown, New Jersey. Examining the wreckage, Eddie found "only a mass of melted aluminum." When another
plane crashed and burned, he determined that the cause of the
crashes was a faulty fuel line.

"I will never understand," he wrote, "how we completed our trip without burning up."

In an attempt to break a transcontinental speed record in early May 1921, Eddie flew a Liberty DH-4, the plane that pilots in the war had named a flying coffin. With extra fuel tanks, he left San Francisco for Washington, D.C., for a celebration of the fourth anniversary of John J. Pershing's departure for France in 1917. Forced to land due to snow over the Tehachapi Mountains, the plane came down in a muddy field, somersaulted, and broke a rudder and both wingtips.

Uninjured and provided with another DH-4, Eddie was airborne again on May 26. His destination was Cheyenne, Wyoming. Because he would be arriving at night, he'd requested that the field be illuminated by automobiles around the edge of the field with their headlamps on and a flaming T-shaped beacon at the head of the runway. As he came in for a landing, he saw that the 'T' was burning at the wrong end of the runway. The plane rolled into a deep ditch and landed on its top, leaving Eddie hanging upside down by his safety belt.

After hitching a ride on a mail plane to Chicago, he was supplied with another DH-4. But his problems weren't over. A storm forced him down into a pasture near Hagerstown, Maryland. After draining gasoline to lighten the plane, he was off again. He arrived in Washington in time for the Pershing anniversary celebration at the Metropolitan Club, but without having broken the cross-country speed record.

While on a visit to the capital in 1920, Eddie was asked by two leaders of the Republican Party, Will Hays, the party's national chairman, and party treasurer Albert Lasker, for his advice "on building an image" of the party's presidential nominee, Warren G. Harding of Ohio. Eddie proposed that Harding be "a flying candidate." The plane would be a DH-4, bought and then customized at a cost of five hundred thousand dollars. The Republicans went for the idea, but when the Democrats accused the GOP of having a $5-million "slush fund," the Republicans decided that having Harding aboard a half-million-dollar plane was not such a good notion after all.

Elected on a pledge to return the United States to "normalcy," Harding called for federal regulation of air navigation that resulted in creation of the Bureau of Aviation and the signing by President Coolidge of the Air Mail Act of 1925. The statute authorized the postmaster general to contract for airmail service with private operators. Among those applying for licenses was Eddie's wartime colleague, Reed Chambers, now president of Florida Airways.

The company was granted Route No. 10, Miami to Jacksonville via Fort Myers and Tampa, at a rate of three dollars a mile per pound of mail. Along with others, Eddie invested several thousand dollars to get the company under way. The rest was raised in a public subscription drive spearheaded by the two world war aces. One of Eddie's tasks was to persuade the city of Tampa to buy a cow pasture and turn it into an airport.

On April 1, 1926, Florida Airways was in business with one Curtiss Lark, augmented later with Ford Motor Company planes. The plane had a Liberty engine and a fuselage made from duralumin. Called the "Tin Goose," it had eight wicker chairs for passengers.

Eddie's dream was to make Florida Airways a north-south airline by first extending its route to Atlanta, Georgia. With the assistance of "an enthusiastic young assistant city attorney," William B. Hartsfield (for whom Atlanta's present airport is named), the infield of Atlanta's auto speedway became an airport. Florida Airways instituted flights from there to Miami by way of Tampa. Unfortunately, Eddie noted, "the public was not ready" to become passengers.

"It was a rare day indeed," he wrote, "when the company had one frightened customer in our wicker chairs."

Florida Airways eventually went into bankruptcy and was bought by a young millionaire from Philadelphia, Harold F. Pitcairn, who got it "for a song." The company was named after him and later became Eastern Air Transport. "And that for the time being," Eddie wrote, "ended my participation in airlines of the East Coast." He would not be involved in aviation again until Charles E. Wilson of General Motors took his advice and entered into the deal with the Fokker Aircraft Company and named Eddie vice president of sales. In that capacity he became a friend of Anthony Fokker, "a colorful individual who liked loud sports jackets and gold knickers." While with Fokker, Eddie negotiated the purchase of Pioneer Instrument company, a maker of precision aircraft instruments that became the Bendix Aviation Company.

When Fokker transferred its operations to Baltimore, Maryland, with the new name General Aviation, Eddie declined an invitation to follow the company and resigned from GM. "Once again I had left a good position with a good future," he wrote. "But I had no regrets."

The decision resulted in him taking an active role in one of commercial aviation's most fascinating episodes and making history as head of a splendid airline.

CHAPTER 19

A Medal and a Peanut

O N BLACK THURSDAY IN OCTOBER 1929, AS THE FORTUNES OF countless investors crashed along with the stock market, Eddie Rickenbacker escaped relatively unscathed, just as Eddie Rickenbacher had walked away from the scary thrill of hairbreadth escapes from sudden death and Captain Eddie had dodged death in the ferocious skies of France, then blithely walked away from several postwar airplane crack-ups. The shrewd manipulator in the rarefied ozone of corporate economics was standing on firm financial ground. He had more wealth in cash than in shares. He had paid off debts associated with the failure of the Rickenbacker Motor Company. His vivacious wife and two adopted sons were comfortably settled in a fine home in Bronxville. He occupied a "good position with a good future" with General Motors. He owned the Indianapolis Speedway. And, as he told city officials from coast to coast, civil aviation offered exciting opportunities.

Although he had been surpassed in the role of America's most celebrated aviator after Charles A. Lindbergh's historic transatlantic solo flight in 1927, he was still hailed everywhere he went as "America's ace of aces." He had earned nine Distinguished

Service Crosses and the Distinguished Service Medal with Oak Leaf Cluster representing the nine DSCs. He lacked only the nation's highest award: recognition of wartime valor in the form of Congress's Medal of Honor. Dismayed by this "oversight," U.S. representative Robert H. Clancy of the Third District of Michigan, encompassing America's "motor city," informed Eddie in December 1929 that he intended to introduce conferring legislation in the House.

While Clancy expressed confidence that the House would endorse it overwhelmingly, he could not guarantee that the Senate would go along. The main stumbling block was a group of Prohibitionist senators. Known as "drys," they were well acquainted with Eddie's drinking and indiscreet patronage of bootleggers. The most outspoken opponent of a Medal of Honor for Eddie was likely to be Sen. Hiram Bingham of Connecticut. He was not only a "dry," but he had gone on record as a critic of what he deemed Eddie's "commercialization" of his war record by putting the Hat-in-the-Ring insignia on the front of the Rickenbacker automobile. He also nursed a grudge against Eddie that dated back to Bingham's service as commander of the Issoudun air base in 1918, when Eddie went public in denunciation of the government's refusal to outfit pilots with parachutes. Eddie's perceived sins against "superior officers" were then compounded when he appeared as a defense witness in the Billy Mitchell trial.

Resentment of Eddie's support of Mitchell also thrived within the War Department. This resulted in a resistance among generals and admirals to supply their required departmental endorsement of awarding Eddie a Medal of Honor. Through bureaucratic delays, the War Department thwarted Representative Clancy's desire to gain congressional approval by March 4, 1930.

Undaunted, Clancy turned for help to the American Legion. Proposed by a small group of officers who had met in Paris immediately after the war and spearheaded by Theodore "Ted" Roosevelt, Jr., the veterans organization with posts all over the United States had become a potent political force. Because of the Legion's backing, support by Michigan governor Fred W. Green, a wellspring of public approval, and the compliance of Senate

Republicans who were nervous about offending voters by deny-
ing the immensely popular Captain Eddie the Medal of Honor,
Bingham was persuaded to withdraw his objection.

When the War Department recognized defeat, all that remained was to justify the medal by citing Eddie's qualifying
deeds. It noted his attack of seven enemy planes on September 25,
1918, in which two had been destroyed. The medal presentation
occurred on November 6, 1930, at Bolling Field, near Washington.
The chief of the Air Corps, Gen. James E. Frechet, read the citation. President Herbert Hoover said:

> *Captain Rickenbacker, in the name of the Congress of*
> *the United States, I take great pleasure in awarding you*
> *the Congressional Medal of Honor, our country's high-*
> *est decoration for conspicuous gallantry and intrepidity*
> *above and beyond the call of duty in action with the*
> *enemy. In the stage of development of aviation when fly-*
> *ing of airplanes was a much more hazardous under-*
> *taking than it is today, you were achieving victories*
> *which made you the universally recognized Ace of Aces*
> *of the American forces. Your record is an outstanding*
> *one for skill and bravery, and is a source of pride to*
> *your comrades and countrymen. Although this award*
> *is somewhat belated I hope that your gratification in re-*
> *ceiving this Medal of Honor will be as keen as mine is*
> *in bestowing it to you. May you wear it during many*
> *years of happiness and continued usefulness to your*
> *country.*

Eddie replied:

> *Mr. President, I should be ungrateful if I failed to rec-*
> *ognize this great honor as a true tribute to my*
> *comrades-in-arms, soldiers and sailors, living and*
> *dead. In peace and in war they have contributed their*

*share. They have perpetuated the traditions and high
ideals of the United States in the air as they have on the
land and sea.*

Awaiting an air show by nineteen planes of the new 94th
Squadron from Selfridge Field, Michigan, five bombers of the 2d
Bombardment Group from Langley Field, Virginia, and nine observation planes from the 9th Group of Mitchell Field, New York,
Eddie seized the opportunity to "put in a word" with President
Hoover on the importance of having a large, independent, and
unified air service. Hoover listened politely and courteously, but
it was apparent to Eddie that the president's "interests were not
in military aviation" at a time when the country was in the worst
economic crisis in its history and people were calling it the
"Hoover Depression."

Long before the show business newspaper *Variety* took note of
the collapse of the stock market with the headline WALL STREET
LAYS AN EGG, Eddie had been keeping an eye on the activities of
"two personable young men on Wall Street." W. Averell Harriman
and Robert Lehman had organized a holding company called
Aviation Corporation, or AVCO. Among its properties were several small airlines that AVCO had combined as American Airways. With operations in the East and West, it had half a dozen
different types of planes, a haphazard basis of operating, and
ledgers showing that it was losing money.

Twenty-nine days after quitting General Motors (March 31,
1932), Eddie joined AVCO (April 29) as vice president of American Airways, charged with the task of developing and maintaining the goodwill of the aviation regulators in the federal
government. Because the job required him to go to Washington
frequently, he used the only airline between New York and the
capital, Eastern Air Transport. Owned by another holding company, North American Aviation, it used a plane called the Kingbird that was built by the Curtiss Aircraft Company (also owned
by North American). Because New York City had no airport,

Eastern Air Transport flew from Newark, New Jersey, in an operation Eddie described as "more or less a gypsy-type." When the weather was good, the Kingbird flew. When it was bad, it didn't.

Climatic conditions were an irrelevancy for railroads. Trains certainly were a far more comfortable way to travel, and a great deal safer. But it would not do for an aviation lobbyist to arrive in the national capital by rail, so Eddie boarded planes that he would rather have been piloting and made his way to Capitol Hill, the Commerce Department, and any other federal office where someone might listen to his gospel of the bright future of aviation. His vision was one in which Americans routinely used airplanes for business and to go on vacations. The view in his imagination was that of an airline that combined the east-west operations of AVCO's American Airways and the north-south Eastern Air Transport. Such an airline could bridge the seasons by concentrating its fleet of planes on the east-west routes in spring, summer, and fall, and provide service to people who might want to escape winter's cold in sunny Florida.

Throughout the Roaring Twenties the state that advertised itself as "the sunshine state" had been gripped by a boom in real estate speculation and a frenzy of building. Between 1920 and 1925, Miami's population more than doubled, going from 30,000 to 75,000. Governor John W. Martin had declared that "marvelous as is the wonder-story" of Florida's achievements, they were "but heralds of the dawn." The evidence was not only in Miami, but Palm Beach, St. Petersburg, and Tampa, a city Eddie had come to know well during his association with Florida Airways in 1926. Six years later he was "positive" that "Florida would attract great numbers of vacationists." To get to its beaches by train from New York required thirty-hours. If an airline established reliable service, passengers could lengthen their time in the sun. And if that airline also operated an east-west service, it would enjoy year-round profits by shifting planes from the Florida route in its off-peak seasons.

If that airline were to be formed by merging east-west American Airways with north-south Eastern Air Transport, Eddie reasoned, the new company would also reduce costs. It would eliminate duplication of facilities, offices, aircraft maintenance operations, and other phases of the business. Planes could be transferred from American to Eastern during the winter months and back to American in Florida's off-season.

The opportunity to fashion a merger of the two airlines presented itself a year after Eddie joined AVCO. Clement M. Keys, the man who held the controlling interest in North American Aviation, the holding company that owned Eastern Air Transport, fell victim to the Depression and declared bankruptcy. Eddie recommended that Harriman and Lehman snap up Eastern Air Transport. "But dealings in high finance," he noted, "are never simple."

What he had supposed would be an uncomplicated business move turned out otherwise. Although Harriman and Lehman controlled AVCO, they held only 7 percent of the stock. The other significant shareholder, Errett Lobban Cord, had obtained AVCO stock and a seat on the board of directors because AVCO had bought Cord's Century Airline. Having known Cord since Cord ran a car-washing firm in Los Angeles, and later as the manufacturer of Auburn and Cord automobiles, Eddie described him as "a sharp and energetic entrepreneur who loved to manipulate stock." As an AVCO director, Cord had learned that the company had $30 million in cash. He wanted it used to acquire properties that would boost the firm's worth, thereby boosting the value of AVCO shares that he held and those he bought in anticipation of such a jump.

To thwart Cord's scheme, Harriman and Lehman exhibited the deft maneuverability of a pair of Hat-in-the-Ring pilots planning a dogfight with the Red Baron's Flying Circus. Rather than employing cash reserves to take Eddie's advice to acquire North American Aviation, they decided to issue an additional 2 million shares of AVCO. This bold stroke would not only bring in funds to buy North American, it would reduce Cord's position in AVCO.

"When E. L. heard about this new plan," Eddie wrote, "he was so angry that he threatened to put not only this particular controversy but also the airline situation in general before the public."

In the formative years of aviation in the United States, some pioneering figures had left behind upright business behavior in order to cross the line into the no-man's-land of flexible ethics and dubious practices of speculators and other fast-buck players who'd fueled the stock market boom of the Roaring Twenties. Painfully aware that "mistakes had been made" and "skullduggery" had been rampant, Eddie felt that because the industry was becoming mature and capable of clean and efficient operation, "washing our dirty linen in public" might provoke an investigation by Congress and bring a flurry of regulations imposed on the industry by the federal government.

Fearing that American aviation would suffer as a result of Cord taking his battle with Harriman and Lehman public, and with a personal and professional stake in the outcome, Eddie dived into the melee with the intention of serving as peacemaker. The fight's arena was the new Waldorf-Astoria Hotel. Relocated to Park Avenue and Fiftieth Street from Fifth Avenue and Thirty-fourth Street to make way for construction of the Empire State Building, it had become the base of operations for Harriman and Lehman. While they maintained two company suites, Cord had an apartment in a separate, elegant, permanent-residents portion of the hotel known as the Towers. This convenient geography made Eddie's mediation a matter of shuttling between separate breakfasts, lunches, and dinners with the contenders.

When Cord seemed to have calmed down and appeared to be in no hurry to carry the battle outside the sedate confines of the hotel, Eddie saw no reason why he should not fly to the West Coast to dispose of long-postponed personal business. Barely settled in Los Angeles, he was informed from New York that Cord "was going to blow the lid off." Before he could get back, a "free-for-all" proxy fight was under way in the full glare of the press. Although his loyalty lay with Harriman and Lehman, he recognized that Cord would triumph.

When the day came that Cord convened the AVCO board of directors and claimed his victory by wresting control from Harriman and Lehman, firing the board members, and choosing his own men, Eddie waited in his office for Cord to come in and confirm that Rickenbacker was out. Never willing to be a fighter who let an adversary get a jump on him and fire the first shot, he greeted Cord's arrival with, "Well, E. L., when do you want it?"

Cord replied, "Want what?"

"My resignation."

"I don't want it."

"You've got to take it," said Eddie.

If Cord were to keep on a man who'd been on the other side in the contest for control of the company, Eddie explained, Cord would lose the confidence of his employees.

After pondering for a moment, Cord said, "Well, all right, but I'd appreciate it if you'd stay around for a couple of months to finish up what you've been doing."

A few weeks later Cord announced that the home office of American Airways would be in Chicago. Informing Cord that he did not want to have to pluck his sons William and David out of school, but really having no desire to leave New York, Eddie again chose to give up a job without one to replace it. But the difference between a youth cavalierly quitting jobs and a forty-three-year-old man leaving American Airways was that the unemployed air line executive had expected the moment would come for him to move on.

All through his life Eddie Rickenbacker had understood that surviving a setback must never be a matter of extemporized reaction. Landing on his feet time after time resulted from anticipating the possibility of a reversal of fortune and coolly formulating a strategy to deal with it. Planning had been the root of his success on the auto track. To become America's ace of aces he'd defeated his adversaries long before he'd met them in the skies by picturing how the battle would begin, unfold, and end. When he did not have a plan, he'd nearly been killed. Finding himself in the middle of the life-or-death corporate struggle fought in the Waldorf-Astoria Hotel, he'd foreseen the probability that Harriman and Lehman would lose and prepared for it by turning to a friend who was sympathetic and resourceful and shared his enthusiasm for the potential of aviation.

The tempting prize that was there for the taking by a man who had no job but plenty of imagination and daring was the cadaver of the aviation empire that had once belonged to C. M. Keys. The holding company, North American Aviation, Inc., was in receivership. Among its parts were large blocks of stock in Pan American, Trans-World Airways (TWA), Western Air Express, and China National Airways. It also owned Sperry Gyroscope Company and Eastern Air Transport Company.

While the fight was raging between Cord and Harriman and Lehman, Eddie posed a tantalizing question to Ernest R. Breech. One of Eddie's "good friends," Breech was assistant treasurer of General Motors. Asked if the company might consider buying and operating North American Aviation, Breech was "interested." Encouraged, Eddie discussed the proposition with vice president John J. Raskob, treasurer Donaldson Brown, and the two top GM figures, Alfred P. Sloan, Jr. and William S. Knudsen. With their assent, Breech presented the plan to the board of directors. The result was a purchase by General Motors of a controlling 30 percent of North American. The deal was announced on the day that Eddie resigned from AVCO. Breech would be president of North American and Eddie vice president.

"Our job was to resuscitate those operations which held some promise," Eddie wrote, "and to unload those that did not."

One of the shed properties was Sperry Gyroscope. Because it was engaged in developing revolutionary aviation instruments, including an automatic pilot that enabled planes to fly in all types of weather, Eddie thought its disposal was a mistake. He noted ruefully that Sperry was let go "at the ridiculously low price" of two dollars a share. He argued, "That's like giving it away. Sperry Gyroscope has almost as good potential as Eastern [Air Transport] itself." History proved him right. Sperry became a crucial part of military aviation in World War II and remains a vital component of America's aeronautical, space, and marine navigation industries.

"You can't have everything, Eddie," explained Breech. "We had to give up something to get Eastern Air Transport and Sperry was the price."

With Eastern in General Motors' hands, Eddie was disappointed that his initial job was not directly running the airline. He was overseer of all of North American's activities. Retained as president of Eastern was Thomas Doe. Harold Elliott was vice president and general manager. Vice president in charge of operations was Charles Dolan. Under the new ownership, Eastern immediately inaugurated a sleeper service between New York and Atlanta and began one-day, thirteen-hour flights to Miami. It also acquired the bankrupt Ludington Line at a bargain price of a quarter of a million dollars. With seven Stinson planes, Ludington had gone broke after a failed attempt to obtain a lucrative New York to Washington airmail contract. It had made an offer of twenty-five cents a mile but had been outpaced by Eastern's bid of eighty-five cents.

When this arrangement in which the U.S. government approved a more costly contract was noted by a Hearst newspaper reporter, Fulton Lewis, the journalism magnate told Lewis to pursue the story, then chose not to publish it, evidently because Hearst decided it was "political dynamite." Frustrated by the refusal to run the story, Lewis conveyed his findings to Alabama Democratic senator Hugo Black. Chairman of a special Senate committee investigating airmail contracts for ocean routes, the ambitious senator from Alabama recognized a chance to expand his probe into all mail contracts that had been awarded by the Hoover administration's postmaster general, Walter Brown. Black studied Lewis's data and reported them to President Franklin D. Roosevelt. Arguing that airlines had conspired with Brown to obtain airmail contracts in a gigantic plan to defraud taxpayers, Black urged Roosevelt to cancel all contracts and turn the nation's airmail system over to the U.S. Army.

The question now was whether the army was able to do so. For an answer, Roosevelt turned to a man who was well known to Eddie Rickenbacker. During the war, Brig. Gen. Benjamin Foulois had been air service commander of the AEF. Now he was chief of the Army Air Service. It was a position in which he had engaged in a squabble over the service's state of readiness with Billy Mitchell. In that battle he'd been embarrassed by Mitchell's assertion that the Army Air Service couldn't lick a South American banana republic. Suddenly asked by the president of the United States on February 9, 1934, if the army was up to carrying the U.S. mail, Foulois had no choice but to reply, "Yes, sir."

At four in the afternoon on the same day, Roosevelt's postmaster general (and one of FDR's chief political advisors), James A. Farley, informed the White House press corps that all airmail contracts would be canceled at midnight February 19. Three days after Farley's bombshell, Roosevelt himself announced that the army would take over the airmail on the twentieth.

On a foggy, rainy New York day in his office in the General Motors building overlooking Broadway, Eddie voiced his opinion on the decision to a group of eager reporters. "The thing that bothers me," he said as he gazed at the terrible weather, "is what is going to happen to these young Army pilots on a day like this. Their ships are not equipped with blind-flying instruments and their training, while excellent for military duty, is not adapted for flying the airmail. Either they are going to pile up ships all the way across the continent, or they are not going to be able to fly the mail on schedule."

On the day of Roosevelt's announcement the entire air service had only three pilots who had logged five thousand hours in the air, and none who were familiar with flying in bad weather. Most army planes were open cockpit. None had instruments for night flying and bad weather. The army had 200 officers and 334 men for ground support. Civil airlines employed pilots with years of experience in better planes in all weather, supported by seven thousand ground technicians.

The cancellation would have a direct effect on three airlines owned by North American Aviation–TWA, Western Air Express, and Eastern Air Transport. It also affected the Douglas Aircraft Company's work on a new transport plane. The DC-1 was a low-wing, twin-engine, all-steel monoplane with stressed-skin construction, a passenger capacity of fourteen, a range of a thousand miles, with ample room for carrying sacks of airmail. (The plane become a workhorse of civil aviation as the DC-3 and a bulwark of the U.S. Air Force in World War II with the designation C-47 and the nicknames Dakota and "gooney bird." After the war, C-47s were flown by civil airlines and the military of other countries all over the world, and many remain in use. In the Vietnam War a version of the plane, the AC-47, was a gunship known as Spooky.)

Interested in the DC-1 for Eastern, Eddie had planned to fly along with TWA's vice president Jack Frye and pilots Silas Morehouse and Capt. Charles W. France from California to New York in March. They hoped to break the transcontinental speed record for a passenger transport while carrying mail. Because of the February 19 cutoff date for civil airmail service, they changed the date of their flight to that day with the intention of landing in Newark before the midnight deadline. Flying with them would be several journalists. But the plan hit a snag in Los Angeles with a report that a tremendous storm was brewing over the Great Lakes and was expected to be over Newark on the evening of February 19. Determined to keep to the original schedule, Eddie calculated that if they made the trip in fifteen hours, they would be in Newark twenty minutes before the storm.

"It was taking a great chance," he wrote, "but, in light of what was happening to the entire air transport industry, it was a chance that we should take."

While having breakfast on the morning of the departure, Eddie read with horror in the Los Angeles newspapers that three army pilots in training for their new jobs had been killed in two crashes. Two reserve second lieutenants had died when their plane hit a mountaintop in Utah in a snowstorm. The other had crashed in dense fog in Idaho. Eddie blurted, "That's legalized murder." A newspaperman asked, "Can we quote you, Eddie?"

He replied angrily, "You're damned right you can." He remained so upset by the use of army pilots to carry airmail that he protested it by resigning his reserve commission in the air force.

When the flight took off at nine o'clock with Jack Frye as the pilot, Eddie could not resist "putting in a few minutes in the copilot's seat" to experience the thrill of handling "the biggest and best plane" he had ever flown. After refueling at Kansas City and Columbus, they flew above and outdistanced the storm over eastern Pennsylvania and landed at Newark after thirteen hours and four minutes, setting a new record for passenger transport. Two hours later the storm closed in and was judged by Eddie among the worst he'd seen in years. At midnight, airmail service passed from civilians to the army.

The decision by Roosevelt that Eddie regarded as folly proved to be tragically so. Just nineteen days after the army began flying the domestic airmail, nine pilots and passengers were dead. This grim reality resulted in a ten-day suspension of Army Air Corps mail operations and a quiet rethinking of the policy in Washington, D.C. The reality was that the army air fleet was undermanned and ill equipped. While civil aviation had carried mail on 27,000 miles of routes, the army was capable of only 16,000 miles. Mail that an airline carried for a fraction of a dollar per pound was costing the government $2.20 a pound. The consequence of the administration's review of the policy was a rare admission from President Roosevelt that he'd blundered.

The remedy was termination of military airmail operations on June 1, 1934. Eleven days later, Roosevelt signed the Air Mail Act of 1934, reopening airmail routes to civilian aviation, but with a ban on bidding by any airline shown to be dishonest or otherwise guilty of misdeeds or shoddy business practices. The law also prohibited manufacturers of planes from operating airlines. This led to corporate reshuffling and giving new names to old airlines. American Airways became American Airlines. United Aircraft & Transport shifted to United Airlines. Western Air Express reorganized as General Air Lines. And Eastern Air Transport turned into Eastern Air Lines.

Although Eddie "disagreed vehemently" with aspects of the Air Mail Act, he decided the changes were "good for the growing air transportation industry." The scramble by companies to meet the law's demands also presented a "challenge" that he disingenuously asserted in his autobiography he "had not wanted," but felt it was his "patriotic duty" to accept.

Flying only 3,358 miles with fewer than 500 employees, Eastern Air Lines was, he said, "a comparative peanut." Its equipment consisted of a mismatched assortment of planes. Salaries were low, and so was employee morale. What bothered Eddie most was the airline's dependence on the government. "As it stands to-day," he told Ernest Breech and the board of directors of North American Aviation when they asked him to run the newly constituted and renamed airline, "Eastern Air Lines is held up by government subsidy. I believe it can become a free-enterprise industry, and I will pledge all my efforts and energies to making it self-sufficient. But if this airline cannot be made to stand on its own feet and must continue to live on the taxpayers' money through government subsidy, then I want to be relieved of that job."

Named general manager of Eastern Air Lines, he commenced work on January 1, 1935.

CHAPTER 20

Captain Eddie Says

FOR EDDIE RICKENBACKER, GENERAL MANAGER OF EASTERN AIR Lines, one thing was certain. He could never understand the company's problems sitting at a desk in New York. Almost from his first day on the job startled Eastern employees at ticket counters, handling luggage, changing a plane's tire, putting a fresh spark plug in an engine, or seated in cockpits found themselves face-to-face with the boss.

In this demonstration of how Eddie intended to run the airline, wrote Robert J. Serling in a history of Eastern, *From the Captain to the Colonel*, the seemingly omnipresent new general manager was like a benevolent tyrant. He could be both ruthless and generous, considerate and arbitrary, amiable and intolerant. Leaving no doubt who was running the show, he "generated fear and respect, hatred and affection, in equal portions."

Combining firsthand investigations with the inevitable paperwork required by the job, Eddie believed he "knew more about the airline, its condition and its problems than did any other man in the company." Workers realized that "they were no longer faceless figures on a payroll sheet, but men and women with distinct names and personalities, members of a team."

To meet Eastern employees he flew from city to city, covering seventy-five thousand miles in 1935. His message was unvarnished: "It makes no difference to me what you think of my ability or my qualifications to run Eastern Air Lines or my knowledge of air transport. There is one thought I wish to register with you, and I hope you will never forget it. That is that my job is to see that you members of Eastern Air Lines are a happy, successful lot, that you get everything that can be given to you. If I do that job properly, I need not worry about the rest of my duties. You men and women will take care of that automatically. We can't help but succeed."

The "greatest fringe benefit" as an airline operator, wrote America's ace of aces, was associating with pilots. Describing the experience, he became elegiac:

> *The very environment of their occupation, high above the vibrations and noises and petty irritations on the earth's surface, is conducive to a broader, wiser, calmer outlook. I know that many a time, when I have been trying to work out some apparently unfathomable problem, I have looked for an excuse to go somewhere, just to take a ride in an airplane. Up in the sky, in the unpolluted air, thoughts come more clearly, and concentration is easier.*
>
> *Yes, there is poetry in the sky. There is poetry in the clouds, in the moon, in the sun, in every phase of the universe. The men who live in the heavens above the world have a spiritual brotherhood.*

Recognizing that Eastern pilots had earthly problems, he set out to help them deal with them, financially and medically. Those who were mired in debt got helpful advice and bigger paychecks. Learning that copilots were forced to make ends meet by working outside jobs, he gave them more money.

Men "who drank a little too heavily" received counseling. To deal with the men's health problems the Eastern Air Lines

Aeromedical Laboratory opened in Miami, headed by "the finest doctor in the United States," Dr. Ralph Greene. When some employees suspected that he was "trying to find their weak spots" in order to "railroad them out of a job later if they didn't toe the mark," he assured them that he was interested only in seeing that they last longer at the job they were working, and that "no flying man can have an alert mind without the help of a good body."

All of this was costly. In the first year the company made one hundred forty thousand dollars, but improvements in the line's operations had cost $6 million. Included in this amount was creation of Eastern's own meteorological department. Eastern planes were also equipped with innovative navigational instruments, and pilots were given the industry's first manual on instrument flying.

To improve living conditions for employees, the operational headquarters was moved from Atlanta to the friendlier climate and lower housing costs of Miami. By increasing the number of flights of the so-called "merry-go-round" between New York and Washington, D.C., pilots were kept busy year-round, ending periodic layoffs. Eastern became the first airline to have a forty-hour workweek, pension plan, and an employee stock-buying plan. He told them, "If it develops that selling these shares on which you have options will bring in a profit and you need the money to buy a home or pay medical bills or take care of some extreme emergency, then I won't object. But, if I find anybody selling his stock to buy a big red automobile or something equally frivolous, I warn you right here and now I'm going to get mad as hell."

Dissatisfied with the obsolete Condor, Kingbird, Stinson, and Mailwing planes Eastern had been flying, Eddie bought five twin-engine, all-metal Lockheed Electras and placed an order to add five Douglas DC-2s to its fleet of nine. This successor to the DC-1 was a sturdy, reliable plane. To demonstrate its qualities and garner publicity for Eastern, Eddie decided to break his own transcontinental speed record that beat the midnight deadline ending commercial airmail service on February 19, 1934. On November 8, 1935, he personally commanded a demonstration flight from Los Angeles to Newark, with a refueling stop at Kansas City, of twelve hours and three minutes, trimming the record by more than an hour. The only pilot to surpass the earlier record had been Maj. James Doolittle. On January 15, 1935, he'd flown an American Airlines plane with two passengers on a nonstop trip from Los Angeles to New York in eleven hours and fifty-nine minutes. Three days earlier Amelia Earhart had made the first solo flight from Hawaii to California in eighteen hours and sixteen minutes in a Lockheed Vega.

While Eddie was turning around the condition of Eastern in 1935, other notable aviation events were establishment of a General Headquarters by the Army Air Corps (March 1), the first launching of a rocket with gyroscopic controls by Dr. Robert Goddard (March 28) that reached an altitude of 4,800 feet and a distance of 13,000 feet at a speed of 550 mph, a round-trip flight by a Pan American Airways "flying boat" Clipper between California and Hawaii in a survey of a possible transpacific air route to the Orient, the death of beloved humorist Will Rogers and aviator Wiley Post on August 15 in a crash in Alaska, and an announcement by Hermann Goering (March 9) that Germany had brushed aside terms of the Treaty of Versailles that had formally ended the Great War by building an air force.

With Eastern reasonably well in hand in the autumn of 1935, Eddie decided to take a vacation in Europe that would include a survey of the state of the continent's airline operations. After a brief stop in England, he and Adelaide began a four-week odyssey by airplane through France and Italy, ending in Germany. At Tempelhof Airport in Berlin they were greeted by two of the men who had been Eddie's hosts at a dinner in 1922. Erhard Milch was now head of the new German air force. Ernst Udet was in charge of design, supply, and equipment. The third figure at the table in 1922, Hermann Goering, was president of the Reichstag and principal aviation adviser to the chancellor, Adolf Hitler. Goering greeted Eddie at a luncheon in his honor at the Air Service Building. It was, Eddie noted, "one big bomb shelter."

"Herr Eddie," said Goering, "do you remember what I told you about the future of our air force when you visited us in 1922?"

"I remember it," Eddie replied, "very clearly."

Beaming and rubbing his hands together, Goering said, "Now we will show you. Udet will take you in charge and show you everything that we have been doing."

For the next several days Udet escorted Eddie through the aviation complex of "the new Germany." In a pine forest, so well concealed that Eddie had no idea it existed until he was in the middle of it, they visited the successor to the Richthofen Flying Circus, Udet's old squadron. Counting only twelve fighters rather than the customary strength of eighteen, along with six two-seater training planes, Eddie asked about the trainers. Udet explained that in their method of training and expansion, they couldn't afford to waste gasoline, manpower, materials, and pilot time. Men waiting to be trained as pilots worked as cooks, clerks, and mechanics. When a trained pilot moved out to a squadron, the next man on the training list took his place.

With Udet's enthusiastic guidance, Eddie visited factories turning out commerical and military planes. He was shown a wind tunnel for testing tailspin characteristics that would prove their worth four years later as Germany launched a blitzkrieg invasion of Poland spearheaded by steeply diving bombers with built-in sirens that produced terrifying shrieks as the planes went nosedown to drop their loads. Laid out for him to study were designs of instruments and engines that left no doubt that Germany was well on the way to fulfilling Goering's 1922 pledge of building a glorious new German empire.

As Eddie looked and listened, he did not question why Udet was revealing to him, "an American, their plans to lick the world." He reasoned that Germany did not consider the United States an enemy, as they did England and France. As to himself, because he'd been a star combat pilot, they "had a compulsion" to awe him "with their Teutonic might."

Returning to England, Eddie and Adelaide were invited to the London home of Lord Beaverbrook. When they arrived at the publisher's townhouse, nearly every member of Prime Minister Stanley Baldwin's cabinet was present. Before Eddie's first cocktail was served, he was drawn into a corner by Robert Gilbert

Vansittart of the Foreign Ministry. He asked, "When are they going to be ready, Captain? The Germans. When will they be ready to fight?"

"In my opinion, a minimum of three years," Eddie answered, "but I lean to a maximum of five years."

Vansittart shook his head and said, "Oh, no, no, no. Two years at the most!"

Convinced that he'd been asked to dine with Lord Beaverbrook so that his distinguished guests could question him about everything he'd learned in Germany, Eddie was surprised that only Vansittart believed the Nazis were hurriedly preparing for another war. All the others were so blunt in disagreeing with Eddie's opinion that Germany would soon be a threat to Britain that he decided there was no point in continuing to sound an alarm to people who were obviously more interested in "petty bickering and keeping themselves in power" than in hearing about the rapidly emerging new German air force.

Receptivity to his report in Washington, D.C., was equally frustrating. When he told his old friend and now general H. H. "Hap" Arnold that Germany was "making pilots of cooks, mechanics, drivers and the like," Arnold evidently forgot that he was talking to a mechanic who become America's ace of aces and a Medal of Honor recipient. He blurted, "It can't be done. You can't make qualified pilots out of mechanics."

Eddie realized he was "talking to deaf ears." The country's military leaders had their own ideas of training. Anything that didn't conform to those ideas could not be allowed.

A man who would have listened was Billy Mitchell, but the officer who had once hoped to keep Eddie as a chauffeur and reluctantly allowed him to train as a fighter pilot in 1918 was in Doctors Hospital in New York's Gracie Square. When Mitchell died of heart failure on February 19, 1936, at the age of fifty-seven, Eddie accompanied Mitchell's sister and a group of friends to place the coffin in a railway baggage car for shipment to Milwaukee for burial. In the "dark and cold catacombs" of Grand Central Terminal, Eddie heard "the eerie echoes" of their footsteps and felt "so bitter, so grief-stricken, so shocked at this ignominious, demeaning end to

a brilliant career." He blamed the absence of a proper military funeral for Mitchell with all honors due an American hero on petty
War Department officials who could never forget Mitchell's blis-
tering criticisms of U.S. military aviation policies that Mitchell saw
as shortsighted and dangerous.

Having encountered the same kind of obstinacy during the
war regarding equipping pilots with second-rate airplanes and
refusing them parachutes, Eddie had developed a suspicion regarding federal government officials who made life-and-death
decisions on the basis of what they saw as political expediency.
That suspicion became conviction with a court-martial directed
at silencing Mitchell and ending his career. Although Eddie had
voted for Franklin D. Roosevelt for president in 1932 because he
felt that Roosevelt's platform "seemed sound and conservative"
and was "what the country needed," he soon decided that Roosevelt had made "a complete 180-degree turn and taken off in the
other direction toward liberalism and socialism." Roosevelt's order to strip airlines of mail contracts, Eddie believed, had been
motivated solely by politics. The appalling result was untrained
army aviators being killed. He also believed that Roosevelt's subsequent reversal of policy to give the airmail back to civil aviation
had been not only steeped in politics, but was intended to give the
federal government a method of regulating commercial aviation.

Wanting no part of what he considered "government subsidy" of
Eastern, he had vowed to operate the airline as "a free-enterprise
company." To underscore Eastern's independence from Washington, he canceled passes that provided politicians free rides. He
then closed Eastern's office in the capital.

"All we were doing there was lobbying, trying to get something
for nothing," he wrote in explanation. "We had more vital operations to spend money on, operations that would develop public
confidence in our business and provide honest earned income. If
we were honestly and fairly entitled to something that Washington could give us, then we would go down there and walk in the
door with our heads up, demand it and fight for it."

Before the Roosevelt administration plucked airmail out of the
hands of the commercial airlines, passengers who flew Eastern

had been tended to by women called "stewardesses." They were registered nurses and "poised young ladies" who would "face emergencies calmly." It was also hoped that they would dispel a fear of flying among women. They certainly proved popular with men. But when Eastern's loss of its U.S. airmail contract cut into the company's operating funds, these flight attendants had been furloughed. In contemplating bringing the women back, Eddie decided that Eastern's and other airlines' experience with stewardesses showed that employing women had created "the greatest marriage market in the world." It had been "almost impossible to keep a stewardess on the job for much more than a year, on the average." At first they married pilots and copilots. Then they married customers. "We would put $1,000 into training each attractive girl," he noted, "and the next thing we knew she would have a ring on her finger."

As a matter of cost efficiency, and Eddie's prejudice against having women in airplanes, Eastern Air Lines would be the only carrier to not employ female flight attendants for years to come. The uniform of Eastern's stewards would be a white double-breasted jacket trimmed with red piping and the title FLIGHT STEWARD embroidered on the breast pocket, dark blue pants, a blue necktie, and a white-and-blue cap. Asked by a chagrined pilot why the stewardesses had been eliminated, Eddie retorted, "Because you bastards are making enough dough to buy your own pussy!"

In a country whose history was rich with individuals who had both a talent and a zest for the art of self-advertising, Eddie Rickenbacker had never been a slacker at promoting his feats and himself as a fascinating figure. The boy had talked his way into jobs. The auto racer was not just a driver, but a personality. He'd marketed Eddie-the-auto-salesman along with the cars he'd been hired to sell. Image always went hand in hand with achievement, whether on the oval track or in the bullet-riddled dogfights in the skies of the Western Front, as his Paris-tailored uniform had proved. It was more important to retain the aura of America's ace of aces than see his face flickering on the movie screens of the United States in return for a certified Universal Pictures check for one hundred thousand dollars. He'd created stories for a cartoon character to fire the imagination of kids about the adventures of flying, but no one was left in doubt that the author of *Ace Drummond* yarns was a real-life exciting and romantic figure.

He had done this instinctively long before the advent of a professional "public relations man." The person credited with that invention was Edward Bernays. An advertising executive, he popularized the Lucky Strike into a cigarette for women and softened the dour image of multimillionaire John D. Rockefeller by suggesting during the depths of the Great Depression that America's richest man give away dimes. Another pioneer in massaging public opinion in order to boost sales of industries turning out consumer goods was Albert D. Lasker. An advertising man based in Chicago, he represented Pepsodent toothpaste, Kleenex, Palmolive beauty soap, the Radio Corporation of America (RCA), Sunkist oranges, and the Republican Party. Bernays, Lasker, and others provided through public relations and advertising an impetus among ordinary Americans to spend their wages on all the things, both necessities and luxuries, that Bernays, Lasker, and the other PR and ad men told them they *deserved* as a reward for their sacrifices during the Great War and their hard work after it ended. Suddenly the average American was being enticed by savvy advertising and PR men to purchase washing machines, electric irons, refrigerators, new furniture, vacuum cleaners, and the two most-desired products: radios and automobiles.

So why, Eddie Rickenbacker wondered in 1936, would these same techniques not be effective in persuading people to travel by airplane? But not with just any airline, of course. They must be persuaded to choose Eastern Air Lines!

While Eddie was pondering how to achieve this result, a man named Beverly Griffith appeared in Eddie's office looking for work. No introduction was necessary. Eddie knew him as a newsreel cameraman who'd covered the auto racing circuit. Griffith was also the first man to take moving pictures from an airplane. He'd filmed General Pershing's 1916 pursuit of Pancho Villa. After stints as general manager of Universal Pictures and Fox, he'd taken his camera to Cuba, Britain, Mexico, Spain, Japan, and

China. Now he wanted to work for Captain Eddie in any job Eddie had to offer. Eddie told him there were no openings, but to come back and see him in a few days. The next day, by coincidence from Eddie's point of view and by luck from Griffith's, the man who held the title of public relations director at Eastern resigned. Whether he did this on his own or at Eddie's urging is not clear. Whatever the impetus, and despite an admission by Griffith that "I don't know a damned thing about public relations," Eddie said, "That's all you've been doing since you were a cameraman. You'll do just fine."

Five-foot-ten in height and weighing nearly three hundred pounds, Griffith withstood his boss's continual beseeching that he lose weight and remained a Rickenbacker loyalist for the next three decades, dedicating his life to burnishing the image of both Eddie and Eastern Air Lines. Among his first "stunts" was parking a Mailwing plane in the sunken plaza of Rockefeller Center for two weeks. (Eddie had situated Eastern's headquarters in a Rockefeller Center skyscraper in the next block.)

To handle paid advertising for the airline, Eddie engaged the Campbell-Ewald Agency, a firm that had done good work for General Motors. The Eastern account was supervised by Brad Walker. His first recommendation was to scrap Eastern's symbol. Opining that a black map on an orange background in roughly the shape of the eastern seaboard "looks like it belongs on the side of a freight car," he proposed a stylized picture of a peregrine falcon, "the fastest-flying bird in the world." He also noted the gleaming fuselages of Eastern's fleet of DC-2s and proposed to advertise the airline as "The Great Silver Fleet," and recommended that each plane's boarding door be painted with a name associated with its route, such as "Florida Flyer."

Although these innovations were Walker's, Eddie's autobiography claimed parentage. "Modesty," said one of Eddie's friends, "was not his strongest suit." But not all of Walker's ideas met with an immediate Rickenbacker embrace. When Walker suggested that napkins have buttonholes so that a male passenger could eat a meal without worrying about getting food on his shirt, vest, and necktie, Eddie shot him down on the basis that a hole in a napkin would raise the cost of napkins by a penny each. A Walker idea to promote Florida as a vacation destination by featuring pretty girls in posters was also vetoed. "No broads in bathing suits," Eddie decreed. "I don't want a flood of mail from rabbis, priests, and ministers." An innovation that he did approve was one of the airline industry's first schedules printed on slick paper with its routes marked in red. That everything had to pass Captain Eddie's muster made sense to Walker. "He was very selfish about his prerogatives," Walker recalled. "He felt, dammit, he was head of Eastern and that was it."

Eager to expand Eastern's reach, Eddie studied a map of the United States and saw that the ideal routes for Eastern would form a figure-eight pattern that encompassed Chicago and New York in the north and New Orleans and Miami in the south, with Atlanta being where the loops crossed. "By using this figure-eight pattern," Eddie wrote, "we could keep our planes circulating constantly, with greatly reduced periods of idleness between flights. Airlines make no money when their planes are not flying."

In addition to fashioning a figure eight for Eastern, Eddie desired a New York–Miami route straight down the coast, and a transcontinental route across the south. But to obtain the Chicago–New York part of the eight would mean challenging the airline that already flew it, American Airlines. When the president of the holding company of which Eastern was a part, Ernest Breech, proved unwilling to take Chicago–New York away from American, Eddie was stymied. This setback was followed by a failed bid to obtain the Atlanta–New Orleans airmail route. This reduced the figure eight to an X, with the additional coastal route.

Undaunted in the desire to expand, Eddie looked to the southwest. But as he pondered extending Eastern's reach to Houston, Texas, he got a phone call that turned out to be a wrong number. The caller was John Hertz. Owner of TWA, he was a formidable figure. Having built the Yellow Cab and Coach Company and an auto rental subsidiary, the Hertz Drive-Your-Self System, he'd sold it to General Motors in 1925 for $43 million and joined Lehman Brothers as a partner. In an attempt to phone the Scarsdale home of Ernest Breech, president of Eastern's holding company, he was mistakenly connected to Eddie's home in nearby Bronxville.

Eddie recalled, "Before I could break in and tell Hertz who I was, he began talking about me. From then on I listened. Hertz went into great detail about how he was going to get that Rickenbacker. He must have talked for half an hour. When he was through, I said gently, 'John, this is Eddie Rickenbacker you are talking to.' There was a very loud silence, and then Hertz hung up."

Eddie's puzzlement over Hertz's misdirected call was dispelled a few months later by the Hearst newspaper chain's financial writer, Leslie Gould. He wanted Eddie to confirm a rumor that Hertz was talking to Breech about buying Eastern. Stunned and alarmed, Eddie felt that if General Motors had given Breech authorization for North American Aviation to divest Eastern, Eddie Rickenbacker was entitled to as much an opportunity as any outsider to bid for it. Meeting with GM president Alfred Sloan, he declared, "If I can't outbid John Hertz, then I'm the loser. But isn't it fair to give me a chance to try?"

Sloan assured Eddie that no slight had been intended and that he would look into it. The result was a thirty-day option on the same terms that had been afforded Hertz—$1 million down and $2 million in long-term notes. Eddie proposed a cash purchase at the end of the option for $3.5 million. Sloan promised that if Eddie could get the financing, Eastern would be his.

Raising the funds from a group of investors was a touch-and-go race against the calendar and the clock to meet the option deadline. But at ten in the morning on the final day in Eastern's hangar at Newark airport, two of Eddie's backers presented him with a check for $3.5 million. Accepting it the next day, Sloan said, "Congratulations, Eddie, and God bless you. I wish you every success in the world."

The agreement between Eddie and his money men provided him with half a million dollars in working capital and gave him an option on 10 percent of the capital stock. A public stock offering would be made of roughly 416,000 shares at ten dollars a share. The issue was oversubscribed three to one. But the timing of the initial date of sale, March 12, 1938, proved untimely. On that very day Hitler launched his storm troops into Austria in an *Anschluss* that not only annexed the country of his birth to Germany, but raised the specter of a new European war. The invasion triggered a seismic shock through the world's governments and financial markets and caused an evaporation of the oversubscription of Eastern stock. Only about half were sold.

To raise the remainder of the money Eddie echoed the postwar Liberty Bond tour by barnstorming the country. In 1919 he was a twenty-nine-year-old war hero of "the war to end all wars," with a trim physique clad in uniform and on his head the jauntily tilted flying cap of America's dashing ace of aces. In the spring of 1938 he was a forty-eight-year-old executive wearing a light gray fedora and business suit by Brooks Brothers of New York in a world made suddenly nervous by the sights and sounds of Germany's jackbooted, goose-stepping soldiers trampling a neighbor's freedom, and wondering which country might be the next prey of the new German empire that Hermann Goering, hero of the Richthofen Flying Circus, had envisioned in 1919 for Capt. Eddie Rickenbacker, hero of the Hat-in-the-Ring Squadron.

With Eastern Air Lines fully capitalized on April 22, 1938, Eddie Rickenbacker was its president and general manager. Realizing "that on that day my life had changed," he wrote what he titled "My Constitution." More than a half century later, when some of America's mightiest corporations and their officers have looted their businesses as a means of personal enrichment by "cooking the books" and defrauding shareholders through nefarious methods of operation, these twelve personal and professional principles and pledges stand as a monument to the man called "Captain Eddie" and offer a standard for measuring anyone who aspires to gain and exercise power in any enterprise:

    1. My goal will be to do a good job and sell, sell, sell Eastern Air Lines at all times.

2. I will plan my work and work my plan each day arranging details in advance as far as possible.

3. I will make a business of arriving on duty on time and then think of nothing but doing my best to help make Eastern Air Lines the best airline in the world.

4. I will spend my time just the same as I would spend my money, as it is the only capital I have to invest, and I will keep a strict accounting of every hour.

5. I will try to do nothing at any time which will undermine my health, as clear thinking and effective action depend on feeling fit.

6. I will stress as well as I can and keep my mental attitude right, never allowing myself to think of my work as a "GRIND" but rather as a pleasure and a privilege.

7. I will endeavor to give careful thought as to the needs of our company and its customers.

8. I will avoid misrepresentation as dishonest and poor policy.

9. I will be fair competition but firm, using diplomacy, remembering "a knocker never wins, a winner never knocks."

10. I will always keep in mind that I am in the greatest business in the world, as well as working for the greatest company in the world, and I can serve humanity more completely in my line of endeavor than in any other.

11. I will become an expert by continuing to study and learn.

12. I realize that most of salesmanship is "MAN" and that success depends on the superiority of Eastern Air Lines's surface.

"A winner never quits and a quitter never wins."

On June 23, 1938, congressional action and presidential assent revoked the Air Mail Act of 1934 and replaced it with the Civil Aeronautics Act. It created the Civil Aeronautics Authority (CAA) with power to regulate air transport rates, foster stability in the industry, and investigate airplane accidents. The law would be amended two years later, turning the CAA into the Civil Aeronautics Board (CAB) to regulate routes, fares, and safety. A new Civil Aeronautics Administration was set up in the Commerce Department with authority over other civil aviation operating matters. Noting that the new law "brought stability and reasonable regulation to an industry that had been walking a tightrope between czarlike controls and government permissiveness," aviation historian Robert Serling wrote that "perhaps the act's major significance lay in the Post Office Department's almost total removal from airline regulatory matters," and that this was "tacit recognition that people and not mail packs controlled the industry's destiny."

Although the Civil Aeronautics Act of 1938 was enacted in June, it would not go into effect until August 1. This presented Eddie with a problem in pursuing his intention to extend Eastern Air Lines operations from an X on the map of the East Coast to the West with a route between Houston and Brownsville, Texas. In anticipation of the move, Eastern had bought a small airline that was operating from New Orleans to Houston.

Because the Post Office Department would soon be out of the airline picture, it came under pressure not to accept bids for a Houston–Brownsville–San Antonio route and leave the matter to the new CAB. Unwilling to accept this "stumbling block," Eddie sought help from Congressman Richard Kleberg of Texas, who was part owner of the gigantic King Ranch. What Eddie desired was a Kleberg-introduced bill to authorize the post office to take bids for the Houston–Brownsville–San Antonio air route. A representative with no lack of clout, Kleberg got the measure passed and presidential signature affixed. The law required the desirable route to be awarded to the airline that would carry mail at the lowest cost to the U.S. government.

The chief competitor was a Texas company owned by and

named for brothers Thomas and Paul Braniff. Sealed bids would be opened in the office of the superintendent of airmail, Charles P. Graddick. When Eddie learned that Braniff Airways planned to place a bid of less than a penny a mile, he prepared a bid of "zero zero zero cents." Although the Braniff brothers claimed that the bid was illegal and sought to have the issue deferred until the CAB came into existence, Eastern's bid was certified.

The added route mileage elevated Eastern to the nation's third largest airline in territory served. Because Eastern would be carrying the mail at no cost to the Post Office Department, Eddie's pledge that his airline would operate with no government subsidy became a reality. The airline also had an unmatched safety record. In 1937, Eastern was the first airline to receive a special award from the National Safety Council for seven consecutive years of flying its DC-2s for a total of 141,794,894 passenger miles without a fatality. The award was given again in 1938.

Three months later, just nine days after winning the Brownsville route, Eddie was told that one of his planes had crashed at Daytona Beach, Florida. Without being warned that a temporary electrical line had been erected between two poles at the end of the airfield following a severe thunderstorm that morning, pilot Stuart Dietz had taken off on what he supposed was an unobstructed runway and hit the power line. He and three passengers died.

Calling the crash "a tragedy of errors," Eddie wrote, "I have never felt more frustrated in my life. Even though I was there on the scene, there was nothing that I could do. The people were dead; the plane was demolished. Although blame was later laid squarely on the electric company by the Department of Commerce, still the airline was responsible. It all came back to the lap of the local manager. He should have known everything that went on at his field."

The company's advertising man, Brad Walker, was ordered to never use the word "safe" in an Eastern ad. "We can say air travel is reliable," Eddie said, "but there's no such thing as absolute safety. The only time anyone is really safe is when he's completely static. If you move, there's always a possibility of an accident."

Although Eddie retained confidence in the DC-2, in which he'd set two speed records in transcontinental flight, Donald Douglas's California aviation company had designed and built its successor. A twenty-one-passenger Douglas Sleeper Transport (DST), it had been put into service by American Airlines in 1936. With a fuselage wider than that of the DC-2, more powerful twin engines, wings at a rakish back-swept angle, and officially called the DC-3, Eddie saw it as the perfect plane for Eastern's booming Florida route. Business had become so brisk that he'd been forced to lease aircraft from United Air Lines. To avoid repeating what he deemed a humiliating experience, he ordered five DC-3s for delivery in 1939. They would become part of the EAL system that grew by more than eleven hundred miles to link Newark, New Jersey, with Atlanta, Georgia; Montgomery and Birmingham, Alabama; Miami, Tampa, and Tallahassee, Florida; Memphis, Tennessee; and Houston, Brownsville, San Antonio, and Corpus Christi, Texas.

After initial resistance that puzzled the entire airline industry, he authorized operations from New York City's new La Guardia Airport, which opened in 1939 in time for the New York World's Fair. The reason may have been a Rickenbacker reluctance to appear to be endorsing the liberal politics of the airport's namesake, Mayor Fiorello H. La Guardia. A blatant friend of President Franklin D. Roosevelt, he was an ardent supporter of FDR's New Deal, which to Eddie Rickenbacker smacked of socialism.

Even without a terminal in New York City, by the end of 1939, Eastern planes were serving 80 percent of the population east of the Mississippi River. When Eddie took over as general manager in 1934, the airline flew a total of 3,360,257 miles on a 3,358-mile route. Five years later the mileage had more than quadrupled to 16 million miles over a 5,381-mile route. The payroll had grown from $876,000 for 473 employees in 1934 to nearly $4 million for 2,000 workers. The company's bottom-line had gone from a $698,539 deficit in 1934 to a 1939 profit of $1,575,456. Eddie's salary was $50,000 a year. It would remain so for the next twenty-five years, making him the lowest-paid airline executive of the 1960s.

Still owner of the Indianapolis Speedway, Eddie was able to steadily increase the purse for the races throughout the 1930s to more than ninety-two thousand dollars. When he first drove on it, he recalled, the race winner had an average speed of 74 miles an hour. During the 1930s the speeds had escalated along with the danger of accidents. Eddie "exulted in the color and competition," but often found himself averting his gaze from the track during the first official lap. When the starter dropped the green flag, it was like pulling a trigger. Drivers jammed accelerators to the floor and barreled down the straightaway to the first turn.

"That was when I would nonchalantly turn and look toward the backstretch from the scene of action," Eddie wrote. "If anything happened, I did not want to see it."

His real gratification in operating the Speedway came from the realization that the races enabled automotive and allied industries to make great strides in improving cars, rubber makers to develop better tires, and petroleum companies to improve gasoline and lubricants. And there were benefits to aviation, including a fuel injection system perfected on the Speedway and the development of low pressure tires.

The owner of the Indianapolis Speedway and president of Eastern Air Lines was also a family man. But by the autumn of 1937 it had been split up. Twelve-year-old David was away at school in Arizona and nine-year-old William was enrolled in a school in Tarrytown, New York. On April 13 of that year the father wrote his "dear pal Billy" a letter that would make its way from Eddie's office in the General Motors Building at 1775 Broadway in Manhattan to the Rickenbacker home at 8 Prescott Avenue in Bronxville by way of the first flight by a Pan American Airways China Clipper from California to China. The first mail shipment to encircle the globe was routed via San Francisco, Hong Kong, Penang, Amsterdam, and Brazil. It was returned to New York on May 25, 1937. Telling William the letter would become "invaluable," Eddie said that as a keepsake "it will be a remembrance of your Daddy's interest in the progress of aviation for your benefit."

The letter was the first of hundreds during the next thirty years. William would publish many of them in 1970 in a book he titled *From Father to Son: The Letters of Captain Eddie Rickenbacker to His Son William, from Boyhood to Manhood.* The second letter, dated July 6, 1939, from Philadelphia, dealt with the inauguration of "autogiro mail service from the roof of the Philadelphia Post Office to Camden Airport," an event that Eddie predicted "will become known as one of the epochal events of air transportation." The letter continued:

> *It is your Dad's good fortune to be President of East-ern Air Lines, which will operate this service–the first of its kind anywhere in the world.*
>
> *As time goes on I prophesy that all large cities will have shuttle service by the autogiro from the main air-port to the roof of the main post office.*
>
> *Further, this will be a stepping stone to the develop-ment of the helicopter which will be used for pick-up and delivery of mail, passengers and express in all large communities between the suburbs and the main airport, increasing the speed of travel tremendously.*

Infatuation with the autogiro soon became disenchantment. In a year of flying the six miles from central Philadelphia to Camden the aircraft "contained many bugs," was "a constant headache," and "never paid for itself." In an article in *Fortune* magazine two years later, Eddie predicted that the future of urban transporta-tion lay with the development of the helicopter. He saw a time not far off when fleets of them would ferry people, mail, and light freight from outlying airports to landing pads on center-city rooftops.

Eleven years before his dalliance with the autogiro, Eddie had "every reason to believe" that the dirigible would "someday pro-vide a major form of long-distance air transportation." In the war years the Germans had used lighter-than-air zeppelin balloons to raid London. While the bombs caused little damage and few casualties, the psychological impact on civilians had been signif-icant. Adaptation of the dirigible to commercial use had also been demonstrated by the Germans. In 1928 he had been impressed with the performance of the gigantic *Graf Zeppelin* in carrying twenty passengers and a crew of thirty-eight from Germany to

Lakehurst, New Jersey, in two days. The next year it flew twenty passengers around the world in twenty days. In 1936 he had been the guest of Capt. Hugo Eckner on the massive airship *Hindenburg*. With the Nazi swastika adorning its rudders, the pride of Hitler and Hermann Goering's Third Reich flew "quietly and comfortably," kept aloft by several interior hydrogen-filled balloons and offering travelers a salon, dining room, and roomettes.

Less than a year later (May 6, 1937), as Eckner and his crew maneuvered the *Hindenburg* toward a mooring pylon at the Lakehurst dirigible port, the hydrogen exploded and the skeleton of the airship collapsed in a flaming heap, killing thirty-six of the ninety-seven passengers and crew who had flown from Frankfurt-am-Main, Germany. Although the third dirigible disaster in the United States in four years brought an abrupt end to expectations of an era of lighter-than-air civilian aviation, when Eddie ruminated on the *Hindenburg*'s fate in his autobiography thirty years later, he offered a prediction. He wrote, "I do not believe, incidentally, that the world has seen the last of the dirigible. We shall soon break through the problem of applying atomic power to dirigibles, and then they may well become great liners of the air." It was a rarity among Rickenbacker's aviation prognostications. He was wrong.

In considering the immediate future of Eastern Air Lines, Eddie recognized the virtues of the new Douglas DC-3 passenger plane and decided it was "the ship we needed in quantity." To get them he persuaded a group of investment bankers to underwrite a stock issue of $3 million. Company stock was selling for $40 a share. The bankers underwrote at $32.50. Again, events in Europe undermined a Rickenbacker plan. Soon after the agreement was struck with the money men, Germany invaded Belgium, stranding thousands of British troops around the port of Dunkirk. While every boat that could be found on the east coast of England dashed across the English Channel to rescue them, stock prices on Wall Street sank.

"I doubt that we could have sold three million dollars' worth to our stockholders for fifteen dollars a share—much less than $32.50," Eddie recalled. "But by that time we had money in the bank, and we did not owe anyone a single dime."

Authorized by EAL's board of directors to buy ten DC-3s, Eddie
offset part of the cost by selling ten DC-2s to Australian interests.
The transaction more than doubled the number of seats on Eastern planes. With the company expanding so rapidly, Eddie followed the DC-3 purchase with a move of the New York office out
of increasingly cramped quarters in the General Motors building
on Broadway to one in Rockefeller Center. While negotiating a
ten-year lease, Eddie persuaded the Rockefellers to name it the
Eastern Air Lines Building. For its dedication on October 15, 1940,
Eddie induced the governors of seventeen states served by Eastern to pose for pictures as they took turns ceremonially pressing
a button that "started" the elevators. A bus service was provided
for passengers flying out of Eastern's terminal at La Guardia
Airport.

Communication with a growing number of employees was
done through a publication called *Great Silver Fleet News* that
featured a column, Captain Eddie Says (later changed to Captain
Eddie Reminds You), which was a mixture of sermons on upright
living, homey advice, and homilies on the value of hard work,
honesty, decency, patriotism, loyalty, marital fidelity, strict child-
rearing, and piety of a sort that had been the hallmarks of Eddie
Rickenbacker's own Horatio Alger–style biography and his life-
long belief in rugged individualism and political and social conservatism. Among them were:

> *None of us here is doing so much work that he can-*
> *not do more.*
>
> *You cannot strengthen the weak by weakening the*
> *strong.*
>
> *You cannot bring about prosperity by discouraging*
> *thrift.*
>
> *You cannot help the wage earner by tearing down the*
> *wage payer.*
>
> *The greatest safety device in this business is a happy*
> *frame of mind, a healthy, happy frame of mind.*

While Eddie's exhortations in Captain Eddie Says illuminated his personality, an insight into his vision of himself as president of Eastern Air Lines was provided in a letter to his son William on October 6, 1939. He quoted a leaflet given by H. Gordon Selfridge to employees of Selfridge's London department store. The subject was the qualities of leadership:

> *The Boss drives his men;* the Leader coaches them.
>
> *The Boss depends on authority;* the Leader on good will.
>
> *The Boss inspires fear;* the Leader inspires enthusiasm.
>
> *The Boss says "I";* the Leader says "we."
>
> *The Boss says "get there in time";* the Leader gets there ahead of time.
>
> *The Boss fixes the blame for the breakdown;* the Leader fixes the breakdown.
>
> *The Boss knows how it is done;* the Leader shows how.
>
> *The Boss makes work a drudgery;* the Leader makes work a game.
>
> *The Boss says "go!";* the Leader says "Let's go!"

CHAPTER 21

Mexican Flyer

O N FEBRUARY 26, 1941, THE BOSS OF EASTERN AIR LINES PRE-
pared for a trip south to make a speech the next day to the
Aviation Committee of Birmingham, Alabama. His purpose was
to gain the committee's support for Eastern's application to operate a Chicago–Birmingham–Miami route. On the 28th he would
attend a meeting of Eastern's board of directors in Miami to garner approval of a purchase of more DC-3s for $5 million. His
plane, Flight 21, known as the *Mexican Flyer,* with the final destination of Brownsville, Texas, would depart New York City at
7:10 P.M. with intermediate stops at Washington, Atlanta, and
Birmingham. The plane was a DC-3 "sleeper transport" equipped
with berths, but he would use a small private room behind the
cockpit called the Sky Lounge.

When the plane passed over Spartanburg, South Carolina, the
boss was comfortably settled in these cozy quarters in a window
seat. Flight steward Clarence Moore was on the aisle. As Eddie
reviewed his speech and his notes for presentation to the board
of directors, the *Mexican Flyer*'s captain, James A. Perry, stepped
into the Sky Lounge.

"Captain Rickenbacker, the weather in Atlanta isn't too good," he said. "We might have some trouble getting in."

"You're the captain," Eddie replied. "Do what you think best."

Looking out the window, Eddie peered through light rain and recognized the lights of the Atlanta Federal Penitentiary. Noting that the ceiling was low, he knew that Perry would follow procedure and make an instrument approach. Having come into Atlanta himself on many another cloudy night, Eddie knew that Perry would follow a radio beam over the airport, fly past it, make a 180-degree turn, and come back on the beam.

As the plane's left wing dipped to go into the turn, Eddie felt a jarring bump and heard a scraping sound. When the left wing swung up and the right went down, he sprang out of his seat and moved swiftly toward the rear of the plane. In the next instant the DC-3's right wing hooked into trees and ripped off. The plane veered to the right and went up on its nose. When the cabin lights went off, he decided that if the plane started to burn, he would open his mouth and invite a quick death by sucking in the flames.

After bouncing around as the plane somersaulted, broke into two pieces, and landed on its tail, Eddie found himself wedged between the bulkhead and gas tank. Wreckage had packed in around his left arm, shattering the elbow. The right arm was clamped too tight to move. He had a dent in his skull, several broken ribs that had broken through the skin, a fractured left knee, and a crushed pelvis. Dead beneath him was Clarence Moore.

Ruptured gas tanks had spilled gasoline everywhere. It mixed with rain that poured into the shattered fuselage. There were groans and cries of pain. In the dark it was impossible to see how many of the sixteen passengers had survived. Most were in night-clothes. A dazed man wandering around and shivering in underwear yelled, "Let's start a bonfire and get warm."

"For God's sake," Eddie shouted, "don't light a match. Just sit tight and wait. Somebody will come and get us."

When a search party reached the wreck at dawn, rescuers spent an hour prying Eddie out of the twisted metal. They found him with an eye dangling from its socket. Four men carried him on a stretcher to an ambulance. At Piedmont Hospital in Atlanta an intern looked at him and said to an emergency room attendant, "He's more dead than alive. Let's take care of the live ones."

To Eddie's astonishment, the head surgeon of the hospital, Dr. Floyd W. McRae, had been an assistant during Eddie's mastoid operation in Paris in 1918.

News that ace of aces "Captain Eddie" Rickenbacker was in a plane crash and critically hurt splashed across front pages in huge headlines in newspapers coast to coast. The afternoon's *Atlanta Journal* blared:

SEVEN KILLED, RICKENBACKER HURT IN
AIRLINE CRASH NEAR HERE

Six columns were given to a photo of the smashed plane lying tangled in a pine thicket. Three members of the crew and four passengers died in the crash. Another died in the hospital, bringing the total to eight. Among the eight who were hurt was Democratic congressman Hale Boggs of Louisiana. (Twenty years later he would be killed in a small-plane crash in Alaska.) Investigators determined that the *Mexican Flyer* had been too low. There was speculation that the plane's instruments had been faulty, but this was unverified because they'd been crushed. Weather was certainly a factor, along with what one expert cited as a long-established Eastern policy of "pushing weather" in order to meet schedules.

Eddie's most serious injuries were to his hip and left leg. The hip was so badly crushed that the ball of the joint had splintered the socket, leaving the left leg shorter than the right. During a discussion among doctors about whether to operate, set it, or leave it alone, Eddie heard Dr. McRae say, "Well, gentlemen, we may let him die on our hands, but we will never kill him."

Eddie refused surgery. "Get me a good osteopath," he declared, "and I'll be out of this place in three days."

He would be in Piedmont Hospital for four months and two days. For ten of the days he hovered so near dying that he later claimed to have felt himself passing away. Long before the phenomenon called "near-death experience" became almost commonplace, he reported, "I began to die. I felt the presence of death. I knew that I was going."

He continued, "You may have heard that dying is unpleasant, but don't you believe it. Dying is the sweetest, tenderest, most sensuous sensation I have ever experienced. Death comes disguised as a sympathetic friend. All was serene; all was calm. How wonderful it would be simply to float out of this world. It is easy to die. You have to fight to live."

Rallying, he "fought death mentally, pushing away the rosy sweet blandishments and actually welcoming back the pain." As he clung to life, he heard the high-pitched, machine gun–like voice of gossip columnist Walter Winchell on the hospital room's radio.

"Flash! It is confirmed," said Winchell with urgent breathlessness. "It is confirmed that Eddie Rickenbacker is dying. He is not expected to live another hour."

Grabbing a water pitcher with his "good right hand," Eddie hurled it at the radio. He turned to his wife, Adelaide, who had rushed to Atlanta with their sons David and William. "Get on the phone and call the top men at the radio networks," he barked. "Tell them to make their commentators quit talking like that. They're not helping me any by telling me I'm dead. I'm not dead, and I'm not going to die."

To doctors, nurses, and orderlies he was as difficult and demanding a patient as he was a strict, cantankerous, and obstreperous boss to the men and women of Eastern Air Lines. He often experienced hallucinations. Attributing them to the effects of morphine and fearing that he would become addicted, he refused to allow continued administration. By will alone he endured the agony of repairs to his leg as surgeons bored a hole through the bone above the knee and put a bolt in it. With the leg braced in steel, he began learning to walk again. Then he graduated to the use of crutches and a pair of canes.

Well-wishes poured into the hospital from people he knew and those who knew of him, famous and not. Indy 500 publicist Steve Hannagan telegraphed, "Get up out of that bed. You can't do this to me." Sportswriter Bob Considine wired, "Keep punching." Wartime aviation colleague Cedric Fauntleroy informed Eddie's doctor, "If Rick needs blood, I've got plenty of it. Will take first available transportation." The mayor who had demanded that New York City build a world-class airport and saw it named after him, Fiorello La Guardia, begged, "Please take care of yourself." The Republican presidential candidate in 1940, Wendell Willkie, wrote, "God bless you old man and take care of you." Director of the Federal Bureau of Investigation J. Edgar Hoover's note said, "I know the indomitable Rickenbacker spirit will pull you through."

By the late autumn of 1941 the Great Silver Fleet had grown by eleven DC-3s to forty. They were flown by 331 pilots and maintained by 500 mechanics. The payroll was $4.7 million per year. EAL was serving forty cities in seventeen states. Having carried more than 300,000 passengers that year, it ranked sixteenth in the number of people conveyed by common carriers, surpassed by seven railroads, American Airlines, and United, but ahead of TWA.

Because of damage to his leg and a severed hip nerve, the president and general manager of Eastern Air Lines would walk with a limp for the rest of his life. Inability to apply pressure with his left foot left him unable to work the pedals of an automobile. Driving had brought him fame and racing had paved the way to flying. Now he could do neither. Nor was he the ramrod straight daredevil of track and skies. He walked with a slightly sideways-tilted torso. In spite of these "several physical mementoes" of an event he would always call "the Atlanta crash," Eddie saw himself "still hard and tough, the indestructible Rickenbacker."

A period of recuperation was spent with Adelaide and the boys in a small cottage at Candlewood Lake, Connecticut, and later in a houseboat at Marathon in the Florida Keys. He and William built a model airplane with a motor. For exercise he rowed a small boat and gave in to the "twisting and turning" of his body by a burly hospital orderly named Mose (today Mose's title would be "physical therapist").

After a month and a half of convalescence, Eddie felt well enough to go to his office in Rockefeller Center for a few hours on

Sundays to "write some letters without interruption." But on Sunday afternoon, December 7, 1941, he had the office's radio tuned to a pro-football game between the New York Giants and Brooklyn Dodgers at the Polo Grounds when the play-by-play was interrupted with a news bulletin. The nervous announcer mispronounced the unfamiliar name of the Hawaiian island of Oahu, calling it "O-ha-oo," as he reported that Japanese planes had attacked U.S. Army, Navy, and Air Force bases at Pearl Harbor in Honolulu.

Fifty-one years old, Eddie was still not fully recovered from the Atlanta crash. He often needed a cane to get around. Having resigned his army commission in 1934 in a snit over the government's "legalized murder" by making air force pilots carry mail, and abiding in bitterness over the army's harsh treatment of Billy Mitchell, he had been a frequently outspoken critic of President Franklin D. Roosevelt's New Deal programs as socialism. Disgruntled that his cries of alarm about the threat of Germany building an air force were ignored, he had no expectation that he would be recalled to arms. Nor did he want to be.

He had not been in favor of the United States becoming involved on the side of Britain and France in the years when another European war seemed to brewing. Like Charles Lindbergh, he had been a supporter of the isolationist America First Committee. A Rickenbacker article in *American Legion* magazine had been titled "Keep America Out." In a radio speech over NBC's Blue Network he had pleaded for statesmanship to "prevent posterity or future generations from condemning or indicting us as having legalized wholesale slaughter, murdered the flower of our youth, and massacred democracy."

He'd told an audience at Kansas City, "We can stay out of war if we want to." Recalling the war that made him famous, he said what the world got from it was "destruction, starvation, depression, and plenty of it." One thing was certain about another war, "that both sides, when the war is over, will be losers, and you and I don't want to be part of that picture."

He believed that his role, and that of aviation and managers

and other leaders of essential industries in the war that began
with the Japanese sneak attack, was to remain on the job. When
his friend William Knudsen, president of General Motors, was offered the rank of lieutenant general in charge of military production, he upbraided Knudsen for considering accepting the post. "If
you take this commission, you'll be through, Bill," he said. "Your
usefulness to the country will be cut in half."

As an act of patriotism, and with the recognition that millions
of young men would be taken into the armed services, including
race car drivers and mechanics, he ordered the closing of the Indianapolis Speedway for the war's duration. (He would sell it in
1945.) Planning was commenced for what he expected to be a requirement by the government that all airlines and their planes be
at the disposal of the armed forces for transporting men and
equipment, and that government and military personnel be afforded top priority in air travel.

A passage of his autobiography about events prior to December 7, 1941, reads as self-flattery, but it captured the essence of a
relaxed military preparedness policy of the American government throughout the 1930s. Eddie wrote, "Of all the services,
land, sea and air, only the Air Corps lacked a nucleus of personnel and the means of training additional pilots. As I pointed out
repeatedly in the 1930s, there should have been a West Point of
the air." Because no such training program existed, he envisioned
that three months of commercial transport flying would provide
an excellent advance training program for pilots and give military fliers "more practical experience than they would gain in a
year with the Army or Navy." The vital bomber command, he believed, "would benefit from this training." Military equipment was
both "insufficient and inefficient compared to that of our commercial airlines."

Convinced that had "our nation's leaders only listened to me
earlier, the entire war could have been prevented" and that a bil-
lion dollars "invested in air power during the five-year period
from 1935 to 1940 would have given us an air force capable of de-
terring both Germany and Japan," he wrote: "For years I had
been the only civilian to utter those thoughts. I had been willing

to stand up and be counted. I had been taking my case to the nation, and the press had been coming to me over the years for comment."

He had proposed 250,000 military airplanes, 1.75 million non-flying personnel, a thousand "master airports," 100,000 parachute troops, and "an Air Force capable of dominating any place within three thousand miles of the United States—and that included Hawaii."

On a Friday evening three months after Japan's attack on Pearl Harbor, Eddie answered the phone in his houseboat in Marathon. The caller was his friend Gen. H. H. "Hap" Arnold. The commander of the U.S. Army Air Forces asked if Eddie was feeling well enough to take a trip up to Washington concerning a job that was so important it mustn't be discussed on the telephone.

When Eddie arrived at the War Department on Monday morning, Arnold explained, "I'm concerned about the reports I'm getting from combat groups in training. I'm told that they are indifferent, that they haven't got the punch they need to do the job they're being prepared for. I want you to go out and talk to these boys, inspire them, put some fire in them. And while you're there, I want you to look around and see what our problems are."

Eddie said he could leave in ten days, after spending Easter with his sons.

"Some of these units will be on the way overseas in ten days," said Arnold. "If you won't go right away, there's no point in your going at all. The situation is that serious."

Eddie's next thirty-two days were spent visiting forty-three air bases, followed by two weeks inspecting U.S. bases in England. After he reported back to Arnold, he was asked to tour combat air bases in the Pacific, questioning the commanding officers, pilots, and ground crews, and making up his mind about what was good and bad. Carrying a message from President Roosevelt to General MacArthur in Australia that was "so secret it couldn't be written down," he boarded an old B-17 bomber in Hawaii with his friend Hans Christian Adamson, a crew of six, and a passenger hitchhiking a ride back to his unit in Australia.

Finding themselves overdue at an island with the code name

X, Eddie realized they were lost, running out of gas, and would have to ditch in the Pacific.

When the B-17 was reported down and everyone aboard was assumed to be dead, Eddie's friend, newspaper sportswriter Grantland Rice, went to the desk in his Riverside Drive apartment in New York to write a poem in tribute to "Captain Eddie" that began, "Danger and Death, have always been your mates." As he penned this sentimental farewell to an old friend on October 24, 1942, Eddie was in his third day in a rubber yellow boat and complaining that whoever figured the size of a raft to hold three men must have had "midgets in mind."

CHAPTER 22

With Danger and Death

WHEN THE B-17 HIT THE WATER IN THE AFTERNOON OF OCTOBER 21, 1942, the crash was a violent jumble of sound and emotions that Eddie had heard and felt when EAL Flight 21 slammed to earth and split in half at Atlanta in the rain. The water soaking him now was the Pacific Ocean. As he struggled out of the plane by way of a broken window, the part of him that would always be a pilot judged that the crash-landing in the sea had been a wonderful demonstration of the skill of the B-17's captain. William Cherry had set her down in the middle of a trough against a waning slope of a swell. From where the ship's belly first grazed the water to where it came to a stop was less than fifty feet. If Cherry had miscalculated, the Flying Fortress would have gone straight to the bottom like a rock, and everyone with it.

Thinking that the entire Pacific was rushing into the plane, Eddie looked around and found Col. Hans Adamson staggering to his feet and moaning about his injured back. The navigator, Lt. John De Angelis, looked okay. So did Cherry, copilot James Whitaker, and the hitchhiker, Sgt. Alexander Kaczmarczyk, who'd told Eddie not to try to pronounce his last name and just call him Alex. The radioman who had been sending out SOS emergency calls up to the last second, Sgt. James Reynolds, had his hands to his face. Blood from a gaping gash across his nose was running through his fingers. Flight engineer John Bartek was struggling to release two three-man rubber life rafts on op-posite sides of the wallowing plane.

Each would inflate automatically to an overall length of nine feet by five feet, but the inside was actually six feet, nine inches long and two feet, four inches across. A third raft had room for two men. When Eddie hauled himself through an escape hatch onto a wing, Bartek was already there, working with hands that had been cut as he untangled a rope line that tethered a large raft to the plane. With the half-submerged B-17 surging and heaving in twelve-foot swells, it was hard to keep a footing in the raft, but with Bartek's help Eddie was able to work the raft next to the wing so that Adamson could get in. Wincing with the pain of his wrenched back, he had to slide from the wing to the bobbing raft. Bartek quickly followed him. Cherry, Whitaker, and Reynolds had cleared the other large raft, but the two-man rig had tipped when Alex stepped in and it had overturned. He and De Angelis splashed wildly in the sea to upright it.

Someone shouted, "Who has the water?"

Another yelled, "And the rations?"

Gazing at each other with horror, everyone realized that in the scrambling to get out of the plane, the emergency water cans and rations packages had been left behind. With the B-17 more than a third under water and sinking, a man who ventured inside would risk being trapped if the plane suddenly went under. This proved to be a mistake. The plane stayed afloat six minutes. As the tail swung upright, appeared to hesitate for a moment, and then slid out of sight, Eddie wrenched a pocket watch from a pocket of his soaked, blue summer-weight business suit.

The time was 2:36 P.M.

Fearing that the pitching waves would scatter the three rafts, Eddie ordered them lashed together. Because Cherry was offi-cially in command, his was first in line, Eddie's was next, and the two-man raft last. All had seawater in them, requiring bailing, only to be swamped again and again by spray from the turgid green waves. Throughout the urgent scramble to get out of the plane, Eddie's gray fedora had remained on his head. Now it was a soaked and floppy bucket for bailing. A pocket of his suit held a chocolate bar. Alex had four. But within hours the candy was a green mush that nobody wanted to touch, let alone eat. In a bit of good luck, Captain Cherry had stuffed four oranges into a pocket.

Knowing that a man could live a long time without food and water, Eddie worried more about clothing. Only he and Adamson were fully dressed, Eddie in a business suit and Adamson in his uniform and army cap. In anticipation of having to swim, the others had shed shoes and socks. None had hats or sweaters. Cherry and Whitaker had leather flying jackets. Bartek was in a jumpsuit. The emergency equipment in the rafts consisted of a first-aid kit, eighteen flares and a flare gun, two hand pumps for bailing, two sheath knives, a pair of pliers, a small pocket compass, two collapsible rubber bailing buckets, three sets of patching gear for fixing leaks (one in each raft), and several pencils. Cherry and Whitaker each had a revolver. Eddie had a map of the Pacific. Everyone had cigarettes. Too wet to smoke, they were thrown overboard. Reynolds had the foresight to grab two fishing lines with hooks from a parachute bag, but they were of no use without bait.

Although half of the exhausted men became violently seasick, Eddie felt less so. Adamson, in agony from his injured back, said that every jerk of the raft made him feel as if he were being kicked in the kidneys. Of most concern to Eddie was Sergeant Alex. In the small raft with him, De Angelis theorized that Alex had swallowed a lot of saltwater.

At the going down of the sun, a bone-chilling mist settled upon the sea. A quarter moon rose and Eddie thought it was a beautiful sight. Wisecracks and small talk petered out as the men began to realize that they were in for hard times. Agreeing that someone had to keep watch in the night, they decided to take two-hour turns. In a burst of optimism, Eddie promised a hundred dollars to the first man to see land, a ship, or a plane. No one slept. Although the ocean's swell moderated and the air was warm, the splash of waves required constant bailing. The surrounding sea seemed to swarm with sharks.

In the gray mist of morning, Eddie was unanimously voted custodian of Cherry's four oranges. They also agreed to divide one that morning and the others on alternate days. As each of the men savored his portion, Eddie and Adamson chose to save theirs to use as bait. By the time the last of the oranges had been consumed, the sea was calm and glassy and the sun beat down fiercely as the rafts stood still with the lines slack between them and the rubber got hot. Faces, necks, hands, legs, and ankles burned, blistered, turned raw, and scorched again. If saltwater got onto flesh, it burned, cracked, dried, then reburned. Mouths became covered with ugly running sores that didn't heal.

Eddie knew that many men had been lost at sea, and that they had spent more time in small boats feeling racked with hunger and thirst, experiencing cold and heat, and knowing the horror of flesh slowly rotting away. He also knew that the greatest danger was giving in to despair. He'd gotten through the Atlanta crash by holding on to the belief that rescue was coming. But nothing in that experience, or in all the bad scrapes of his harum-scarum youth, in a racing car, and cracking up in a rickety secondhand French Nieuport had prepared him for this. Being on the Pacific in a tiny, crowded rubber raft under a broiling sun felt as though he were being turned on a spit. His only relief was to fill his battered hat with water and jam it down over his ears. He also had handkerchiefs that he soaked and passed around. Folded bandit-fashion, they gave some protection to the lower part of a face. But there was no sparing one's eyes. The ocean reflected billions of sharp splinters of light. Yet he came to hate the nights. During the day he could see the men, the play of the water, seagulls soaring, and life. Nights brought fear, groans and moans, a man crying, and someone whispering a desperate prayer.

One day when Bartek took a New Testament from his jumper pocket and began reading it, Eddie wondered if everyone might profit by his example. Although religious ritual had not been a significant part of his life, he believed in prayer and attributed his narrow escapes from death to God's design. He proposed that the men join in morning and evening prayers. With the rafts drawn together, each man read a passage from Bartek's New Testament.

But religious practice did not keep Eddie from cursing whoever had decided that a raft could comfortably hold five men. He vowed that if they should ever meet, he would either revise his opinions, or prove them on a long voyage, whose conditions would be set by Eddie Rickenbacker. Because Adamson was in severe pain, Eddie and Private Bartek gave him one end of their raft to himself while they lay facing each other, or seated back to back. He found that whenever he turned or twisted, he made Bartek do the same. A foot or hand or shoulder, moved in sleep or restlessness, was bound to rake the raw flesh of the other man. For Alex and De Angelis in a two-man raft the size of a very small bathtub, it was worse.

What bothered Eddie most was not knowing where they were, other than at some point on the equator. In this location the familiar stars of the northern hemisphere, the Big and Little Dippers and the North Star, were in different positions. Although Adamson had been in charge of the Planetarium in New York for several years, he could not say with certainty where they had gone down. Eddie and Cherry agreed that they were west or northwest of Island X and drifting.

In hope of killing a passing shark for food, Whitaker used pliers to fashion a spear from one of the aluminum oars. But when a shark glided close to the raft, its skin was so tough that the point of the makeshift harpoon bent flat. Cherry fired his revolver in vain at seagulls until exposure to the damp, corrosive salt air left the gun inoperable. He cast it overboard. Heat also wreaked havoc on the oranges, forcing Eddie to abandon the one-every-two-days rule. The last shriveled hunks of fruit were consumed on the sixth day, leaving the men with only the food of their imaginations. For Cherry it was chocolate ice cream. Reynolds described the soda pop he intended to drink for the rest of his life. Although Eddie had not had a chocolate malted milk in twenty-five years, he suddenly could not get his mind off the memory of its taste. Talk by men with voices made raspy by thirst also turned to their lives' hopes and dreams, ambitions attained and those that were not, their achievements and mistakes, and what might lie beyond death. No one talked about the war.

Day eight was like the hot, flat, and calm previous seven, except that dolphins swam by amid a cluster of sleek, fat, foot-long mackerel and a swarm of thousands of smaller fish, all out of reach. But as Eddie dozed with his hat pulled down to shade his eyes, he was jolted out of his lethargy by something settling on his head. Opening his eyes, he saw the men in the other rafts staring at him. Realizing that some sort of bird had chosen him as a perch, Eddie slowly lifted his right hand.

Breathless and acutely conscious of famished, almost insanely expectant men watching him, he knew that if he failed to grab the bird, he would never have one land on him again. Trembling fingers gently touched feathers, then snapped like a trap around the neck of a plump seagull. Moments after the neck was wrung and the feathers plucked, the gull was cut into seven equal chunks of stringy, fishy food. Even the bones were chewed and swallowed.

Entrails became fish bait on a wire hook with Whitaker's gold ring as a shiny lure and weight. The immediate result was a rather small mackerel that was divided and eaten. A sea bass was saved for the next day.

As the sun went down, the sky clouded, the air cooled, a soft wind rose, and the sea roughened, signaling an impending squall. Shirts came off and were spread out to catch rain that would be wrung out into bailing buckets. It came down like a waterfall. But the wind and waves rolled one of the rafts over. Pitched out, Cherry, Whitaker, and Reynolds struggled to right it and scramble back in, but lost were oars, a few flares, the flare gun, and a bailing bucket.

Day nine. The sea bass was eaten and each man was allowed half a jigger of water. But the condition of Sergeant Alex worsened. In a stupor, he mumbled phrases of prayers in Polish.

On day ten Alex was given two jiggers of water, one in the morning, one at sundown. The sea turned rougher. Increasingly worried about Alex, Eddie asked Bartek to change rafts with Alex in the hope that in a larger raft Alex would rest better. He remained in Eddie's raft the next day and night. On the twelfth day he was weaker but more rational. After the evening's prayer, he asked to be returned to the little raft he'd shared with De Angelis. Eddie consented. A few hours later De Angelis reported that Alex was dead.

On the morning of day thirteen, Alex's wallet and jacket were kept in expectation that one day they would be given to his family. De Angelis murmured all he could remember of Roman Catholic burial prayers. Rolled over the side, Alex's body did not immediately sink, but floated away facedown.

Day fourteen: All watches but Whitaker's were no longer working. The compass needle was rusted motionless. Eddie's map was too deteriorated to be of use. A St. Christopher's medal and crucifix that he had carried in a small case since a ten-year-old French girl had given them to him in 1917 were corroded and the case was crumbling. The condition of Adamson's back gave him no peace. Silver colonel's eagles on his collar were corroded black. His clothes were rotting, his beard was gray stubble, and his eyes were bloodshot and swollen. Eddie feared his old friend would be the next to die. The night brought a series of squalls. Rain that was wrung from shirts and socks was added to caught water in a bailing bucket. It amounted to a gallon.

Since leaving the B-17, Eddie had insisted that the three life rafts be kept together. On the fifteenth day he decided that their only hope of rescue would be for one raft, manned by the strongest three, to row to the southeast where they might have a better chance of being spotted by a plane or ship. Cherry, Whitaker, and De Angelis volunteered and set out in early afternoon. At dawn they were still in Eddie's sight. The current had proved so strong that paddling against it had been impossible. For the next three days squalls pounded the rafts and blew them in all directions. The interminable slap-slapping of waves caused constant pitching and swaying that left everyone exhausted. Eddie worried that the lines linking the rafts would break. But the collected rain had provided each man with three jiggers of water.

The seventeenth day was heavily overcast, but out of the clouds in the afternoon came the drone of an airplane engine. From a squall off to the left Eddie saw it flying low and fast. About five miles away, it was a single-engine pontoon craft. Bartek jumped up. While Eddie steadied him in the rocking raft, he waved arms and shouted. Everyone joined in. But the plane came no nearer. Too distant for its markings to be identified, it disappeared in clouds and the noise of its engine faded away. The yelling stopped.

Yet to have seen a plane, and the first sign of other human life in two and a half weeks, meant that land was near, or that a ship equipped to launch a pontoon plane was in the vicinity.

The next afternoon two similar planes appeared, about six miles away, but they flew off without their pilots noticing rafts with men frantically waving shirts in them. On the morning of day nineteen there were four planes. A pair to the north and two in the south, they flew about four thousand feet high and disappeared beyond the horizon.

When no planes were seen in the afternoon, Eddie wondered if the rafts had drifted near a string of islands and were now moving into the open ocean. Though deeply disappointed that they'd not been seen, he rationalized that the situation could have been worse. They had a supply of water and the rafts were floating in the midst of huge schools of sardinelike fish that were caught simply by scooping them into a hand and trapping them against the side of a raft, then eaten whole and alive.

Around six o'clock in the evening on day twenty, Eddie heard Cherry and De Angelis arguing. He paid no attention until he heard Cherry demand that he be left alone in the raft. He declared his intention of trying to make land by himself.

"Staying together is no good," he said. "They'll never see us this way."

Joining the argument, Eddie said that Cherry had no way of knowing which way to go. The planes they'd seen had come from all directions. If the pilots hadn't spotted three yellow rafts, what chance was there that one raft would be observed? Cherry was adamant.

As he set out, carried by the swell and a light breeze, Whitaker and De Angelis made up their minds to also venture off. Unable to talk them out of it, Eddie watched both rafts until they were out of sight. They left him with Adamson and Bartek, who seemed more dead than alive. If, as he believed, the rafts had drifted past land, their chances of holding out much longer were not good. The likelihood of Cherry, De Angelis, and Whitaker succeeding in separate odysseys seemed even more remote.

During the night the sky cleared. The sun rose blazing as Eddie searched the flat ocean for seaweed, floating debris, a seagull, anything suggestive of land. Stirring from semicoma, Bartek muttered, "Have the planes come back?"

Eddie answered, "There haven't been any since day before yesterday."

"They won't come back, I know," said Bartek. "They won't come back."

With Bartek falling silent and Adamson lying as still as a corpse, Eddie gave up looking for any sign that might spark hope and drifted into a restless doze. Late in the afternoon he felt a tugging at his shirt and awoke to Bartek saying excitedly, "Listen, Captain. Planes. They're back. They're very near."

Approaching from the southwest, there were two. A couple of miles away, a few hundred yards off the water, they disappeared into the setting sun, evidently without anyone on board having seen Eddie seated in the yellow raft and waving his battered, misshaped fedora. With night only a few hours away, despair swallowed elation. But half an hour later he heard planes, much closer than before. Scanning the dimming sky, he turned toward the sun and saw them coming out of it. Like Fokkers of the Red Baron's Flying Circus above the Western Front, they swooped straight toward him, but the plane that flashed over and past the raft bore the white star of the United States Navy and the man in the cockpit had a grin that seemed brighter than the sun itself. After a full circle around the raft, the plane set off after the second plane.

Bartek kept asking, "Are they coming back?"

"Yes," said Eddie. "They know where we are and will certainly come back."

The sun was setting and a dangerous looking squall was forming to the south. He had supposed that the planes had returned to
their base and that a Navy PBY Catalina flying boat would soon
appear to pick up the three sorry looking wretches in their little
yellow rubber raft. As minutes passed, confidence waned. Half an
hour went by, then three-quarters of an hour, with no sign of returning planes. But as he gazed toward the worrisome forming
squall, he saw the two planes a mile or so off. Skirting the squall,
a Catalina veered into a low cloud, then burst out and headed
toward him. After gliding down and circling, one PBY went off and
the other stayed overhead, circling again and again while Eddie
waved and waved and wondered what the pilot had in mind. Was
he waiting for someone else? Might he be planning to bring down
his seaplane and do the rescue himself? As the sun set, he feared
that the plane might run low on fuel and have to return to base,
leaving him, Adamson, and Bartek to another night at sea. If the
squall caught them, only God knew where they might be blown.

A white flare flashed below the plane. Then a red one. Far off
on the southern horizon, two lights blinked. Suddenly Eddie understood why the plane had been circling. The pilot had been
waiting for a boat but was now coming down to land on the dark-
ened sea. After it taxied to within a few yards of the raft, the pilot
shut off the engine.

Eddie paddled the raft to the plane and grabbed on to a wing
strut. Radioman L. H. Boutte of Abbeville, Louisiana, climbed
down to help, followed by the pilot, Lt. W. F. Eadie of Evanston,
Illinois. Eddie thought how clean and handsome they were, and
how proud he was to have them as countrymen. Eadie said they'd
have to hurry. Because Japanese were nearby, he explained, it
was too risky to wait for a rescue boat. They also had welcome
news. Captain Cherry had been sighted the previous afternoon
about twenty-five miles away by a navy patrol plane in which
Eadie had been the radioman. Cherry had given the navy the location of Eddie's raft. As to Whitaker, De Angelis, and Reynolds,
an English missionary had found them on the beach of an unin-
habited island and radioed his discovery. A navy plane carrying a
doctor had been sent to get them.

By Eddie's reckoning, he'd been rescued on a historically significant date–the eleventh of November–World War I's Armistice
Day. But because the three rafts had drifted across the International Date Line, he and his six companions were actually picked
up on November 12, a few hours into what Eddie figured was
their twenty-first day, but it was actually their twenty-fourth
since the B-17 ditched.

On Saturday, November 14, 1942, nearly every newspaper
front-page editor from coast to coast wrote the same headline:
RICKENBACKER FOUND ALIVE. To an Associated Press writer in Washington, D.C., the "dauntless" American ace of aces in the First
World War was the country's "embodied proof that you can't keep
a good man down." On the United Press news ticker he was "the
man who always came back" and "iron man Eddie Rickenbacker." William Randolph Hearst's International News Service
called him "the death-cheating pioneer of the world's airways." A
Boston Globe picture editor's caption under a file photo of Eddie
exclaimed "The Great Indestructible." In New York, Grantland
Rice became a poet again to hail the man who "whipped the Pacific and shoved Death aside, as part of the job that he takes in his
stride."

Announcement of the rescue by the navy made it clear that it
had been accomplished by its aviators, but it was Gen. Hap
Arnold who quickly informed the nation that a special plane being dispatched to the Pacific to bring Eddie home from the island
of Samoa would belong to the air force. Secretary of War Henry
Stimson sent Eddie a message promising him there would be "a
warm reception" awaiting him at home. Eddie let Stimson know
that he intended to go on with his mission. He would see General
MacArthur when his doctors declared him fit.

At the start of the mission he'd weighed 180 pounds. At Samoa he
was down to 126. On his sunken cheeks was a dirty brown beard
about an inch and a half long and a drooping Fu Manchu–style
mustache. After both were removed by a pharmacist's mate with a
straight razor, who informed Eddie that he had never shaved
another man, Eddie regretted that he hadn't had a picture taken of

how he looked that day. Well groomed and crisp in khaki clothing, he boarded a B-24 bomber that had been converted to a transport. Arriving in Australia, he was informed that at MacArthur's insistence the hop to Port Moresby, New Guinea, would be in an armed B-17.

Recalling that the last time he'd seen MacArthur was at the Billy Mitchell trial, and that they'd "disagreed vigorously and had said some unpleasant things to each other" and wondering what kind of reception he'd get from the U.S. commander in chief of the Pacific, he resolved to keep a mental armor plate about him at all times to prevent him from saying anything that would be derogatory or argumentative, regardless of what MacArthur might say. After the plane landed on a metal runway in the hills and taxied toward a group of men, MacArthur took a dramatic stance. As Eddie came forward with a limp, MacArthur met him halfway. "God, Eddie," he exclaimed, "I'm glad to see you."

Mental armor abandoned, Eddie delivered the message from President Roosevelt that was too important to be written down. MacArthur invited him to be his weekend houseguest and then tour the scene of battle in the U.S. fight to drive the Japanese off New Guinea. After eleven days of "hard going day and night," Eddie began a return flight to Samoa on December 11. After checking on the condition of the men who had endured more than three weeks on rafts with him, he was ready to place a telephone call to Adelaide. The first attempt failed. He was told the Bronxville number had been so swamped with calls by reporters and others that it was changed. When he got through to the new number, he was so emotional that he could barely speak. He told Adelaide, "I hope you will never have to go through such an ordeal again." She agreed.

Although Hans Adamson remained in frail health, he accompanied Eddie on the special air force plane to Los Angeles. Greeting Eddie were brother Dewey and their mother. She told Eddie that she had never given up hope. Eddie wrote, "It was a wonderful reunion, for Mother had always been the greatest inspiration in my life."

Awaiting Eddie's arrival in Washington, D.C., on Saturday,

December 19, were Adelaide and the boys, along with Hap Arnold and a contingent of army and air force officers. The first to greet him was Bill. He ran to the plane crying, "Oh. Daddy, I'm so happy to see you again."

In the thirty-six days since the navy plucked Eddie Rickenbacker from a raft in the far Pacific, no reporters or civilian photographers had been allowed near him. Consequently, on December 19, 1942, they swarmed to accept Secretary Stimson's invitation to a press conference in his office. Seated at his desk, Stimson reminded the correspondents and cameramen that he'd promised to produce Captain Rickenbacker "as soon as he came to see me." Rising, he turned to Eddie and said, "Captain Rickenbacker, the chair is yours."

While flashbulbs popped, the office erupted with applause from the reporters. It was an outburst of affection and admiration that today would be unlikely from a Washington press corps that generally considers any such demonstration of patriotism by journalists as unprofessional. But on that Saturday afternoon in the third week of the second year of the war, Eddie was able to speak without interruption by questions, to explain why he'd set out on a mission to the Pacific, the ordeal he and the others had endured until they were rescued, and how God had answered their prayers. After noting that America's fighting forces needed "more and more of everything," he concluded with a hope "that the trip, and whatever hardships we had to accept or endure, may prove to be a lesson to our people at home and a stimulus to drive them on to greater things because, without their effort and the material they are producing, our boys can't do the job they are so willing and anxious to do in the four corners of the world."

After lunch with Stimson, Eddie, Adelaide, and the boys flew to New York and were met by Fiorello La Guardia at the airport named for the feisty thrice-elected mayor known to the people of New York City as "the little flower" and "Hizzoner" and by editorial writers of the *Daily News* as "Butch." After "more press conferences," Eddie and family headed for home. The next day he was on all the radio networks from his apartment on East End Avenue in New York. He implored listeners to more effort "because you can never approximate the sacrifices our men are making on the battlefront for you and me."

The president of the American Shoe Brake and Foundry Company, William B. Given, Jr., was so moved when he read Eddie's remarks to the press in Stimson's office that he had them published in a slim hardbound book titled *Captain Rickenbacker's Story*. In a foreword, Given wrote, "Few stories of War can compare for drama and courage, and epic quality with that of Captain Eddie Rickenbacker and the men who spent [24] days with him on emergency life rafts in the South Pacific. Many of us will want to read this story, as Captain Rickenbacker himself tells it, and to draw from it the inspiration of the will to win that these men demonstrated. We will want to keep it, and show it to our children, as an example of American courage, American faith, and American ideals in 1942."

Given knew what he was talking about. Awaiting Eddie at home was a pile of offers from newspapers, magazines, and book publishers eager to pay him to write his story. But he felt that he had no right to do so because everything had happened while part of his expenses were "paid by the American taxpayers." When General Arnold granted permission, Eddie said, "I'll sell the story to the highest bidder and donate every penny of whatever I receive to the Air Force Aid Society." (The organization had been founded by Arnold's wife but had collected only five hundred dollars.)

The winning bid of twenty-five thousand dollars from Henry Luce, owner of *Time* and *Life* magazines, was for a three-part serialization in *Life*, with a full-page pitch by Eddie for contributions to the Air Force Aid Society. The first part in the January 25, 1943, issue was titled "Pacific Mission." The cover was a photo of Eddie above the headline EDDIE RICKENBACKER TELLS HIS OWN STORY. A picture on page 19 showed Eddie and General Arnold with fingers pointing to the route of the mission on a huge world globe. The next page had pre-mission photo portraits of Adamson, Cherry, Whitaker, De Angelis, Bartek, Reynolds, and Alex. Also pictured on the page were "Rickenbacker's relics," consisting of Eddie's battered shoes, the crucifix and case, certificate of Eddie's membership in the Elks Club, a folder of ruined traveler's checks, and what was left of Eddie's fedora. A *Life* artist provided drawings of the men on the rafts and a sketch of Eddie reaching for a seagull perched on his head. Four photos simulated "how three men can crowd into large 'five-man' raft." A full-page had photographs of "The Career of Eddie Rickenbacker from Racing Driver to Head of Airline."

The day that *Life* went on sale across the nation, Eddie's official report on his mission to the Pacific was given to Secretary Stimson.

When book publisher Doubleday, Doran and Company published the three-part *Life* account with the title *Seven Came Through: Rickenbacker's Full Story*, Eddie provided a postscript "Message to America." It reviewed his prewar visit to Germany and quoted Goering's boast that Germany would create a new empire based on airpower. He then analyzed the status of the war and concluded, "Unless the statesmen are able to deal with the issues raised by airpower, they cannot hope to deal with the old and troublesome institutions [on earth]. I venture to say, there will be no peace if the air is left in chaos."

An unexpected result of Eddie's being lost at sea and finding himself considered a hero for the second time in his life was a suggestion by officials in both political parties in Ohio that he run on their respective tickets for the U.S. Senate. Captain Joseph Medill Patterson, publisher of the *New York Daily News*, went further. He saw Eddie as president of the United States. Eddie shot down the suggestion. "Even if I were qualified for the job," he said, "I wouldn't have a chance of being elected. I'm too controversial a figure."

Three months later he found himself taking the longest airplane odyssey of his life. As an unofficial emissary to Russia, he would also do a bit of spying.

CHAPTER 23

Willful Old Warbird

O N APRIL 27, 1943, CIVILIAN EDDIE RICKENBACKER BOARDED AN
Air Force C-54 transport plane in Miami along with a few
military passengers and a doctor. A "special consultant of military morale" of the War Department, Dr. Alexander Dahl of Atlanta was an osteopath. He had helped Eddie recover after the
crash of the *Mexican Flyer*, and Eddie wanted him on hand to
keep him "physically ready for the hard work that lay ahead."

What this work entailed was explained in a letter in Eddie's
pocket. From Secretary of War Stimson, it informed "To Whom It
May Concern" that Capt. Edward V. Rickenbacker "will visit the
stations and installations of the Army Air Forces in the North
Africa, European Theater, U.S.A. Forces in the Middle East, U.S.A.
Forces in India, Burma and China, European Theater, and any
other areas he may deem necessary for such purposes as he will
explain to you in person" in his capacity as "Special Consultant to
the Secretary of War."

To accomplish this itinerary Eddie would fly in a C-54 (civilian DC-4 and later DC-6) from Miami to the West Indies, then to
Natal, Brazil, across the Atlantic to Dakar in West Africa, and on
to Algiers, where he would be provided a reconfigured B-24 to

take him to Cairo, Egypt; Tehran, Iran; India; Burma; China; and across the Union of Soviet Socialist Republics to Moscow. The "Russian mission," as Eddie termed it, was justified on the basis that the Russians were receiving hundreds of U.S. planes, and there was no American more qualified than he to advise on their maintenance and use. Nor was there an American pilot more admired in the Soviet air force, not only because of his aviation expertise, but for his heroism against the Germans in 1918 and during twenty-four days adrift in the Pacific Ocean.

As the eastbound journey of inspections of U.S. airpower and consultations with the commanders and men who were fighting the war in North Africa, the Middle East, and the Asian continent unfolded according to plan, Eddie was confident that with his credentials the Russians would surely be pleased and eager to let "Comrade Eddie" see anything of the Soviet Union's air force and its air defense system that he wished. In Moscow he had a favorable meeting with Foreign Minister Molotov and the chief of staff of the Red Army, Georgy Zhukov. He grew even more optimistic about the visit when he was greeted by the commander of one of the most sensitive of Russian military operations. The officer who gave him a pounding on the back and a bear hug was Andrei Youmachev, and Eddie knew him. He had been treated to a dinner by Eddie when Youmachev had visited New York in 1937 after copiloting a Russian single-engine plane from Moscow over the North Pole to California.

Although the Germans were only a few miles from Moscow in June 1943, Eddie was convinced by all that he observed that the Red Army and the Red Air Force "were growing stronger every day." He found military leadership "excellent." He was confident that Russia's "capable" military machine would "fight to the very gates of Berlin."

While in Moscow, Eddie was informed in a cable from Adelaide that their son David had joined the marines. Awaiting him in New York was a note from David. It pleaded that Eddie not embarrass him by visiting him at boot camp. His brother Bill was on summer vacation from Asheville School in North Carolina. But after a few weeks of relaxation, Eddie was soon off on another inspection tour. This one took him to U.S. outposts in the Aleutian Islands.

In carrying out these missions, Eddie flew halfway around the world and back, some fifty-five thousand miles. For three months and seven days he'd inspected U.S. Air Force units and seen what was going on in Russia. He talked to approximately three hundred thousand American troops, the great majority of them in units made up of heavy, medium, and light bombers and fighters. He came back with so many items given to him by the men to be passed on to loved ones at home that he had to order an Eastern Air Lines truck to take them to the airline's shipping department.

Although he had sent interim reports to Stimson, he prepared a detailed summary of the trip for the War Department. He hoped to discuss his findings with President Roosevelt, but was not surprised that FDR chose not to meet with a man who had been a constant Roosevelt critic.

Recalling the events of the summer of 1943, Eddie wrote in his autobiography:

> *And so my observations on the Soviet Union and my recommendations for dealing with this vast country were never carried by me personally to the President. If they had been, they might never have been considered or applied. But that fact remains that, owing to a unique and fortuitous set of circumstances, I was able to see more in Russia and talk more frankly with that country's political and military leaders than could all the emissaries, both British and American, sent to Russia during that period.*
>
> *I strongly believed that Roosevelt and Churchill could and should get together and negotiate with Stalin, with both understanding and strength. I believed that positive concessions should be made but that they should be based on justice, not on any effort to buy Stalin off. I believed that Stalin would listen and meet us halfway.*

But we did not negotiate from strength, and Stalin,
wily and suspicious, got the better of us at the confer-
ence table.

Before leaving on the journey that took him to Moscow, Eddie
had signed a contract with Twentieth Century–Fox. He wrote to
Bill on April 24, 1943, that writers were "on the job putting my
life's indiscretions together," expecting the movie would be ready
for the screen in December.

That forecast was optimistic. The film was released in the
summer of 1945. It began in the cockpit of a B-17 as preparations
were being made to ditch in the Pacific. Alternating with the lost-
at-sea drama, flashbacks depicted Eddie's life story, with Fred
MacMurray as the race driver who became "Captain Eddie" and
Darryl Hickman playing him as a boy. Charles Bickford was Eddie's father. Lynn Barry portrayed Adelaide. Directed by Lloyd Ba-
con, it was scripted by John Tucker and took a few liberties with
the facts. Advertising for *Captain Eddie* promised, "Here is a man
who pinned his dreams to machines and their bright danger.
They never failed him."

Two years to the day after writing to Bill about the Twentieth
Century–Fox contract, Eddie's letter to his son at school in
Asheville, North Carolina, noted that the sudden death of President Roosevelt eleven days earlier (April 12, 1945) "had surprised
a lot people, but not me because I had understood how seriously
ill he has been for months past." Clearly shedding no tears over
the demise of the president he believed had been trying to bring
socialism to America and who had brushed off meeting with him
after his expedition to Russia, Eddie expressed confidence that
President Harry S Truman would be "a real" president. He viewed
Truman's succession as an "an act of fate that will level out our
future and get us on an even keel again."

Concerning Eastern, Eddie told Bill that "things are going
ahead nicely, but headaches are beginning to develop and will
multiply as time goes on" because of "the rapid expansion we are
making." A year after the end of the war, the workforce reached
6,000 and the route system had grown to 9,000 miles. The fleet

consisted of forty-nine DC-3s and nineteen DC-4s, a modification of a wartime transport, one of which had become the first presidential plane, called the *Sacred Cow* until President Truman renamed it *Independence* for his hometown in Missouri. But the plane that Eddie longed to add to Eastern's fleet was a sleek, four-engine, triple-tailed beauty that had been developed before the war for passenger service by Lockheed. Called the Constellation, it had been flown in the latter years of the war by the Air Transport Command, primarily as a cargo transport. Eddie bought fourteen for $2 million each. The plane was so complex that it needed a third man in the cockpit, a flight engineer. Noticing that crews called the plane "the Connie," he griped that it was "like calling your wife a floozie." But the nickname stuck.

To call attention to the new plane, advertising man Brad Walker came up with another slogan, "The world's most advanced airliner." Eddie approved a promotion budget of half a million dollars, with another two hundred thousand provided by Lockheed. What the ads could not promise passengers was extra room in their seats. The Constellation sat them five abreast. Because the Connie would be a mainstay of the Florida route, the plane's proud promoter bridled at the idea that its use be limited as a vehicle for northerners who spent their winter months in the Sunshine State. He saw no sense in the acceptance by Floridian hotel and beach resort owners that there was one "season," when the calendar consisted of four. He argued that it was "shortsighted" to pay "a fortune to close down each spring, turn the hotels back to the jungle for six months, and then go through the expense of redecorating, cleaning, and reorganizing." Stay open year-round, he said, and "Eastern would bring down the customers." Dubious hostelries agreed to give it a try in 1949, with Eddie's pledge of a $1.5 million advertising blitz that proclaimed, "Visit Florida in the Summer." The first off-season result was modest profits, but enough to persuade everyone that Florida should open for business in all seasons. Miami acknowledged Eddie's contribution by naming a four-mile link between the city and Biscayne Key "Rickenbacker Causeway."

Two other Rickenbacker postwar innovations shocked the airline industry but thrilled Eastern's employees. He instituted a forty-hour workweek and the first retirement plan. But not without a Captain Eddie Says lecture. "There are only two places where absolute security exists with free clothing, food, and lodging," he said. "In jail and the poorhouse."

An advertising slogan approved by Eddie in 1946 bragged that Eastern was "Tried and Proved." When a Harvard University English professor shot off a note to EAL's public relations office that it should be "Tried and Proven," Eddie said to the PR vice president, "Tell that big brain from Harvard the slogan is selling seats and we're keeping it."

Almost as romanticizing and fancifully embroidering of Eddie's success story as the 1945 movie *Captain Eddie* was a biography of Eddie published in 1946 by his pal and raft mate, Hans Christian Adamson. Eddie was so pleased with the book that he distributed copies to "My friends and associates of Eastern Air Lines." He noted on a wrapper that it was his "wish that you receive this book, the story of my life, as a personal gift from me." Noting that the special edition was "dedicated to you [in a note by Adamson titled "To the Gang That Made Eastern"], he wrote, "I send [it] with the hope that you may profit in some way from the lessons I have learned through the years without yourselves having to endure all of the bitter shocks, trials, and disappointments. If you can benefit by these experiences even in a small degree, the preparation of this edition will have been very worthwhile to me."

Adamson dedicated the book to his wife, Helen, to Adelaide, and "A Great American Mother," Elizabeth Rickenbacher. Eddie recalled her "attempting to keep together our family of seven" after the death of their father. "With the help of the three oldest children, Mary, William and me," he wrote, "she managed to keep the wolf from the door until the younger ones, Emma, Louis, Dewey and Albert, were able to do their share."

But in the spring of 1946, the Rickenbacker family matriarch was in failing health. After visiting her in mid-March, Eddie wrote to Bill, "It is rather pathetic to have one grow so old—one who had done so much in the world and given so much to others.

She seems to have arrived at the end of her rope so to speak, being extremely thin and having no body resistance. She is more or less living on her will power."

Having seen her children "become good American citizens" and Eddie honored for his heroism in two world wars and esteemed as a leader in commercial aviation, Elizabeth died at her home in Los Angeles at the age of eighty-three on the last day of March.

Nine months later, Eddie lost the man who'd taught him how to write and give a speech. After a long struggle with throat cancer, Damon Runyon died at 6:10 P.M. on December 10. In 1942, Runyon and newspaperman Walter Kiernan had written Eddie's "Complete Life Story."

Published as a "ten-cent magazine," it provided thirty-four pages of biographical data "illustrated with the most complete collection of pictures of Rickenbacker and his fabulous career that has even been assembled."

As "King of the Dirt Track," noted the authors, "Eddie didn't believe in recklessness. He asked only a fifty-fifty chance for safety and though he played with death, Eddie knew what he was doing." In "Rickenbacker Goes to War," he was the "No. 1 Target of the German flying force" who "wore his uniform with quite an air" and "looked his reputation." "Rickenbacker in Action" was a double-page assembly of pictures taken in September 1918 by a Universal Newsreel titled "Cavalcade of the Air."

"New Futures in the Air" noted that after the war Eddie was "offered the moon," but he had "no time for glory." Instead, he "settled for a lecture tour and for writing," built a car "which was to flop dismally," went "back to the racing world again" as owner of the Indianapolis Speedway, took over Eastern Air Lines and with "his skillful and loving guidance" made it "the marvel of the air industry."

"Rickenbacker–Prophet" was portrayed "drawing a picture of the war which was to come, the war he saw gathering–the war which broke over us, *in the air.*" In "Rickenbacker the Indestructible," Runyon and Kiernan recounted the ditching in the Pacific and the twenty-four days when the world feared he was dead.

The biography's final words wished Eddie many more "happy landings."

Although ALFRED DAMON RUNYON was etched next to Runyon's wife's name on a tombstone in Woodlawn Cemetery in The Bronx, Runyon was not laid to rest in the grave. In a last note to his son, he had asked that his ashes be given to Eddie to be strewn over Manhattan. Accordingly, Eddie took off from La Guardia Airport in a twin-engine Eastern transport a few days before Christmas and headed north. Above the cemetery, he banked left and flew down the Hudson to the Statue of Liberty, then circled to go uptown above Broadway to Times Square. Over the "crossroads of the world" in the heart of the city of "guys and dolls" that Damon Rynyon had called "Baghdad on the Hudson," Eddie slid open the cockpit window and let the ashes go. They fell in a clump for a moment, then scattered in the wind.

Eight days after Runyon's death, Eddie was at the White House to receive the Medal of Merit. The citation specified his "exceptionally meritorious conduct in the performance of outstanding services to the United States from December, 1941 to December, 1944" as "Special Representative of the Secretary of War and Commanding General, Army Air Forces" that had "contributed substantially to the fund of knowledge which ultimately brought about the defeat of the enemy." The medal was also for Eddie's civilian work as president of Eastern Air Lines.

Five weeks after receiving it, he was back in Washington under different circumstances. A congressional committee had called him to testify on the subject of air accidents, including an Eastern crash at Galax, Virginia, caused by a faulty guidance beacon.

He wrote to his son Bill, "Unfortunately, the newspaper fraternity, the railroads, the steamship people, and the ironic critics who get paid for putting words together have lumped all of the accidents that took place from one end of the world to the other, including those in China, India, England, military, private, charter and contract carrier accidents, and we, the transport industry have been given credit indirectly for all of them."

Coincidentally, before he wrote this letter on January 26, 1947, he had learned that a Dutch airliner had crashed in Copenhagen,

killing nineteen, including American singer Grace Moore and
Prince Gustaf of Sweden. "This, of course," he wrote, "will make
new headlines by the hour for a few days and radio flashes every
hour on the hour–all of which will cause an awful lot of people
to quit traveling by air as a great number already have done, as is
evidenced by the low load factor, and in general multiply our
headaches." The letter continued, "Generally speaking, business
has been terrible in the air transport industry. Many of the companies are in bad financial condition and growing worse and the
list is growing longer."

As for Eastern, he noted, bad weather, accidents, and negative
publicity had cut the load factor to the point that the line's operating performance was the lowest in company history for the
month of January. He glumly reported that January 1946 was the
first January in the red since 1936. But by "saving cash through
the years and keeping our costs down and not spending as much
as we make," he went on, "we are able to weather the storm without being drastically hurt, providing we can keep control of the
situation during this trying period for the next year or two which,
in all probability, will leave us in the position of being the only
one [airline] who has been able to weather it."

Despite displeasure over press treatment of airplane crashes
and his criticism of reporters who seemed to relish providing detailed accounts of accidents, Eddie recognized that because he
was always deemed "good copy," the coverage afforded him was
a golden opportunity to push the airline industry in general and
Eastern in particular. As a race car driver and then as ace of aces,
he had learned that if he held a press conference, it was invariably thronged. Fascination in him and his exploits had increased
dramatically because of his twenty-four days "lost at sea" and the
sensational rescue, especially when the public heard about a
seagull landing on his head. Along with two poems penned by
Grantland Rice had come a ballad written by a thirteen-year-old
girl named Phyllis Beckman that read in part:

> *On the eighth day a seagull*
> *Lit on Rickenbacker's head;*

It didn't take them very long,
To eat that bird, he said.

If Captain Rickenbacker was scheduled as the speaker at a public meeting of any kind, a contingent of reporters and photographers could be counted on to be there, whether the subject was the need for improvements at the local airport, a pep talk to youths about the value of hard work, or the future of Soviet-American relations in what was now being called a "cold war" by everyone, and the division between East and West an "iron curtain" by Churchill.

Before the United States entered the Second World War, Eddie had been an "America First-er," but never a believer that the country ought to declare a policy of "isolation" from the world. As head of an airline, he was an internationalist and wanted Eastern Air Lines to have a healthy share of the world-traveling passenger pie. From his earliest days with Eastern he'd set a goal of expanding to Puerto Rico, Mexico, and the southern transcontinental route. Feeling that "the entire Caribbean area was ready to bloom," he saw that its "logical heart" was Puerto Rico. The island was an American possession, centrally located, and populous. The challenge was to persuade the American people to go there. After gaining the right to establish both New York–San Juan and Miami–San Juan routes, he launched a massive advertising campaign, including a map. He soon noted that "the run was profitable." To claim lucrative routes to Canada and Bermuda, Eastern acquired Colonial Airlines. Considering Mexico City "a natural," a route was opened from New Orleans to the Mexican capital.

He then looked even farther south. In 1949, with a group of newspapermen, Eastern officials, and CBS radio's most popular radio star and aviation promoter, Arthur Godfrey, he took a thirty-one-day tour through Latin America aboard a Constellation. They met with government officials, industrialists, civic groups, and airline operators.

That Eddie Rickenbacker had become a potent personality as the calendar changed from the 1940s to the 1950s was signified by the April 17, 1950, issue of *Time* magazine. Two weeks earlier Eddie had announced that Eastern's profits were $2 million, "making 1949 the airline's fifteenth consecutive year in the black."

With his portrait in color on the cover, backed by a rendering of the Hat-in-the-Ring Squadron insignia and a superimposed Eastern falcon, *Time*'s National Affairs section gave him four and a half pages. Under the heading "Heroes," an article titled "Durable Man" began:

> *Heroes, like the Hudson River shad, are a notably perishable commodity; no matter how brightly they may gleam when they are hauled into public view, they have a disconcerting tendency to spoil if they are left in the sun. Those who do not go gracefully to an early grave often fall easy prey to baldness, fallen arches and the horrors of earning a living. Even if they avoid the relief rolls, and skid-row bars, they are still apt to end up squirting old ladies with water pistols at American Legion conventions.*
>
> *By all the rules of fate and chance, that scarred and willful old warbird, Edward Vernon Rickenbacker, should have been back home in Columbus, Ohio last week with a cane, a bad temper, a book of yellowed clippings and a half interest in a suburban gas station. Instead, after 38 years of derring-do, he was one of America's most famous and successful men—not only a kind of Buffalo Bill of the gasoline age, but an intimate of rulers, and a self-made captain of industry as well.*

At age fifty-nine, six-foot-two, spare, and graying, Eddie Rickenbacker was "far more than a bemedaled old soldier with a game leg and a good press." As the president and general manager of Eastern Air Lines he was "one of the shrewdest, toughest, most highly admired and ferociously damned of U.S. businessmen, and the only living human soul who had ever been able to wring consistent profits from that debt-ridden peacock of modern transportation, the airline industry. As such, he was a completely individualistic and often baffling combination of Daddy Warbucks, Captain Midnight, Scrooge and Salesman Sam."

Noting that his "violent years have left their mark," that he "limps stiffly with his left leg, and at times his weatherbeaten face is lined and drawn," the article recorded that Eddie drank his last highball in 1947 but "he still goes to cocktail parties, and stands amid the crush to babble amiably while he holds a glass of ginger ale." With a "look of cocky assurance to his big nose, his grin, the set of his heavy brows," he remained "Rickenbacker, the battered invincible" who "still flies endless miles along his system, still gets up before dawn to study reports of planes, weather, passenger revenues."

To underscore that Eastern operated without government subsidy, and "galled" by the "spendthrift methods" of airlines that were bolstered by taxpayers, Eddie sent a letter to the chairman of the Senate Commerce Committee, Sen. Edwin C. Johnson. Naming five lines—National, Delta, Capital, Colonial, and Chicago and Southern—he wrote, "Eastern Air Lines, Incorporated, hereby offers to operate the entire domestic system of any or more of the five above-mentioned air carriers at a non-subsidy rate." According to his calculations, he said, the five carried 2,701,000 ton-miles of mail in 1948 and received an average of $4.45 per ton-mile, aggregating $12,077,000 from the government. His offer was that Eastern would do so at 60 to 65 cents a ton-mile over the same distance, or $1,676,000, thus saving taxpayers $10,401,000. The challenge was ignored.

In addition to resentment of federal subsidies going to competitors, the president and general manager of EAL bristled over the cost of providing meals to passengers. He was especially irked that National and Delta began serving filet mignon, forcing Eastern to do the same at a cost of an extra fifteen thousand dollars a month. Free alcoholic drinks offered by competitors compelled Eddie to set aside his belief that alcohol did not belong on airplanes. His attempt to persuade the industry to charge for drinks failed when transcontinental and international operators balked. Eddie then set a limit of two drinks per passenger. An amenity provided to EAL passengers that other airlines did not offer was a free Gideon Bible. A blind traveler could also get a braille *Reader's Digest.*

When Houston, Texas, opened a new airport terminal, Eddie guaranteed press coverage of Eastern's participation in the celebration and upstaged the other airlines by announcing that EAL would invite physically handicapped children to take rides on special Eastern flights, and that the kids would be conveyed to and from the airport on fire engines. The stunt succeeded so well that Eastern announced "demonstration flights for teachers." Called "Eastern's Educators' Air Lift," it was tried out in Charlotte, North Carolina, and continued for two and a half years in every Eastern city but New York and Chicago.

In running the airline, Eddie was what later generations of businessmen termed a "micromanager." He had been doing so since the outset of his control of the company in the form of holding quarterly meetings in different cities. Suspended during the war, the conclaves resumed as semiannual events for vice presidents, department heads, regional managers, field supervisors, city traffic and sales managers, chief mechanics, and foremen.

"It was at these meetings that Eastern's management corps saw Rickenbacker at his best–and at his worst," wrote Eastern historian Robert J. Serling. "Without a doubt they *were* beneficial in many ways, giving every manager knowledge of problems and policies affecting other departments." They could also be intimidating. Everyone in EAL management knew that their boss had a fearsome temper and was not fond of being challenged. "You didn't argue with Captain Eddie in front of 500 people," recalled one veteran of these meetings. But the bursts of temper were usually brief, he continued. "If he saw a man was extremely nervous– and I've known a couple of them to actually faint–he'd pat him on the ass and whisper, 'Slow down, son–you're going just fine.' "

Another Rickenbacker employee relations device, though briefly used, was an essay contest. The first subject was "My Job and How I Like It." The next (and last) was "How I Can Help

Make My Company Successful." Prizes ranged from General Motors autos to washing machines and radio-phonographs. Seven thousand employees were eligible to enter.

Life in the Rickenbacker apartment on East End Avenue was similarly managed, but to Adelaide the marriage was "a union of equals." Strong-willed, she admitted to possessing a "volcanic personality." Rather than sit at home while Eddie was away on missions for the War Department, she had traveled extensively with golfing champion Bobby Jones to raise funds and morale for the Air Force Auxiliary. While Americans were being urged to contribute "Bundles for Britain," she started "Bundles for America" and raised $4 million to aid families of U.S. servicemen overseas. In undertaking these projects, she was not neglecting their sons.

In 1943, David had joined the marines and served with distinction in the Pacific. After the war he attended Worcester Academy for a year before entering Hamilton College in upstate New York. Like David, William had gone to boarding schools. Too young for the military during the war, he enrolled at Harvard. He immediately celebrated and "managed to get on probation." This brought a stern letter from "Daddy." On March 7, 1947, Eddie wrote:

> *Do not let youthful influences surrounding you get the best of you or your judgment, and do not let prejudices and likes or dislikes for the instructors and professors ruin your common sense or judgment. You are there to learn, and they are there to teach you. I would abide by their judgment and, certainly, above all, by the rules of the school. Otherwise, the penalty might be so severe that you will regret it all your life—particularly after you grow older and have sense enough to look back and recognize your mistakes and your failure to appreciate advice from elders.*

Two and a half years after graduating from Harvard, Bill joined the air force. Eddie wrote to him, "With your departure to enter the military services of your country as a cadet in the Air Force of the United States of America, Mother and I hope that you will remember and follow a few of the simple rules of life which will be beneficial to you as time goes on." The rules were those that Eddie had learned as a boy and practiced and espoused as a man: a million friends are worth more than a million dollars, be respectful to superiors and elders, benefit from exercise, appreciate being an American, with faith "in the Power Above you will have faith in yourself."

He also offered advice on flying. "To become a good pilot and remain one," he advised, "never forget that an airplane is like a rattlesnake; you must keep your mind and eye in it constantly or it will bite you when you least expect it, which could prove fatal."

As Bill trained at Randolph Field, Texas, and with David nearing his graduation from Hamilton, they had their eyes and hearts set on buying a ranch in Texas. Eddie saw "many years of pleasure, health, and happiness through the opportunity to help build something deeply rooted in the soil of this great land which you [Bill and David] can build upon, benefit by, and develop for your family and yourself in the true traditions of the sound principles laid down by our forefathers, which have made this country great."

While spending a few days at the Texas ranch in February 1952, Eddie suddenly faced a crisis that presented an immediate threat to Eastern's operating structure. He was awakened at three in the morning by a phone call from his secretary, Marguerite Shepherd. "Sheppy" reported that a plane had crashed at Elizabeth, New Jersey, killing twenty-eight passengers and crew along with four people in an apartment house. Although it was not an EAL plane, she said, because the accident was the third serious one in a few weeks involving a plane from Newark, the airport had been ordered closed by the government. This meant that Eastern's operations were being forced to shift to Idlewild Airport in New York City. Although negotiations had been under way between Eddie and the New York Port Authority to establish service at Idlewild, Eastern did not fly from there and therefore had no hangar and ground facilities.

Rushing to New York, Eddie contemplated the ramifications of the calamity of closing Newark. It was the base for 65 percent of Eastern's operations and maintenance facilities for all New York–based planes. The shutdown of Newark came at the peak of the New York–Florida season. After a 1,650-mile flight from Houston to La Guardia Airport, Eddie arrived in time for an emergency meeting of airline operators, government officials, other parties who had interests in the situation, and Port Authority chairman Howard Cullman. The result was the formation of a fifteen-member committee that had the purpose of preserving Newark Airport. The group, later named the National Air Transport Association, devised a program to deal with the safety concerns and a major complaint by residents in areas around airports about the noise of planes taking off and landing. In the meantime, Newark stayed shut at a cost to Eastern, during a year, of $1.5 million in lost revenue, higher fuel costs, overtime, and the expense of transportation for employees displaced from Newark.

As spokesman for the National Air Transport Association, Eddie found himself engaged in a battle to promote favorable publicity for the entire airline industry. On the issue of safety, he answered that there was a risk of accidents involving anything mechanical that moved. He cited statistics on automobile crashes, train wrecks, and even ships that sank. As to airplanes, he noted that in 1951 there had been sixteen million takeoffs and landings in the United States with no fatalities. America's future, he said, depended on a vigorous air transport industry.

Asserting that the airplane had become as crucial a part of American life as the car, he recalled his boyhood when people had told him that the automobile could never replace their safe, reliable, good old horses and buggies. People had been even more dubious about the place of the airplane in their future, but the day was approaching when the children of those skeptics would routinely get on jet-powered airliners to cross the country in a quarter of the time required by propeller-driven planes.

Although Eddie saw air travel's future in jets being developed by Boeing and Douglas in the United States and De Havilland in England, he found no wisdom in Eastern Air Lines rushing to exchange propeller planes that were "giving excellent economical service" for the "far more expensive" jets that he felt needed further development. After a flight in a Boeing prototype jet, he ventured the opinion that if it were ever to make money, it would need a wider cabin to seat more passengers. In a demonstration of De Havilland's Comet he found a structural flaw that "scared the living daylights out of me." Not long after this, he noted that three Comets crashed, resulting in "a great blow to British prestige."

Eddie's belief that jets were in Eastern's future had been stated at a news conference in Atlanta in 1948. He said that "within five or six years Eastern will be flying jet-propelled planes from Atlanta to New York in a maximum of an hour and a half." But in 1952, when the last of Eastern's DC-3s made their final runs, the replacements were a mixture of turboprop Martins and thirty Super-C Constellations. Since the Douglas DC-3 became the backbone of the Great Silver Fleet, sixty-three of the indomitable twin-engine airliners adorned with the Eastern falcon had flown 83.5 million miles, equivalent to 3,343 trips around the world, and 254 years in the air. In the quarter century since Eastern began operating in 1927 with a Ford trimotor, its planes had carried an average of a million passengers a month. To mark Eastern's silver anniversary in 1953, twenty-two more Super Connies were ordered. They and other types of planes with improved designs and performance, including Douglas DC-7s and the Lockheed Electra, would operate over nearly thirteen thousand route miles.

Discussing expansion of Eastern's fleet in *Business Week* magazine, Eddie cited "the tremendous potential for air transportation." Because young Americans were "born in the lap of aviation" and "the airplane is their most natural and preferred means of travel," he forecast that by 1965 airlines would have progressed more in ten years than in the past twenty-five. He was replacing equipment, he explained, "because of the rapid obsolescence of plane design, we don't want to be caught with outmoded planes on our books."

For airline historian R.E.G. Davies, author of *Airlines of the United States Since 1914*, the first, faint glimmerings of the dawn of jet-powered passenger planes marked the beginning of a third phase in the history of civil aviation and airliners. He wrote, "First there was the era during which an aeroplane–almost any aeroplane, it did not matter what type–was the subject of awe. Then came the intriguing period when development proliferated to such an extent that different types of aircraft were recognized by quite a large section of the public." (The automobile had gone through the same phases.)

During the airplane's evolution from fascinating to common-place, Eddie Rickenbacker had ridden the wings of ambition, fame, luck, confidence, will, and ability to build the biggest air-line in the country. While achieving this, he shared the aviation industry's limelight with four other pioneers: William "Bill" Pat-terson of United, Cyrus R. "C. R." Smith of American, Juan Trippe of Pan American, and TWA's Howard Hughes. With one exception they had been totally dedicated to air transport since it had taken root in the U.S.A. "Except for Hughes [who had inherited a for-tune and owned TWA outright]," Davies wrote, "none of these great men had a substantial financial interest in the airline they served so well. With advancing years, their touch was still sure, although eventually age and chance began to overtake them."

In 1954, with his sixty-fourth birthday approaching, still in firm control of Eastern but thinking about age and chance, Eddie decided that the best place for him and Adelaide to reside was not in an apartment, but in a fine hotel. After trying New York's Park Lane and the Carlyle and finding them unsatisfactory, they set-tled in the smaller, quieter Stanhope, just across Fifth Avenue from the Metropolitan Museum of Art. When the rent was raised 15 percent, they moved to an "ideal" penthouse in the Regency on Park Avenue. Deciding that the Texas ranch was "too far away," Eddie donated its buildings and twenty-seven hundred acres to the Alamo Area Council of the Boy Scouts of America.

When Bill was discharged from the air force in 1955 and re-turned to New York with the intention of going into the investment business, Eddie gave him the names of a number of friends "down in Wall Street." Bill joined Smith, Barney and Company and within a year was in charge of the aviation research department. He later

opened his own firm in Tarrytown and married his childhood
sweetheart, Alexandra Harriman Leys of Yonkers. After meeting
William F. Buckley, Jr., publisher of a new magazine of conservative political opinion called *National Review,* he joined the staff
and rose quickly to be a senior editor. Their home was in Briarcliff
Manor. They had two sons, James and Thomas. With the ranch
gone, David and his wife Patty also came back to New York. He
joined the United States Trust Company. They settled in Upper
Montclair, New Jersey, and raised three children, Brian, Marcia,
and Nancy.

Proud of his sons and pleased with the direction of their lives,
Eddie also pointed with pride to Eastern's combined profits in
1957 and 1958 of more than $16 million. Part of it went to the pur-
chase of forty Lockheed Electra turboprops. Eastern's firm financial structure enabled him to launch Eastern toward a place in
the jet age by striking a deal with his old friend Donald Douglas
for the purchase of forty Douglas DC-8 jets.

With his eyes on a bright future, Eddie appeared to give no attention to rumblings from some passengers that Eastern's current
planes were showing signs of wear and tear. One group of regular
fliers began wearing celluloid lapel pins printed with the initials
WHEAL. They meant "We Hate Eastern Air Lines." What mattered
was not the gripes of a few, but that the seats were filled and the
planes departed and arrived on time, safely. Yet he was not indifferent to the state of the planes he was buying. The DC-8s would
have handsome interiors done in "stratosphere blue." Walls would
be adorned with shields representing the coats of arms of the five
countries that Eastern served. In 1959 the airline employed 18,000
men and women and reached 128 cities in twenty-seven states
with 228 planes making 1,400 trips a day for a total of half a million miles every twenty-four hours. Eastern planes linked every
major city from New England and the Great Lakes to St. Louis,
mid-Texas, Florida, the eastern seaboard, the Gulf Coast, and
Puerto Rico.

For a quarter of a century Eastern's emblem was a falcon in
flight. But its real symbol was the man who had built the airline
and compiled a record of twenty-six years of profit with not a cent

of government subsidy. Irascible and strong-willed, he'd been a benevolent tyrant, just as he'd been a demanding boss in garages that built racing cars, as a flight leader and commander of the Hat-in-the-Ring Squadron, and as owner of the Indianapolis Speedway. Long on ego, he was unstinting in asserting opinions on every topic as forcefully as he wielded authority.

At no time since he first attracted the attention of the press as a dashing daredevil in a stripped-down car on a dirt race track was he not famous. He was exactly the man America imagined a hero should be. He had become the figure expected of a leader of an industry. He had risen to prominence in step with two machines that remade a country and welded it into a nation. A king of the road and the skies, he had made his name synonymous with the car and the plane. With American grit and common sense, he'd exemplified courage, patriotism, and every virtue held dear in the country's mythology. He'd led the good life. And lived one.

On October 1, 1959, Eddie was one week away from his sixty-ninth birthday. He was also at a point in his illustrious life, as Eastern Air Lines historian Robert J. Serling rightly observed, when he had held power too long. In such a man, he wrote, power becomes addictive "and among the symptoms is the delusion of omnipotence. Beliefs and prejudices congeal into rigidity. Reasoning becomes inflexible. Decisions are inevitably arbitrary. And the most tragic aspect of this condition is that a strong leader seldom realizes what has happened to him—he deludes himself into believing that the glory of the past is all he needs to meet the present and the future. Unhappily for Eddie Rickenbacker, someone *did* see what had happened—and he was not among those officers [of Eastern Air Lines] who were either afraid of him, overly fond of him, or helpless to challenge his power. That was Laurence Rockefeller."

Since playing a vital role in Eddie's taking over Eastern Air Transport, Rockefeller had increased his investment through stock splits and options to become Eastern's largest individual stockholder and a significant influence on the board of directors.

It was Eddie's close connection with Rockefeller that motivated him to establish Eastern's headquarters in Rockefeller Center. Another demonstration of the closeness of their relationship had occurred in 1946. A member of the socially desirable Sleepy Hollow Country Club, Eddie was asked by Laurence to recommend admission of Laurence's brother David. Biographer Finis Farr noted the irony that "the shabby kid from [Columbus] had arrived at a place where he could do a social favor for a Rockefeller."

Because social courtesies were always kept distinct from business, a friendly gesture thirteen years earlier could not outweigh Rockefeller's concerns in 1959 about decisions that Eddie made concerning the future of Eastern Air Lines. The discreet, low-key, behind-the-scenes businessman felt uneasy about Eddie's brusque managerial methods, his leave-it-to-me method of decision-making in buying new equipment, and a belligerence regarding the government in general and the Civil Aeronautics Board (CAB) in particular. Rockefeller blamed Rickenbacker's "arrogance" for "an excessively long period in which lack of support in Washington and a lack of friends" hurt Eastern's attempts "to improve our route system."

Rockefeller also worried that to the public "Eastern Air Lines" and "Rickenbacker" had become one and the same, that its employees were fanatically devoted to "Captain Eddie," and that in running the company Eddie believed you were either on his team or against him. He was, in Rockefeller's view, "the epitome of a monolithic leader. He wanted your support and if you didn't give it to him, he'd get it from someone else."

As majority stockholder, Rockefeller proposed bringing in as a consultant on equipment purchases a highly respected official of American Airlines, Richard "Dick" Johnson. Eddie knew him well, but he did not suspect that Johnson's true purpose was to provide Rockefeller with an evaluation of Eddie's executive competence in leading Eastern into the jet age. Johnson found that "there hasn't been anything new in this company for four or five years." He voiced his opinion that "as you look into the next decade, there will have to be changes made."

Keenly aware that as a venerated hero in two world wars, an

esteemed public figure, and a colorful personality, Eddie Rickenbacker was not a man who could be simply sent on his way with
a pat on the back, a testimonial dinner, and a gold pocket watch
engraved with platitudes of praise for a job well done, Rockefeller
pursued a strategy that had been a mainstay of business in America for his grandfather, John D. Rockefeller, and other wily ty-
coons and "robber barons" of the industrial Gilded Age: Never
kick an icon OUT; kick him UP.

Rockefeller's first choice to replace Eddie as Eastern's president was Najeeb Halaby. A Texan of Arab descent, he'd fallen in
love with flying as a boy when he went to a parade honoring
Charles A. Lindbergh in 1927. Five years later he made his solo
flight from an airfield in Los Angeles. He had been a navy test pilot in World War II and the first American aviator to fly a jet
plane. Between 1948 and 1952 he served as a foreign affairs advisor in the Defense Department. Directed by Rockefeller to ana-
lyze the Rickenbacker management style by observing Eddie at
meetings of Eastern executives, Halaby reported, "I had never
seen a more dictatorial example of centralized management nor
such public humiliation of employees, to say nothing of the waste
of time." What Eastern needed until such time as Eddie retired,
Halaby said, was a strong number-two man who would have real
authority as president. Eddie would be chairman of the board,
but with reduced power. Halaby also told Rockefeller that he had
no interest in taking on the presidency of EAL. The decision
proved a sound one. Halaby later became chief of the Federal Aviation Administration and head of Pan American When his
daughter Lisa married King Hussein of Jordan, she shared his
palaces in the Hashemite Kingdom as Queen Noor.

With Halaby unavailable, Rockefeller turned to Malcolm A.
MacIntyre. A former lawyer for American Airlines and undersec-
retary of the air force, he became president of Eastern on October
1, 1959. Putting the best face on the involuntary power shift in his
autobiography, Eddie said that because of a trend "toward more
and more bureaucracy," as exemplified by regulations imposed by
the CAB, he had become "so disgusted with this trend toward
socialism" that he "felt like stepping out of the airline business

completely, provided that we could find the right type of executive to take over [for] me." Noting that in October 1959 he was seventy years old, he explained, "Some of our directors felt that Eastern should have a younger executive officer, to which I agreed."

A year and a half before Eddie was stripped of the presidency of Eastern, he received a memorandum from William L. Morrisette, vice president for traffic, sales, and advertising. It proposed that Eastern Air Lines consider "a no advance telephone reservations plan applicable to commuter service." The genesis of the idea was fierce competition between nine airlines on the New York–Washington route. Describing the situation in his autobiography, Eddie asked, "How could any one line show a profit in such a situation?"

Read in the context of the deregulation of public services that gave birth to unrestrained competition in the 1980s and 1990s, the following lines in Eddie's autobiography proved to be prescient. "Imagine the chaotic state, the lack of service that would result," he wrote, "if there were nine separate telephone companies in New York or Washington, nine utility companies, nine water companies." One wonders what he would make of today's multiplicity of choices in telephone companies, electricity suppliers, brands of bottled water, cable television systems providing hundreds of channels, and computers through which air travelers who have no loyalty to any airline can routinely search for the lowest-priced tickets. And what might the man who had resented having to provide free meals think of giving away seats to passengers who had accumulated "frequent-flyer miles"?

The "no advance reservation" idea envisioned Eastern planes flying round-trip between New York and Washington several times a day regardless of how many people were on board, and should there be an overflow, rolling out another plane to accommodate them. Eddie was dubious at first, calling it "nothing but a bus service." But as he thought about it, he realized that for years he had been shuttling planes between cities for economic advantage in the "merry-go-round," even if it meant that a plane carried only a few passengers and sometimes none.

Debate over the viability of an "air shuttle" and the planning that followed the decision to attempt it delayed introduction of the revolutionary service until 1961. Unveiled on April 30, its route had been extended to include Boston. Flights departed every two hours. The planes were ninety-five-seat Constellations. On June 12, the first "second section" was required to accommodate an overflow of one passenger. The result was a financial loss but a harvest of invaluable publicity and an upsurge in shuttle passengers that necessitated the introduction of hourly flights. By June 11, 1962, the shuttle had carried a million passengers. CAB chairman Alan Boyd pronounced the air shuttle "the greatest thing that has happened in air transportation in years."

Although the shuttle operated at a loss for the first few years, the service eventually made Eastern a new force in the northeast corridor market. Newark was added in April 1962. On December 1, 1963, the shuttle set a one-day record of twenty thousand passengers. By the close of 1965 the number of shuttle users totaled 10 million a year.

"By this time," wrote U.S. airline historian R.E.G. Davies, "the air shuttle was as much a part of the New York, Boston, or Washington transport scene as the Triboro Bridge or the Jersey Turnpike." If identified as a separate, autonomous airline–which effectively it was–the air shuttle ranked as the sixteenth-largest airline in the world, measured in passenger boardings.

But "Captain Eddie" was no longer a part of the company that he had built and run with a hand as iron as his will.

CHAPTER 24

Slipping the Surly Bonds of Earth

Informing Eddie Rickenbacker that he "had to go" as Eastern's chairman fell to four members of the board of directors. It happened on December 19, 1963, in the Hampshire House hotel suite of board member Harper Woodward. The blow was softened by the announcement that Eddie's nemesis, Malcolm MacIntyre, would also be going. In doing this, the board was following the business and military logic that if the top man were to be replaced and a clean break made with the past, the man below him also must go. Eddie was told that MacIntyre would be replaced by Floyd Hall, a senior vice president and system general manager of TWA.

After reminding the firing squad that without Rickenbacker there would not have been an Eastern Air Lines, Eddie accepted his fate gracefully. "Okay. I'm willing to leave the whole damned thing to Floyd Hall," he said. "I'll move out of my office like you guys want. No more arguing, no more fighting. I'll do what you want me to do."

The change would become official on December 31, 1963. That day, a message written by Eddie was teletyped to all Eastern offices, officers, and "all members of the Eastern Air Lines family."

Noting that "Floyd Hall takes over as president and chief executive officer" and "we are fortunate to have the services of one of the industry's outstanding young leaders," Eddie said, "I ask all of you—you youngsters who have more recently joined our ranks as well as you veterans who helped me build Eastern Air Lines through the years—I ask all of you to give Floyd Hall the same full measure of loyalty and cooperation you always gave me in the past."

The retirement dinner was held at Eddie's favorite restaurant. A former speakeasy two blocks uptown from the Eastern Air Lines building in Rockefeller Center, Jack and Charlie's 21 Club took its name from its address, 21 West Fifty-second Street. Cousins Jack Kriendler and Charlie Berns had gone into selling liquor and food at the start of Prohibition, operating at various locations before buying the townhouse at a bargain price during the Great Depression. By charging outrageous prices for food and drinks in the downstairs back room, they limited the club's patronage to the well-heeled and business executives. To maintain the atmosphere of a "men's club," women customers were confined to upstairs dining rooms to shield them from a decor in the barroom that consisted in large part of drawings, paintings, and cartoons of thinly clad young women. The revealed beams of the ceiling of the room were festooned with dangling representations of corporations and other enterprises whose employees gathered at the long bar.

The youngest of the four Kriendler brothers, Peter, known to customers as Mr. Pete, recalled that when Eddie discovered that Howard Hughes had contributed a model of a TWA plane to the ceiling, a miniature example of a Great Silver Fleet airliner went up the next day. As an early and continuous 21 patron, Eddie was a charter member of a group of celebrities and business movers-and-shakers called the Skeeters. Organized by sports broadcaster Ted Husing, the group always gathered at the east end of the long bar. Members were "admirers of the breed" who ventured to racetracks in the wilds of New Jersey, a state notorious for its vast swarms of large mosquitoes, hence the group's name. That horse racing was either an avocation of the 21 clientele in the form of betting or a business to stable owners such as the Vanderbilts and the Whitneys was acknowledged in front of the club by a line of cast-iron jockey figures painted in the colors of their contributors.

Among other clubs and groups eager to boast that Capt. Eddie Rickenbacker belonged (usually because they simply declared him a member) were the Confederate Air Force of Tulsa, Oklahoma; Historic Order of Owls; Tall Cedars of Lebanon; the Love 'em All Club; Royal Order of Groundhogs; Ancient Order of the Himalayas; and the National Association of Screwballs. His serious memberships were in the American Legion; the 29 Club, consisting of twenty-nine corporation executives; the Links Club (golfers, of course); and the Hole in One Club of the Sleepy Hollow Country Club, for one he scored on July 7, 1946.

Evidence that Edward V. Rickenbacker was considered on a par with the men in the top echelons of business and politics who had a conservative viewpoint came in July 1958. He received an invitation to attend the annual conclave of such men at the "Festival" of San Francisco's Bohemian Club. Gathered in rustic surroundings and quartered in sylvan lodges, they discussed national and world affairs and what ought to be done about them. (Such men still do, although the nature of today's attendees is not limited solely to conservatives.) Among those present when Eddie arrived were "the chief," former president Herbert Hoover; radio commentator Lowell Thomas; Dr. E. Wallace Sterling, president of Stanford University; DeWitt Wallace, publisher of *Reader's Digest*; Roy W. Howard of the Scripps-Howard newspaper chain; a San Francisco oilman, Albert C. Mattei; Arizona newspaper magnate Eugene Pullman; and a U.S. senator from Arizona, Barry Goldwater.

Six years later in reviewing the life of Edward Vernon Rickenbacker from the hindsight perspective of an obituary, the *New York Times* would opine, "While his successes came in fields that were developed in the 20th century, his philosophy seemed to many a carryover from the 19th century." He was "an individualist of the old empire-building school." But in the long run, the *Times* obituary would continue, "it will not be his material successes that will be remembered. Rather, he will be recalled as a

larger-than-life figure cast in the same mold as legendary folk heroes of the past."

Had Eddie been able to look ahead from his last day with Eastern Air Lines and read what the obituary writer forecast as his
legacy, he certainly would have found no reason to argue. His entire life had been a relentless quest for glory in the present, the future, and in the memory of America. As a race car driver, ace of
aces, airline builder, indomitable survivor of crashes and twenty-
four days "lost at sea," implacable foe of anyone who tried to re-
strict the reach and the success of Eastern, and believer in his
America he had indeed been larger-than-life.

He was by no means finished.

In his letter resigning the chairmanship of Eastern, he'd
vowed, "I am going to expand my crusade to save the American
way of life for future generations, as I want our children, our
grandchildren, and those who follow them to enjoy the opportunities which have been mine for seventy-three years."

He was not optimistic about the direction the country seemed
to be taking. "Since the early days of the Roosevelt administration," he recalled in his autobiography, "I had been observing our
country steadily becoming a socialized welfare state. I was bitterly opposed to this trend, but I was hesitant about standing up
on my hind legs and stating my views and the reasons for them.
I was afraid that the general public had not had the time to as-
similate what was happening to the country and would not understand what I was talking about."

He'd tried in a speech in 1951. He warned:

> *We are now living in a garrison state, or a state of
> armed neutrality, although few of you realize it. I doubt
> very much whether any of us present here tonight will
> ever again see and enjoy the peacetime periods in this
> land of ours, as we have known them during our life-
> time up to now. For one thing, we are going to get taxes
> on top of taxes, resulting in a lower and lower standard
> of living as time goes on. With those taxes will come
> controls on top of controls, which means the loss of*

*more and more of those liberties we cherish so dearly. I
say these things as a realist, which I have always been
throughout my life—and the American people must become realistic too, and face the facts. . . . Knowing that
the life of man is pledged to higher levels here [America]
than it is elsewhere, are we striving to hold aloft the
standards of liberty and hope? Or are we disillusioned
and defeated—feeling the disgrace of having had a free
field in which to do new things in the cause of freedom
and not having done them?*

In May 1960, it was not Eddie Rickenbacker who did something "in the cause of freedom," but William Rickenbacker,
investment counselor and member of the staff of William F.
Buckley, Jr's *National Review.* Along with what the conservative
opinion magazine said were 30 million "other exasperated Americans," Bill received two questionnaires from the U.S. Census Bureau. Most recipients got one white form, but he also received a
Blue Questionnaire that asked, among other questions, how
many bathrooms were in his house, his phone number, where
he'd been born, what language was spoken in his parents' home,
if he had worked last week, and for how many hours?

Considering the blue form "uncivilly inquisitorial and absolutely unconstitutional," Bill shot off a letter to the Census Bureau. "I have studied this snooping questionnaire," he snapped.
"It does not relate to any constitutional requirement I know of, it
has not been addressed to the population as a whole; and I shall
not answer it. Indeed, I have already torn it up. Some day, when
the summer satrap of the Snooper State comes to ask me why I
refuse to contribute my share of statistics to the national numbers
game, I shall call for my lawyer." Eddie's offer to pay Bill's legal
expenses was declined. Eddie said, "Give the bastards hell."

The government issued a summons demanding that Bill appear before a grand jury in answer to a charge of violation of Section 221, Title 13, U.S. Code, requiring citizens to cooperate with
the Census Department of the Department of Commerce. Bill appeared with a constitutional expert, attorney C. D. Williams, who

at times had served as general counsel to the Commerce Department. Bill told the prosecutor and grand jurors that he "did faithfully and gladly complete" the white form, but that he'd rejected the blue "on the ground that it violated my rights under the Fourth Amendment and was otherwise an unnecessary violation of my privacy." He added that the American Civil Liberties Union had come to conclusions similar to his own "regarding the legality of demanding an answer to such questions." The grand jury returned an indictment. An appeal to the Second Circuit Court of Appeals to quash the indictment was rejected by Judge Thurgood Marshall. Bill was tried, found guilty, sentenced to sixty days in federal prison (suspended), and fined one hundred dollars.

Four months later Eddie accepted an invitation to address the Chicago Economic Club. The weather in Chicago on that April evening in 1961 was inauspicious. Driving to the Palmer House hotel on icy streets through snow and sleet, he expected a small turnout. He found more than one thousand hardy Chicagoans, mostly men, packed into the banquet hall.

As daringly as he took up auto racing and as fearlessly as he'd zoomed across the skies of the Western Front, he ventured into political combat with all guns firing in an early salvo of an ideological struggle for the soul of the Republican Party. It would begin in earnest four years later in the party's nomination of Sen. Barry Goldwater for president, culminate in 1980 with the election of Ronald Reagan, and continue into the twenty-first century with George W. Bush. Eddie's title for the 1961 speech was "Conservatism Must Face Up to Liberalism."

Interrupted twenty-four times and given a four-minute standing ovation at the finish, Eddie spoke for an hour. He saw an opportunity to start "a new chapter" of his life and with a "resolve" to say what was really on his mind. He began by declaring that "the liberals were no longer firmly in the saddle," that "the winds had shifted," and that conservatives "were rising up across the land, finding new strength in their old convictions, making their voices heard and winning at the polls." Modern liberals, he said, had "forsaken the original meaning" of the word "liberal." Instead of advocating freedom, they were striving to pile up power in Washington.

It was conservatives, Eddie said, "who must take individual freedom as their battle cry and resist encroachment of federal power." The government must be taken out of "competition with private enterprise" to eliminate "the billions of dollars in expenditures annually being poured down a rathole." In an all-out attack on the federal income tax, he sounded a theme that would be echoed by Ronald Reagan in his inaugural address. "The taxing power," Reagan would say, as Eddie believed, "must not be used to regulate the economy or bring about social change."

Eddie received so much favorable response to the Chicago speech, with requests for copies, that he had it printed as a pamphlet. Invitations to speak flooded in from other groups that were so eager to hear him that they proffered money. If an honorarium were to be paid, he directed that the funds go to "uplift" organizations, including the Boy Scouts of America, Big Brothers, the Boys' Clubs of New York, and Children's Village of Dobbs Ferry, New York.

Financially secure in retirement and with more free time on his hands than at any period of his life, Eddie soon felt an urge to travel, but now his companion would not be someone in an air force uniform, but his wife. The route he chose for their extended vacation was across the ocean that had nearly claimed his life. Beginning in Alaska, they flew to Japan, Okinawa, Korea, Taiwan, Hong Kong, Bangkok, and Australia. From there the odyssey went to the Fiji Islands and the speck of land that the B-17 hadn't been able to find in 1942, Canton, and onward to Hawaii and Seattle. Thronged by reporters on his return, the man who'd run Eastern Air Lines could not keep himself from taking a crack at American organized labor. "One thing about those people out there," he said, "they aren't plagued with union regulations and hours of labor as we are. Most of them work fifty or sixty hours a week."

Resuming making speeches, Eddie found that not all of his audiences were as warm as the one in Chicago. After addressing a women's group, one of the ladies said, "You scare me." Eddie answered, "I meant to."

After a speech in Nashville, Tennessee, in early October 1962, the local newspaper ran a scathing editorial. Under the headline

MR. RICKENBACKER RANTS, it said, "For an aging public figure who has enjoyed a glamorous and successful career, Mr. Eddie Rickenbacker seems to be a most unhappy gentleman." What Eddie found insulting about the editorial and the headline was not being called "Captain." But the newspaper was wrong in stating that Eddie "seemed" to be an unhappy gentleman. He *was*, in fact, *very* unhappy. Not with his own life, but with the direction his country was going in in the mid-1960s–politically, economically, socially, culturally, morally, and in an upheaval in race relations.

He found little to approve.

His unrequested advice to President Lyndon B. Johnson on the war in Vietnam was that the United States win it. He enjoyed a joke about a Republican who said that he'd been told that if he voted for Sen. Barry Goldwater in 1964, in a year the United States would be at war in Vietnam. "Well, I voted for Barry," said the Republican, "and we were."

On the United Nations: "I have no confidence in it as it has worked out."

Anticolonial movements in Africa: "Dark folks don't like white supervision."

American race relations: "We [whites] are fortunate in that we number around ten to one. But the rate that the blacks breed and multiply, that will constantly go down, because we have birth control in America because of intelligence on the part of whites. It benefits the colored people not to have it, in order to multiply to the point where they are a greater influence than the whites. It's that simple, and that is true of any minority. If the time ever comes when they outnumber, then they will rally themselves with colored peoples in all parts of the world."

President Truman: "Well, he knew how to swear. He knew how to drink bourbon. He knew how to make up his mind, and unfortunately made it in the wrong direction."

John F. Kennedy: "Overrated."

Richard Nixton: "A better man than people give him credit for."

An Eddie Rickenbacker custom at Christmastime was a chatty letter to his friends and business associates in which he summed up the previous year and looked forward to the new. In 1965 the

letter was shorter than usual and took a farther look back. He
wrote that since he had crossed "the three quarter century milestone on October 8," he'd been thinking of his countless bless-
ings. "Yes the Lord has been kind to me," he said, "and I am very
grateful!"

Two years earlier, at age seventy-three, wanderlust had enticed him and Adelaide to go to Europe. When nostalgia beck-
oned him to visit the graves of Ernst Udet and the Red Baron, the
officials of Communist East Berlin were reticent about granting
permission. But his lasting fame as America's ace of aces and
their trepidation about insulting the United States government
carried the day. The gate to the cemetery was rusted shut. A
guard broke it open. Udet's grave was unkempt. The resting place
of the Red Baron, a monolith rising from the uncut grass, needed
no more identification than the name RICHTHOFEN. Wondering
how many Germans remembered him, Eddie photographed the
monument, but the picture "turned out not good."

Shortly after returning to New York, Eddie lost the friendship
of the man he'd always called "the chief." Herbert Hoover, who'd
presented Eddie's belated Medal of Honor in 1930, died in his
suite in the Waldorf Towers on October 20, 1964. To Adelaide,
Hoover and Eddie were "Model T Americans." Symbolic citizens
whom everybody knew, they personified "the good American" of
a time past for whom one could proudly "claim some kinship."

Deciding that it was time to put his adventuresome life be-
tween the pages of a book, Eddie began working on it in 1967.
Like all authors, he wrestled with a title. Among contenders that
would leave no doubt about how he viewed himself were *The Indestructible Captain Eddie Rickenbacker*, *The Man Who Has Lived
Many Lives in One*, *The Autobiography of a Great American*, *The
Man Who Is Alive Today Because of His Faith in God's America*,
The Man Who Has Cheated the Grim Reaper Many Times, *The
Man Who Wants to Live Forever*, *I Had to Fight to Live So Long*,
and *The Indestructible American*. Going for simplicity, but confident that his name alone was sufficiently compelling to sell it, he
called it *Rickenbacker*.

Dedicated to his mother and wife, it began, "My life has been filled with adventures that have brought me face-to-face with death." After 443 pages, it ended in true Rickenbacker style:

> *It is not old-fashioned to wave and love the flag of our country or to worship God in heaven. Let us acknowledge and be grateful for the blessings of freedom that God has given us. Let us dedicate our lives to the perpetuation of the American principles of freedom with confidence. Let us stop and analyze ourselves to find out what life means to us.*
>
> *I want nothing further in material value or personal prestige—no power, no wealth, no political plums. But I do pray that this exhortation in the name of freedom and liberty will spread to every nook and cranny of this land of ours for the benefit of future generations.*
>
> *Let us therefore pray every night for the strength and guidance to inspire in others the gratitude, the love, the dedication that we owe our beloved country for the sake of our posterity.*
>
> *Then, and only then, can we say when the candle of life burns low—Thank God, I have given my best to the land that has given so much to me.*

The book was received according to how Eddie Rickenbacker was perceived. It was the autobiography of a significant, even great American who gave his all in war and peace in the skies and on the ground. Or it was an exercise in self-flattery and an inflated estimation of his contributions to aviation. Readers and reviewers who saw him through the prism of the Eddie Rickenbacker of 1968 saw his hawkishness on the Vietnam War, conservative politics, and racist outlook and held them against the auto racer, ace of aces, and airline builder found in the book. Admirers of Captain Eddie discovered what they were looking for: bravery, heart, adventure, strength of convictions, common sense, rugged individualism, love of wife and pride in sons, patriotism, and belief in God. Those who didn't like him didn't

buy his book. Those who loved him and what he stood for bought
it by the thousands and stood in long lines to get him to autograph it.

This act, Bill observed, was "a full ceremonial" in which "Captain Eddie sat down, hunched over, worked hard, and in the silence of concentration produced this unmistakable mark—while
the petitioner drank in the silence and observed the man's energy
and honesty pouring in his direction." He wrote with a controlled
flourish, Eddie V. Rickenbacker.

An organization called America's Future, based in New
Rochelle, New York, gave copies to 32,352 public and parochial
schools and college and university libraries and 500 to the Boys'
Clubs of America. Every book had a pasted-in black-and-white
portrait of Eddie in his World War I uniform against a background of a dogfight with a German plane going down in flames.
The bookplate read:

This book is the gift of the following:

CAPT. EDDIE RICKENBACKER

HIS FRIENDS

AMERICA'S FUTURE

The strain of a book tour and signing thousands of autographs
that might have taken a toll on a younger author finally caught up
with seventy-eight-year-old Eddie. He came down with pneumonia and was briefly hospitalized. But he was well enough to write
in his 1968 Christmas card note, "Another year has passed and
what a year!" (He was referring to the election of Richard Nixon
as president.)

Eddie now had two homes. A cottage at the Key Biscayne Hotel in Florida had an ocean view. A small suite in the Dorset Hotel in midtown Manhattan on Fifty-fourth Street between Fifth
and Sixth Avenues was an easy walk to the 21 Club, where he
was an old friend, and to the Eastern Air Lines Building in Rockefeller Center, where to people of the jet age he would have been
a relic of the past as quaint as a DC-3 or a Connie.

His sons were prospering and had given him and Adelaide daughters-in-law and grandchildren. In September 1972 he and Adelaide celebrated fifty years of marriage. On October 8 they marked his eighty-second birthday. Four days later he had a stroke. Fluid caused pressure on his brain that required surgery. When he developed pneumonia, doctors held little hope that he would recover, but he rallied. Then came kidney failure. He pulled through, but soon lost the ability to speak. Transferred to a nursing home in January 1973, he amazed everyone again by recovering his voice and seeming to completely recover.

He began talking about a trip to Switzerland to visit the places where his parents had been born. Although Adelaide was having problems with her eyesight, she agreed to make the trip with him in the summer. He was feeling well enough on July Fourth to appear in public at an Independence Day parade in Miami. Unrecorded was whether he thought back to a Fourth of July parade in Paris in 1918 and that on the next day he had commandeered a coveted Spad that became the instrument of his glory days as America's ace of aces.

On July 12, 1973, Eddie, Adelaide, Marguerite Shepherd, and a medical orderly arrived at the Hotel Barlach in Zurich, Switzerland. But the plans to visit the birthplaces of Father and Mother Rickenbacher had to be postponed. Adelaide developed pleurisy. This was followed by Eddie experiencing irregular breathing.

A doctor ordered Eddie to a hospital for chest X rays.

At 4:15 on the morning of July 23, he died of heart failure.

The obituary in the *New York Times* on July 24 noted, "Edward Vernon Rickenbacker was a man whose delight in turning the tables on seemingly hopeless odds took him to the top in three fields." It recalled his "daredevil pre–World War I days" of automobile racing; being the "ace of aces"; and his success in "the highly competitive airline business" as "the first man to prove that airlines could be made profitable, and then the first to prove that they could be run without a Government subsidy and kept profitable."

The Atlanta crash of February 1941, said the *Times*, was followed by "the still greater test of his courage" as "the commander of rafts" in October 1942 when the world believed he was dead somewhere in the vast reaches of the Pacific Ocean.

The obituary noted, "A self-made man whose formal education ended with the sixth grade, Mr. Rickenbacker was a driving leader. He put the stamp of his dominant personality on everything he touched."

Captain Eddie was saluted with three memorial services. The first was on July 27 at the Presbyterian Church on Key Biscayne. The second took place in New York City at the Marble Collegiate Church on Fifth Avenue on August 7. Three days later he was cremated, and his ashes were buried next to his parents' graves at Greenlawn Cemetery in Columbus, Ohio.

Four jets flying over in the missing leader formation were from the 94th Squadron.

NOTES

FOR ANYONE WHO MIGHT UNDERTAKE HIS BIOGRAPHY, EDDIE RICKEN-backer provided a compass in three exceptional memoirs. Published within months after he came home from the Great War as America's ace of aces and returned to print in 1965, *Fighting the Flying Circus* is a vivid and exciting chronicle. Drawn from a diary that he kept with "religious regularity," it provided not only a portrait of himself in aerial combat, and occasionally on the ground with the top brass of the AEF and the Army Air Service, but details about personalities and exploits of comrades and rivals in scoring victories. Twenty-four years later, first for *Life* magazine and then in the book *Seven Came Through*, he plunked readers into tiny rubber life rafts bobbing in the Pacific Ocean with him and six other courageous men thought lost by the world. In 1967 he plumbed an astonishing memory for an autobiography. So famous was he by then that he had entered a rare world of people whose last names were the only identification needed—Valentino, Garbo, Ike, Patton, MacArthur, and Roosevelt. In relating his life, he was assisted in considerable measure by faithful secretary Marguerite "Sheppy" Shepherd, who diligently preserved letters, speeches, souvenirs, and other memorabilia from his automotive and aviation careers between the world wars, through the fiercely competitive 1950s as airlines battled for dominance, emergence as an outspoken political conservative with a dubious view of the 1960s, and his twilight years.

The greatest trove of ephemera—consisting of correspondence sent and received, articles by and about him, the first draft of the autobiography, Christmas letters, speeches and the notes he made in preparing them, and office records amounting to 36,000 items in 262 file boxes—would be archived at the Library of Congress. Items from his military career were conveyed to the Air Force Museum at Wright-Patterson air base, Dayton, Ohio, and the Smithsonian Institution's National Air and Space Museum, including his battered fedora and other relics of the twenty-four days adrift in the Pacific. Eddie Rickenbacker as auto racing hero and racetrack owner is enshrined at the Indianapolis Motor Speedway Museum. Domestic memorabilia and artifacts were donated by the family to the library of Auburn University. Among this material are letters saved by Bill, some of which were reproduced in Bill's 1970 book *From Father to Son: The Letters of Captain Eddie Rickenbacker to His Son William, from Boyhood to Manhood.* Spanning the decades from April 1937 to August 1965, they provide insights into Eddie's thinking on politics and war, his opinions of leading public and business personalities, and his philosophy of life.

Bill died of cancer on March 21, 1995, at age sixty-seven at his home in Francestown, New Hampshire. He and his wife, the former Alexandra Harriman Leys, had two sons, James and Thomas. Eddie's son David died in February 1983 in White River Junction, Vermont. Fifty-eight years old, he'd worked for fifteen years as a representative for the firm Shearson–American Express. Married to the former Patricia Bowen, he had a son, Brian, and two daughters, Marcia and Nancy.

Blind and in failing health, ninety-two-year-old Adelaide took her own life with a pistol on February 2, 1977, at Key Biscayne, Florida.

The Rickenbacker biographies are *Rickenbacker's Luck: An American Life* by Finis Farr; a thirty-six-page sketch by journalists Damon Runyon and Walter Kiernan published as a tribute after the 1942 rescue at sea; and *Eddie Rickenbacker* by Hans Christian Adamson, his friend and companion during that harrowing experience. Published in 1946, it is therefore not a full life story and goes beyond affection to worshipful. But it presented aspects of Eddie's life up to then that were drawn from their personal relationship and interviews with a subject who was very cooperative and sympathetic. While not a Rickenbacker biography, *From the Captain to the Colonel: An Informal History of Eastern Airlines* by Robert J. Serling was an invaluable source on EAL from its beginnings and on the intricate and sometimes cutthroat business of airlines. Eastern's history is also found in *Airlines of the United States Since 1914*, by R.E.G. Davies.

The airline that Eddie built no longer exists. As a result of deregulation of the industry in 1978, Eastern encountered troubles with labor strife, the rise of "no frills" lines offering low fares, and attempts at takeovers until it was sold in 1986 to Frank Lorenzo, whose chief interest was the Eastern shuttle. After it was bought in 1989 by real estate magnate Donald Trump and Lorenzo disposed of the remains of Eastern in bankruptcy proceedings, Eastern ended all flight operations in 1991.

Eddie's name and legacy were memorialized with a 1995 U.S. postage stamp (60 cents), part of the Great Americans series of commemoratives, issued in his hometown, Columbus, Ohio. The city also honored him through the Rickenbacker Port Authority and the five-thousand-acre Rickenbacker International Airport, which is the base for a consolidated Navy and Marine Corps Air Reserve Center and Rickenbacker Air National Guard 121st Air Refueling Wing and 160th Air Refueling Group.

Helpful in my understanding of military aviation during World War I were *The First Air War, 1914–1918*, by Lee Kennett; *Hostile Skies: A Combat History of the American Air Service in World War I*, by James J. Hudson; *The United States in the First World War: An Encyclopedia*, edited by Anne Cipriano Venson; and *The First World War: A Complete History*, by Martin Gilbert. Lieutenant Colonel Gene Gurney, USAF, compiled an invaluable resource, *A Chronology of World Aviation*, published in 1965 by Franklin Watts, Inc. in the Watts Aerospace Library.

Eddie's exploits as a racing star, World War I ace, carmaker, automotive executive, aviation prophet and advocate, builder and boss of Eastern Air Lines, survivor of plane crashes (including a ditched B-17 in the Pacific), advocate of conservative politics, and always fascinating public personality and celebrity, received extensive and continuous attention in the American press. As a self-appointed prognosticator on the future of aviation, he saw most of his predictions come true, though not his forecast that one day atomic power would allow dirigibles to become "great liners of the air" and a nuclear-fueled "rocket flying belt" would become "a routine means of individual transportation." Among innovations he predicted were electronic banking and shopping by television. He foresaw purchase orders being flashed electronically and the bought items delivered by air the next day, although his vision of such commerce did not anticipate that it would be done through devices called the personal computer and "the Internet."

There is no doubt that if Eddie could return to "the surly bonds of earth," he would be pleased to find that "Captain Eddie Rickenbacker" items, from his books, autographs, and shots of him standing beside Spad No. 1 to pictures of him smiling proudly as he posed next to a DC-3 or Connie of the Great Silver Fleet, are put up for bidding on Internet auction sites.

He would also be pleased to note that as America's ace of aces, he was an exception. He never went, as he feared he might, "from hero to zero."

BIBLIOGRAPHY

Adamson, Hans Christian. *Eddie Rickenbacker*. New York: Macmillan, 1946.

Baldwin, Hanson. *World War I: An Outline History*. New York: Harper & Row, 1962.

Barrett, William F. *The First War Planes*. Greenwich, Conn.: Fawcett Publications, 1960.

Bishop, William. *A Winged Warfare*. New York: George H. Doran, 1934.

Buckley, Harold. *Squadron 95*. Paris: Obelisk Press, 1933.

Davies, R.E.G. *Airlines of the United States Since 1914*. Washington, D.C.: Smithsonian Institution Press, 1972.

Farr, Finis. *Rickenbacker's Luck: An American Life*. Boston: Houghton Mifflin, 1979.

Gilbert, Martin. *The First World War: A Complete History*. New York: Henry Holt, 1994.

Gurney, Lt. Col. Gene, USAF. *A Chronology of World Aviation*. New York: Franklin Watts, 1965.

Hall, James Norman, and Charles B. Nordhoff. *The Lafayette Flying Corps*. Boston: Houghton Mifflin, 1920.

Hudson, James J. *Hostile Skies: A Combat History of the American Air Service in World War I*. Syracuse, N.Y.: Syracuse University Press, 1968.

Kennett, Lee. *The First Air War, 1914–1918*. New York: Free Press, 1991.

Mitchell, William. *Memoirs of World War I*. New York: Random House, 1960.

Mondey, David, ed. *The Complete Illustrated Encyclopedia of the World's Aircraft*. London: New Burlington Books, 1978.

Nordhoff, Charles B., and James Norman Hall. *Falcons of France*. Boston: Little, Brown, 1929.

Oughton, Frederick. *The Aces*. New York: G. P. Putnam's Sons, 1960.

Renahan, Edward J., Jr. *The Lion's Pride: Theodore Roosevelt and His Family in Peace and War*. New York: Oxford University Press, 1998.

Rickenbacker, Edward V. *Ace Drummond*. Racine, Wis.: Whitman Publishing Company (a Big Little Book, fiction), 1935.

———. *Fighting the Flying Circus.* New York: Frederick A. Stokes, 1919.

———. *Rickenbacker.* Englewood Cliffs, N.J.: Prentice-Hall, 1967.

———. *Seven Came Through.* Garden City, N.Y.: Doubleday, Doran, 1943.

Rickenbacker, William. *From Father To Son: The Letters of Captain Eddie Rickenbacker to His Son William, from Boyhood to Manhood.* New York: Walker and Company, 1970.

Robinson, Anthony. *Dictionary of Aviation: An Illustrated History of the Airplane.* New York: Crescent Books, 1984.

Serling, Robert J. *From the Captain to the Colonel: An Informal History of Eastern Airlines.* New York: Dial Press, 1980.

Sweetser, Arthur W. *The American Air Service.* New York: D. Appleton, 1919.

Venson, Anne Cipriano, ed. *The United States in the First World War: An Encyclopedia.* New York: Garland Publishing, 1995.

Whitehouse, Arch. *Air Battles of the First World War.* New York: Duell, Sloan & Pearce, 1963.

INDEX

ABOUT THE AUTHOR

H. PAUL JEFFERS is the author of more than fifty books. They include *Theodore Roosevelt Jr.: The Life of a War Hero*; *Commissioner Roosevelt: Theodore Roosevelt and the New York City Police, 1895–1897*; *Colonel Roosevelt: Theodore Roosevelt Goes to War, 1897–1898*; *The Bully Pulpit: The Teddy Roosevelt Book of Quotations*; and *Roosevelt the Explorer*. Other biographies are *An Honest President: The Life and Presidencies of Grover Cleveland*; *The Napoleon of New York: Mayor Fiorello La Guardia*; and *Diamond Jim Brady: Prince of the Gilded Age*. Works of crime nonfiction include an anecdotal history of Scotland Yard, two studies of the FBI, and a true-crime bestseller, *Sal Mineo: His Life, Murder, and Mystery*. A former broadcast journalist, Jeffers lives in New York City.